Alameda

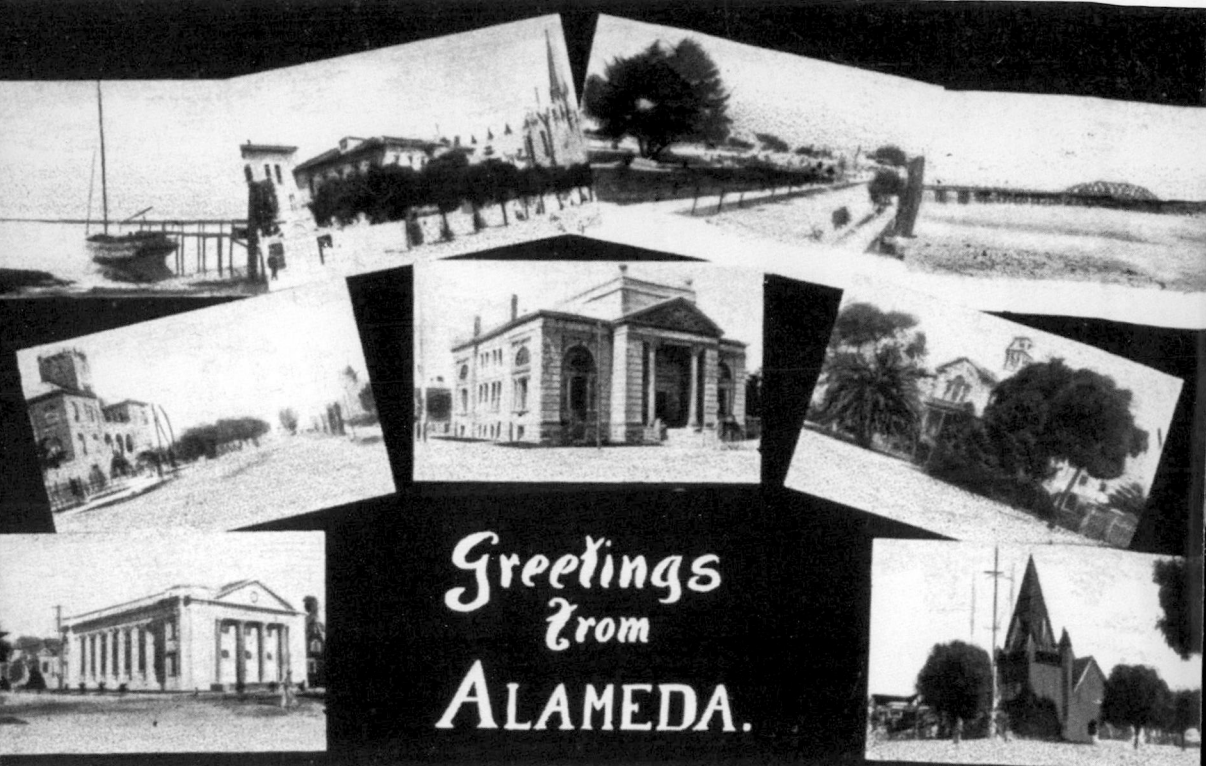

Early in the 20th century, Alameda was referred to as the "City of Beautiful Homes" and the "Dahlia City." This *c.* 1907 multi-view postcard shows, from left to right, (first row) First Presbyterian and Christ Episcopal Church; (second row) city hall, Carnegie Library, and Haight School; (third row) the bay shore, Notre Dame Academy, Jackson Park, and Bayfarm Island Bridge.

POSTCARD HISTORY SERIES

Alameda

Greta Dutcher and Stephen Rowland

Published by Arcadia Publishing
Charleston SC, Chicago IL, Portsmouth NH, San Francisco CA

Printed in the United States of America

Library of Congress Catalog Card Number: 2005929106

For all general information contact Arcadia Publishing at:
Telephone 843-853-2070
Fax 843-853-0044
E-mail sales@arcadiapublishing.com
For customer service and orders:
Toll-Free 1-888-313-2665

Visit us on the internet at http://www.arcadiapublishing.com

Dedicated to Frances Nachbar Avanzino (1919–2005), friend and lifelong Alameda resident.

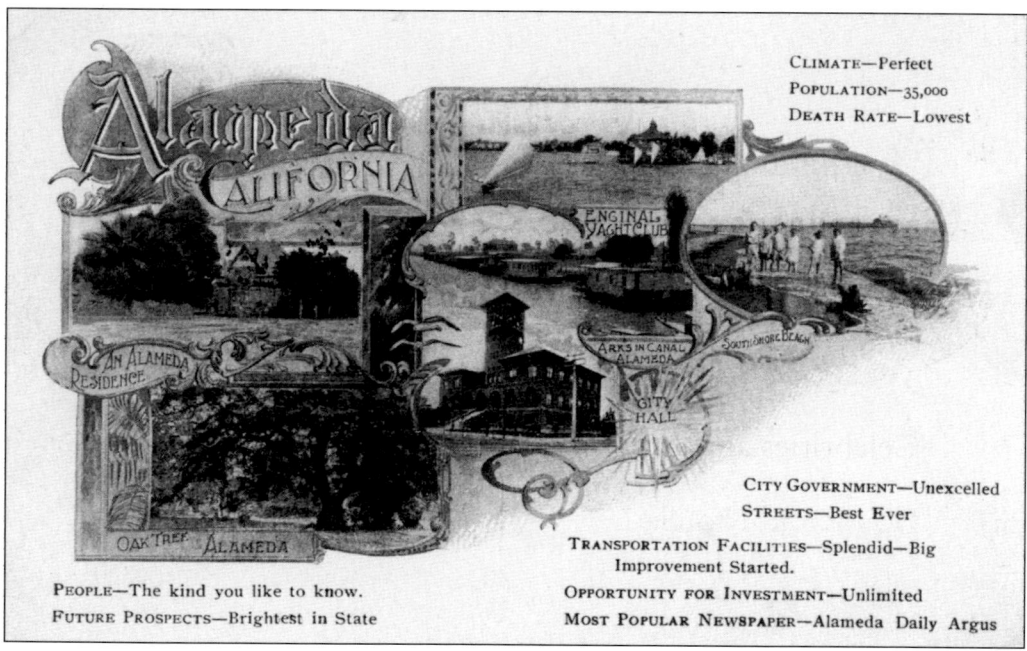

Alameda's charms are advertised in this *c.* 1908 postcard. The chamber of commerce described it as "A summer Mecca for those seeking an ideal vacationland," with its ideal climate throughout the year, beaches offering bathing, boating, dancing, and many other amusements, as well as unsurpassed industrial facilities.

CONTENTS

Acknowledgments

I wish to thank Ed Clausen for generously loaning his wonderful postcard collection; historian Woody Minor for taking time away from his own projects to help, and whose vast knowledge solved many mysteries; my dear friend Dave van Hulsteyn, for assisting with research; Jeff Geier, my kind and understanding employer; George Gunn and the Alameda Historical Museum; and librarians Robyn Gaskill, Patti Itano, Karin Lundstrom, Jane Pratt, and Lynda Williams at the Alameda Free Library, who provided direction and materials that were extremely useful.

INTRODUCTION

Alameda is unlike any other city or town in the San Francisco Bay Area. That's not an exaggeration from two proud residents, but something that's been acknowledged by many outsiders, as well. Where else will you find such a large concentration of Victorian architecture? Where else are you so shielded from sprawling freeways and strip malls that grow next to them? How many other physical islands in this area can you actually live on?

Alameda has, for the most part, avoided the temptation to become another wasteland of tract housing and shopping centers. The fact that it is an island (and trying to access it from the freeway is convoluted for the uninitiated) lends Alameda just the slightest bit of isolation, making it the unique, charming town it is today—one we have dubbed "The Island Paradise."

All that being said, Alameda is no stranger to change, as the postcards in this book demonstrate. Over time, we were surprised to find how many different Alameda postcards were made. For such a small place, the island sure had a lot to say in pictures. We have painstakingly selected the most unique, interesting, rare, and relevant postcards we have been able to get our hands on. Given the enormous amount of subject matter printed on postcards in the early 1900s, we hope that you'll find exactly what you're looking for. You may even find your house.

With all the change that has taken place, however, the handwritten notes on the backs of these postcards prove that, even with the passage of time in a rapidly evolving world, people haven't changed very much. As these images and their messages attest, our basic wants and needs are the same as they were 100 years ago, and our desire to connect with each other continues.

As a peninsula, Alameda really came onto the map when William Chipman and Gideon Aughinbaugh purchased the land from Antonio Maria Peralta in 1851. Although filled with dense oak groves, meadows, and marshlands, San Francisco residents found the peninsula ideal for orchards and residences and, working with other local landowners, they created the Alameda we all know and love today. Their work paid off as the population boomed during the late 1800s and early 1900s, being the catalyst for the creation of schools, churches, houses, and businesses with awe-inspiring architecture. A large number of these early buildings still exist today. We've worked to include as many lost buildings in this book as possible, so that everyone may be aware of and remember them.

Once the canal opened in 1902, finally making Alameda an island, businesses burgeoned along the waterfront, boosting the population and economy. World War I only helped to perpetuate this expansion. You could call this period Alameda's glory days, and browsing through this book, you'll find that a good deal of the postcards included are from this era.

The other key player in Alameda's growth was the Naval Air Station. Although not complete when America entered World War II in 1941, the Naval Air Station evolved with the war. For over 50 years, it was a key player in Alameda's expansion of business, economy, and population.

Although businesses along the canal have dwindled since the early years of this century, and the Naval Air Station fell victim to downsizing in 1997, Alameda still thrives. These postcards help to document Alameda's fascinating history during its busiest era—small, personal souvenirs that, after all these years, ensure we never forget the origins of this place we call home.

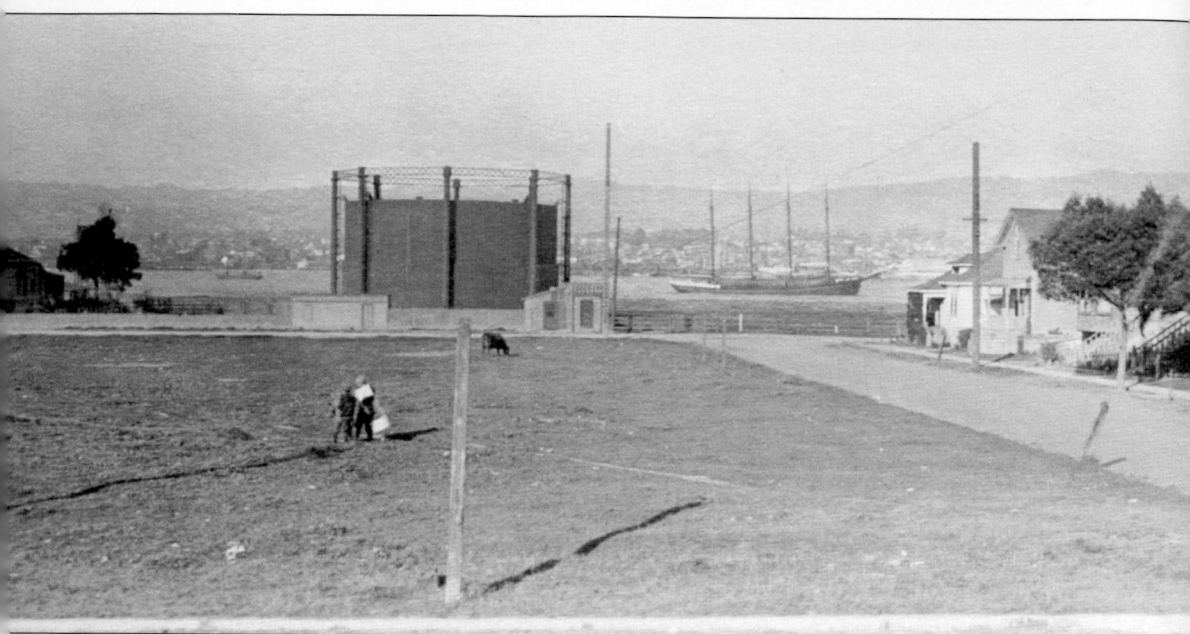

Dated October 8, 1912, this postcard shows three boys borrowing a cow's pasture to fly their box kite on a windy day. According to the message written on the back, this photograph was taken from the writer's front porch, and her son Robert was one of the boys pictured. Note the large sailing ship passing by on the estuary.

One

THE ESTUARY

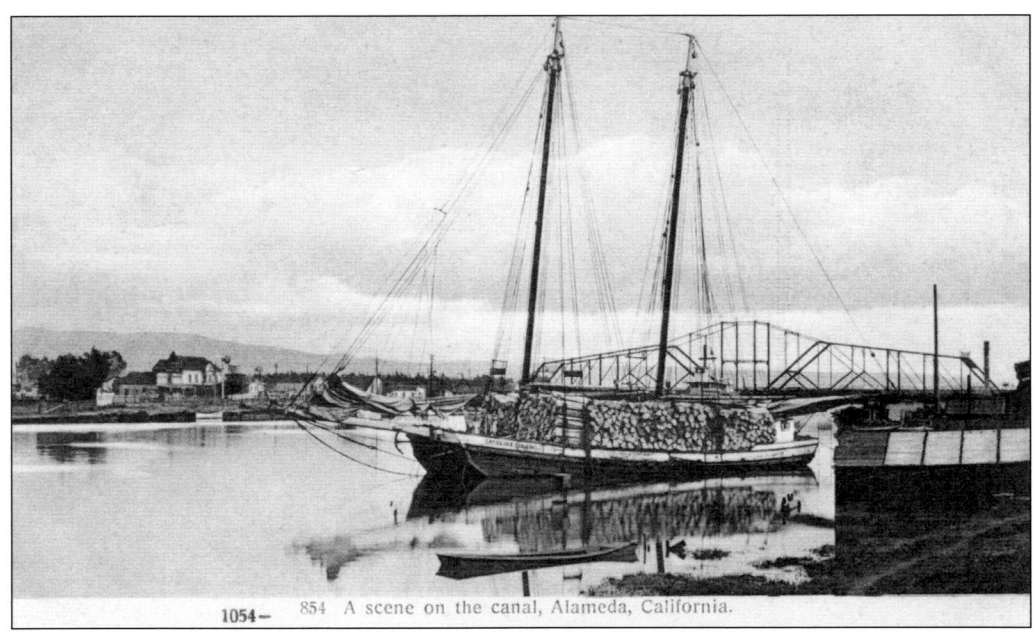

1054— 854 A scene on the canal, Alameda, California.

Water first flowed through the canal on August 7, 1902. The first craft to navigate the canal was a rowboat carrying three children. On the evening of September 15, 1902, an extravagant parade marched through the streets of Alameda, ultimately finding its way to the Park Street Bridge. An elaborate fireworks display was then held along the canal, and a carnival and celebration continued for two more days. At the end of the festivities, a procession of 200 decorated ships made its way down the canal, and more than 35,000 people watched and cheered. World hammer-throwing champion Tom Carroll entertained the crowds with an exhibition of his skill, which culminated with a hammer being thrown across the canal. Alameda was finally an island. (Published by Cardinell–Vincent Company, Oakland, c. 1907.)

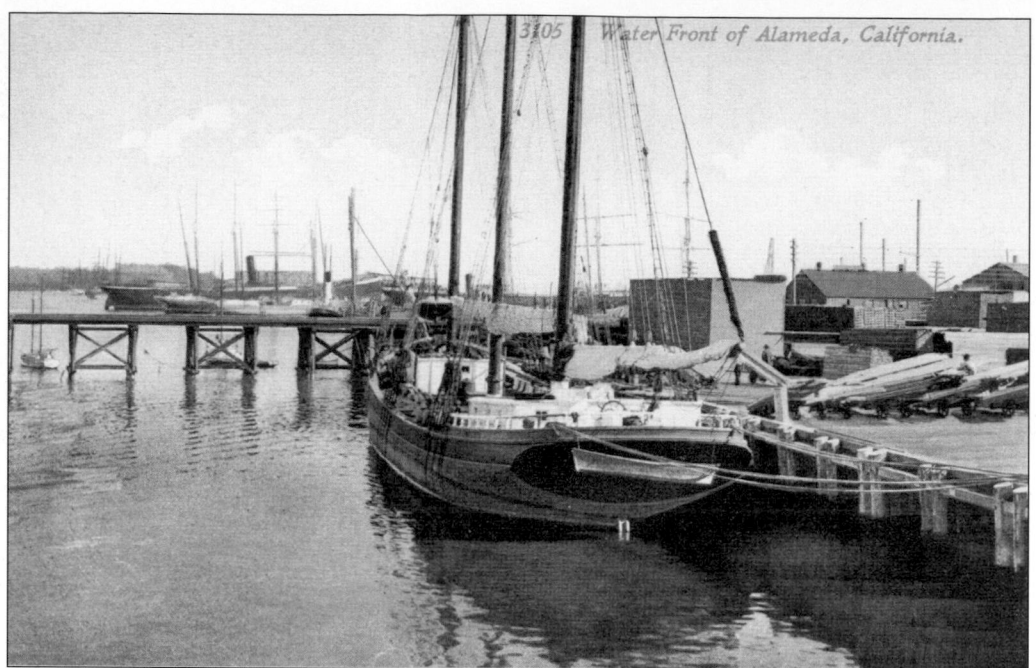

Before the canal was created, waters in the estuary were often low, and ships ran aground. Plans to create the waterway were formalized as early as 1873, yet due to legal and governmental problems, the project was not completely finished until the summer of 1902, nearly 30 years later. (Published by Edward H. Mitchell, San Francisco, *c.* 1912.)

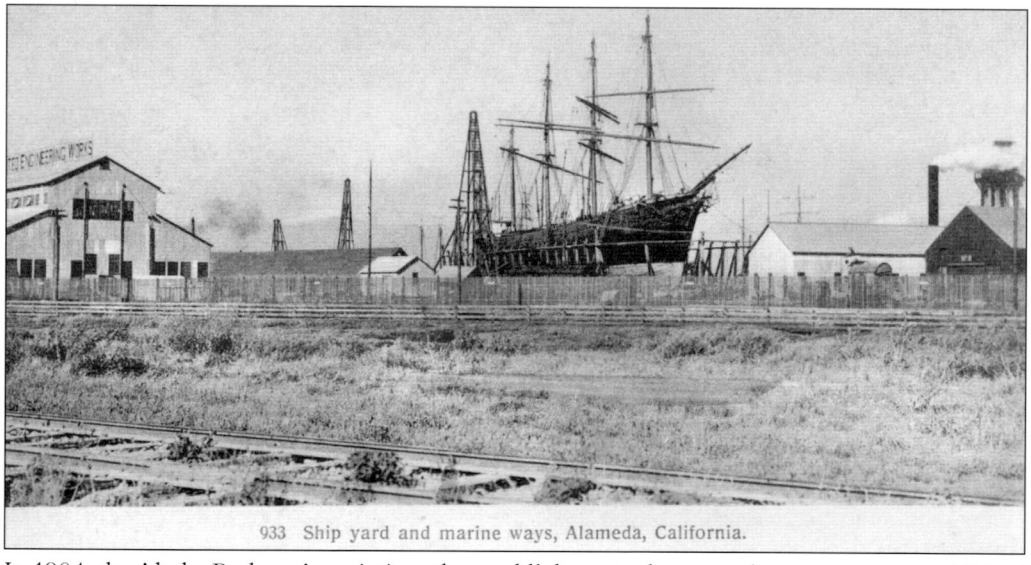

933 Ship yard and marine ways, Alameda, California.

In 1904, the Alaska Packers Association, the world's largest salmon-packing company, established its winter mooring basin and repair yard on the waterfront at Grand Street. A large sailing ship is seen in this *c.* 1912 postcard view of the now quite busy Alameda waterfront. Other business along the waterfront during that era included the Dow Pump Works, established 1905 at the foot of Oak Street, and the shipyards of the Atlantic, Gulf, and Pacific Company, which were established in 1906 at the foot of Walnut Street. (Published by Cardinell-Vincent Company, Oakland, *c. 1907.)*

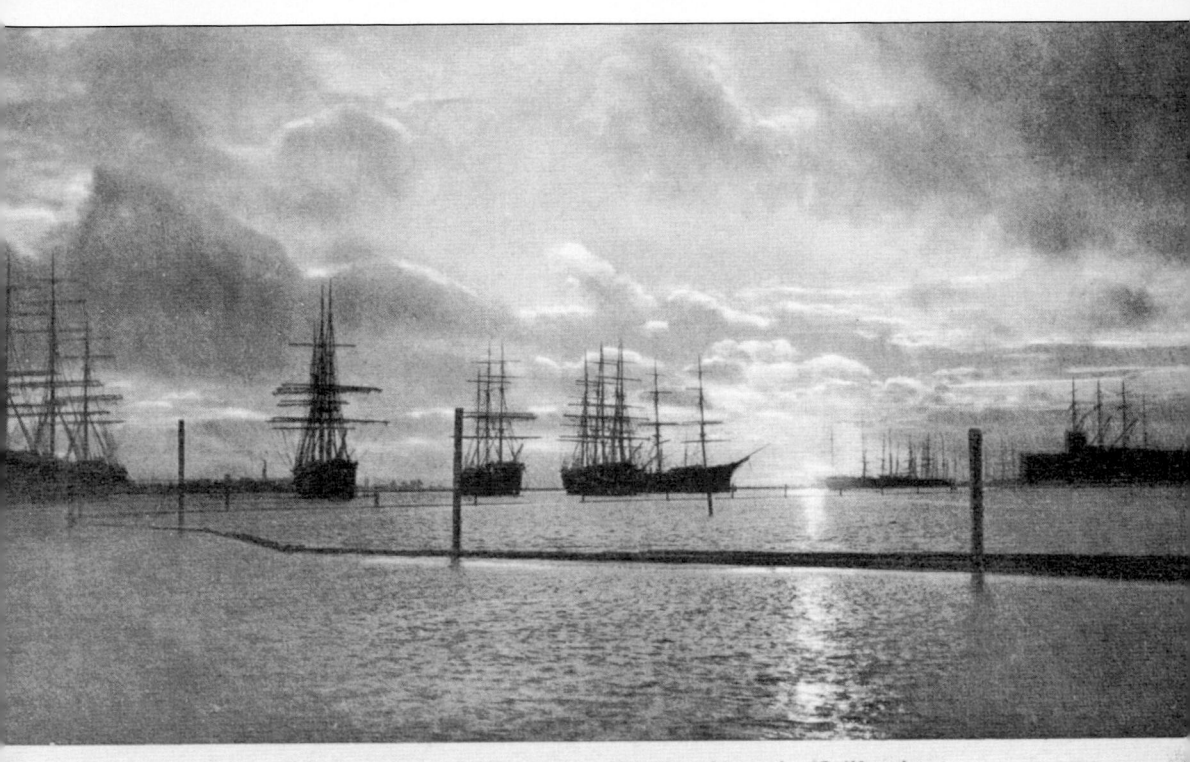

943 Evening scene on the Estuary, Alameda, California.

After 1902, industry boomed along the waterfront and continued to expand as a result of World War I. World War II, of course, brought even more business. This *c.* 1907 postcard shows the sun setting on the estuary, an analogy to the inevitable decline of business after the war was over. (Published by Cardinell-Vincent Company, Oakland.)

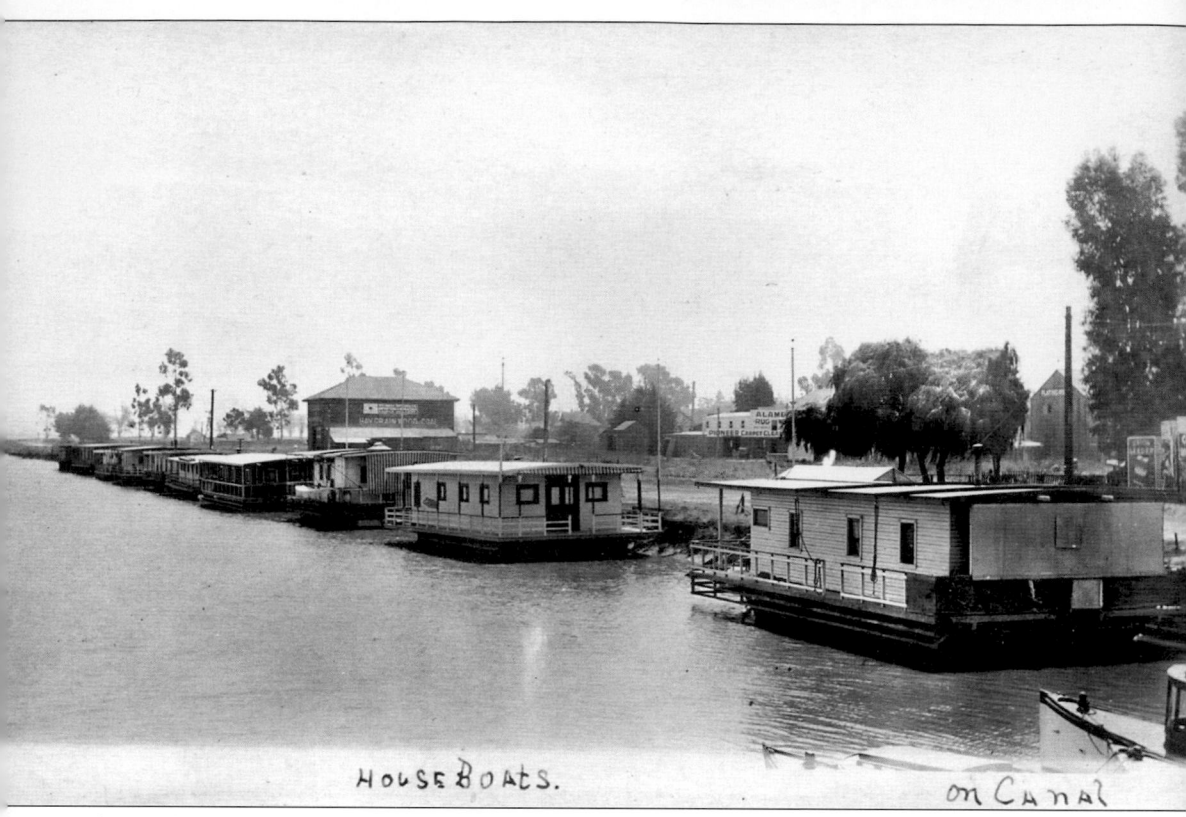

HOUSEBOATS.   on Canal

The tidal canal opened in 1902. The channel, which began at Oak Street, ran approximately southeast for 7,000 feet, making an open waterway from the harbor in Oakland to the San Leandro Bay. This photographic postcard shows a collection of houseboats on the estuary near the Park Street Bridge, *c.* 1906. The building on the left advertises hay, grain, wood, and coal for sale. Alameda Rug and Pioneer Carpet Cleaners are toward the right. Some of the houseboats were owned by residents, but rentals were common.

Two

COMMERCIAL DISTRICTS

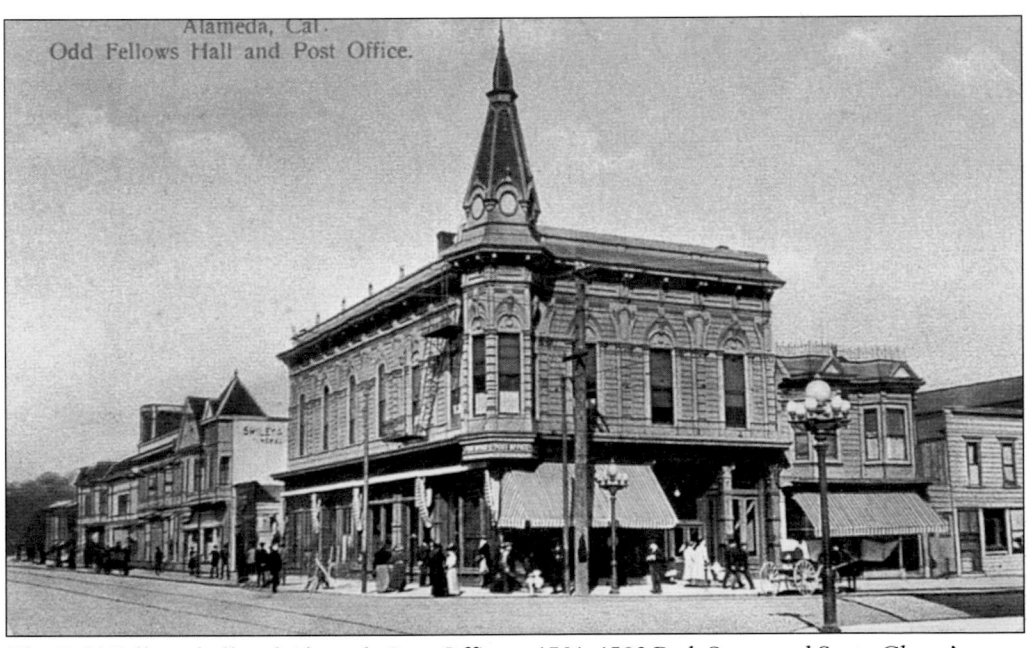

The Odd Fellows hall and Alameda Post Office at 1501–1503 Park Street and Santa Clara Avenue was designed by William Patton and built in 1878. In 1909, the postmaster was Theodore W. Leydecker. Bayfarm Island's Leydecker Park now carries his name. This Odd Fellows hall was demolished in 1926 and replaced with the present Jorgensen/Amandes-designed structure in 1927. (Published by Pacific Novelty Company, San Francisco.)

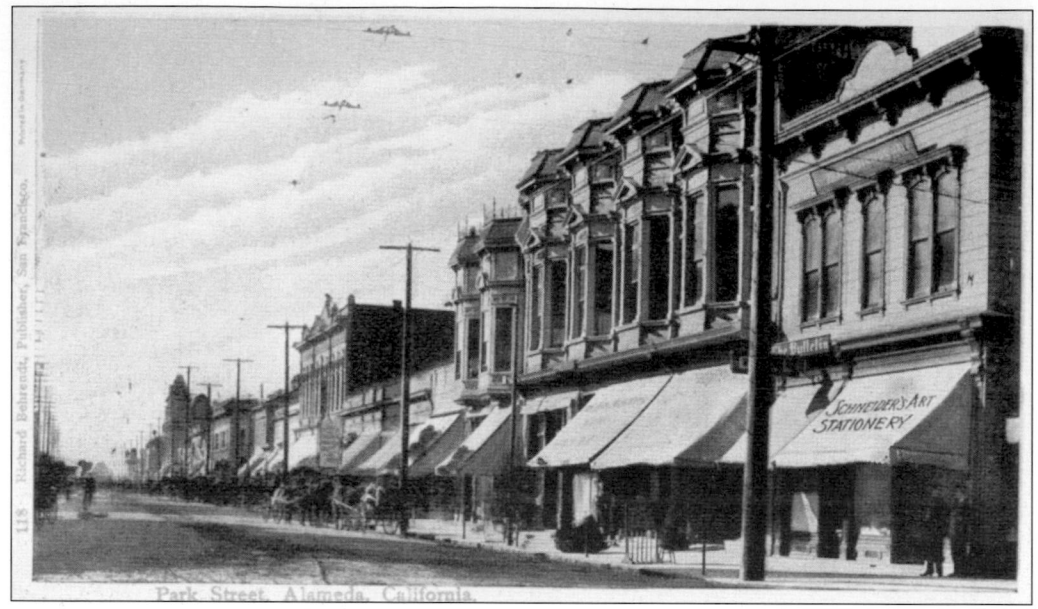

This *c.* 1908 image of the 1400 block of Park Street just past Santa Clara Avenue heading southwest, shows the Bulletin building on the right and Schneider's stationery store at 1435 Park. Proprietor Henry Schneider lived on the island as well, at 2310 Central Avenue. (Published by Richard Behrendt, San Francisco.)

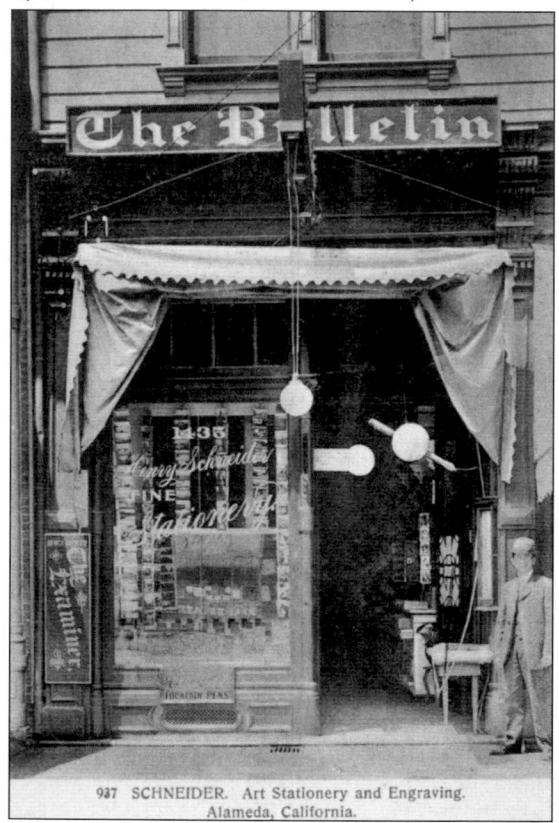

937 SCHNEIDER. Art Stationery and Engraving. Alameda, California.

The man on the right in this *c.* 1908 picture of Schneider Art Stationery and Engraving at 1435 Park Street is most likely the proprietor, Henry Schneider. The front window displays a selection of postcards, some of which probably appear in this book. The building that housed this store was constructed in 1873. (Published by the Cardinell-Vincent Company, Oakland.)

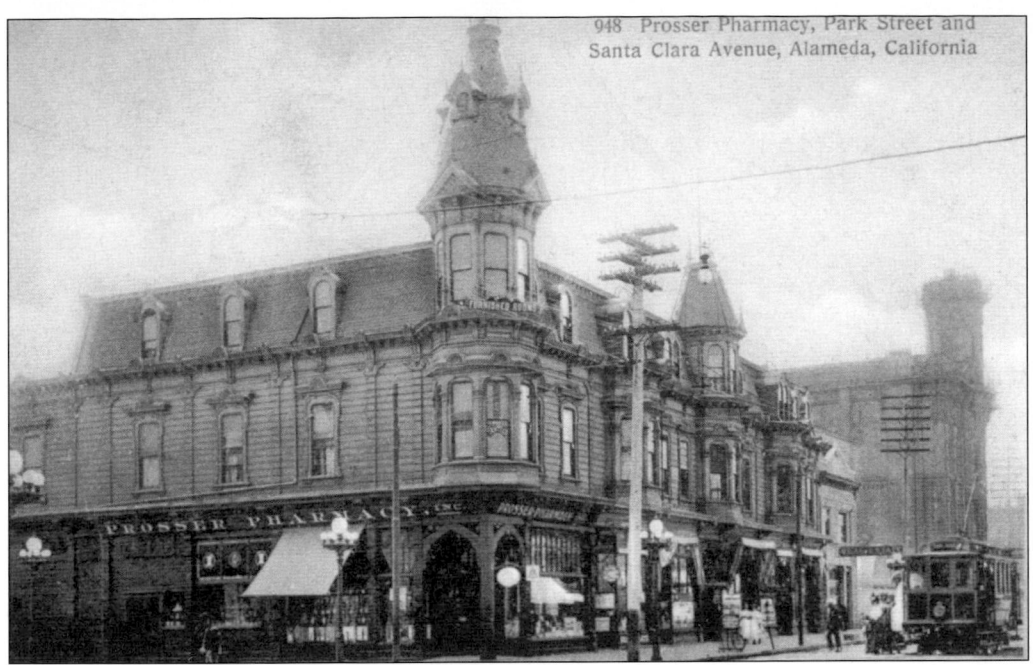

948 Prosser Pharmacy, Park Street and
Santa Clara Avenue, Alameda, California

The Prosser Pharmacy building at Park Street and Santa Clara Avenue heading southwest and shown here *c.* 1907, was also known as the Tucker Building. Named for original owner Dr. Joseph Tucker, it was designed by local architects Sherwin and MacKenzie and built in 1879. It contained retail space at street level, offices on the second floor, and furnished rooms for rent on the third floor. In 1933, the building was remodeled in the Streamline Moderne style, designed by H. A. Minturn, and exists as a restaurant today. (Published by the Cardinell-Vincent Company, Oakland.)

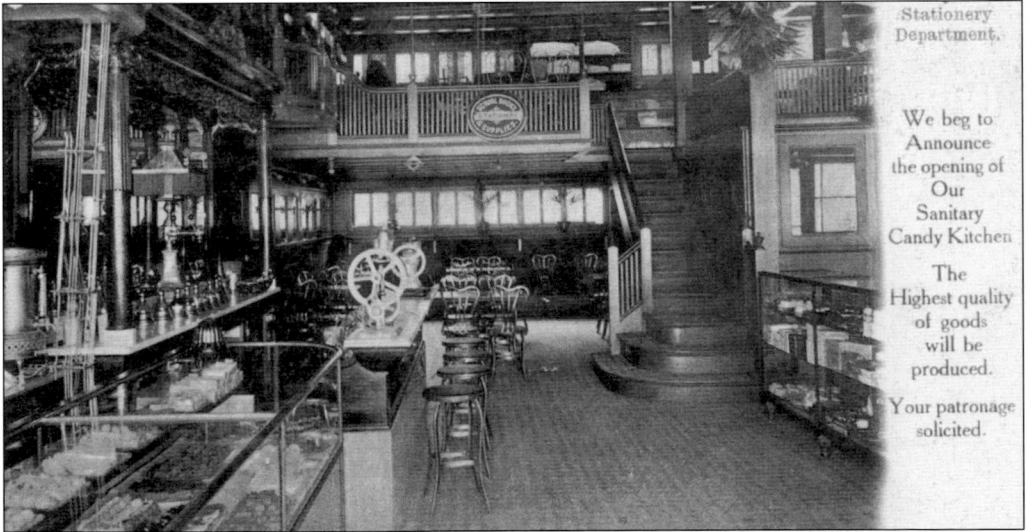

Stationery Department.

We beg to Announce the opening of Our Sanitary Candy Kitchen

The Highest quality of goods will be produced.

Your patronage solicited.

This interior view of the candy, ice cream, and stationery department of the Prosser Pharmacy was taken *c.* 1905. To advertise a new venture, the card states: "We beg to announce the opening of our sanitary candy kitchen. The highest quality of goods will be produced. Your patronage solicited." In this rare image, the glass display cases hold a variety of candies, and a sign on the upper-floor railing announces the availability of stationery, schoolbooks, and supplies.

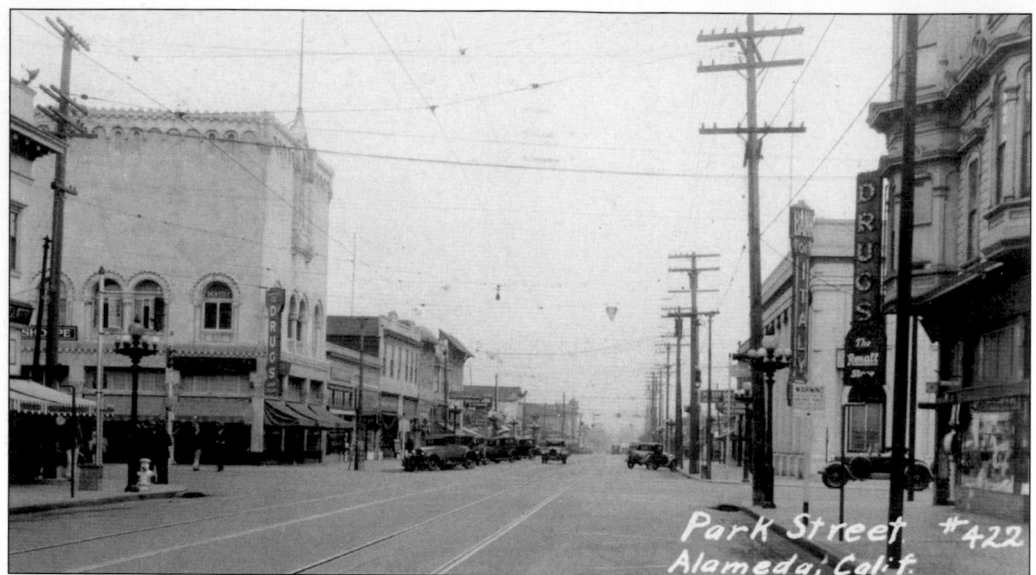

This 1928 photographic postcard view is of Park Street at Santa Clara Avenue, facing northeast. Past the Rexall drugstore on the right is 1500 Park, the Bank of Italy. Originally the Citizens Bank of Alameda, it was designed by architects Oliver and Foulkes in 1906 and enlarged in 1923–1924.

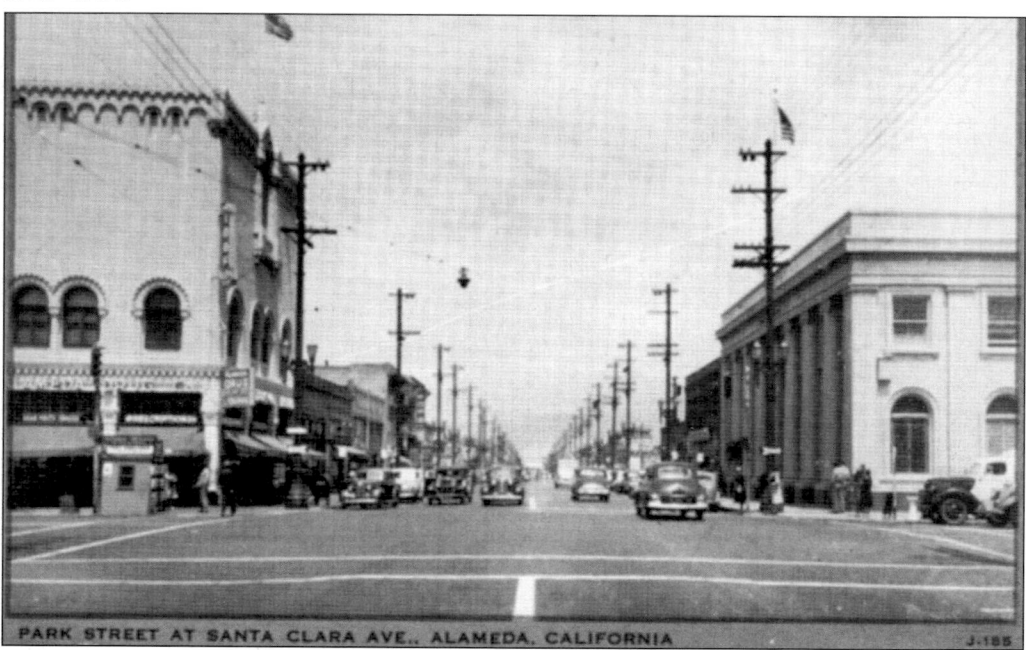

The intersection of Park Street at Santa Clara Avenue, looking toward Oakland, is seen in this *c.* 1950 view. On the left is 1501 Park, designed by Mark T. Jorgensen and F. F. Amandes of San Francisco to house the Odd Fellows Encinal Lodge No. 164 and dedicated on December 9, 1927. Lodge rooms were located upstairs, and a banquet hall occupied the basement. The ground floor was leased for retail. Unfortunately the exotic decoration has been stripped from the outside of the building. (Manufactured by Wayne Paper Box and Printing Corporation, Fort Wayne, Indiana.)

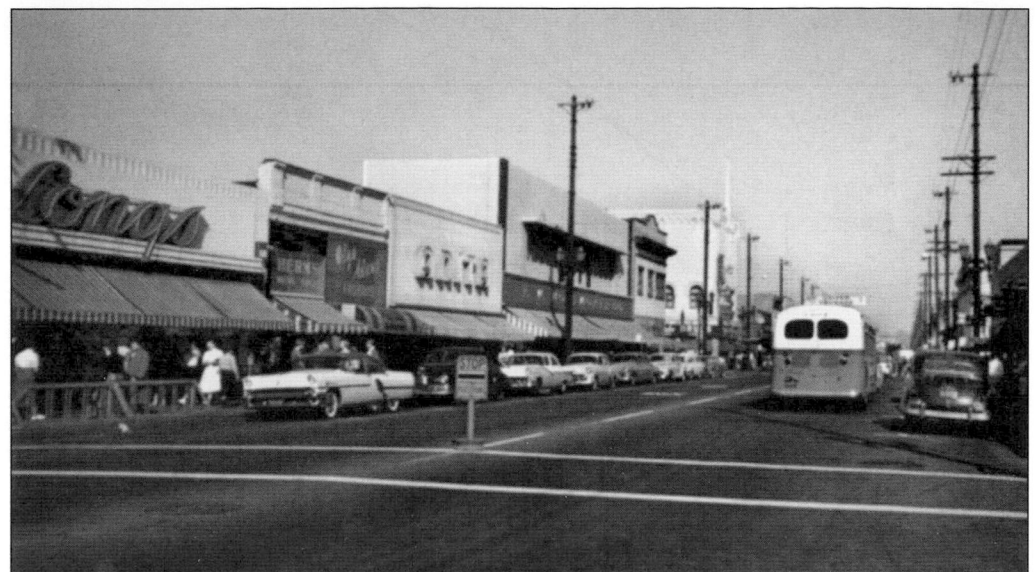

A 1950s postcard provides a view of Park Street, heading northeast. Customers had many drugstores to choose from in this busy shopping district, including Longs, J. J. Newberry, Alameda Drug Company, and more. The brief caption on the back of the postcard describes it as "a popular shopping section in this city of homes." (Published by E. F. Clements, San Francisco.)

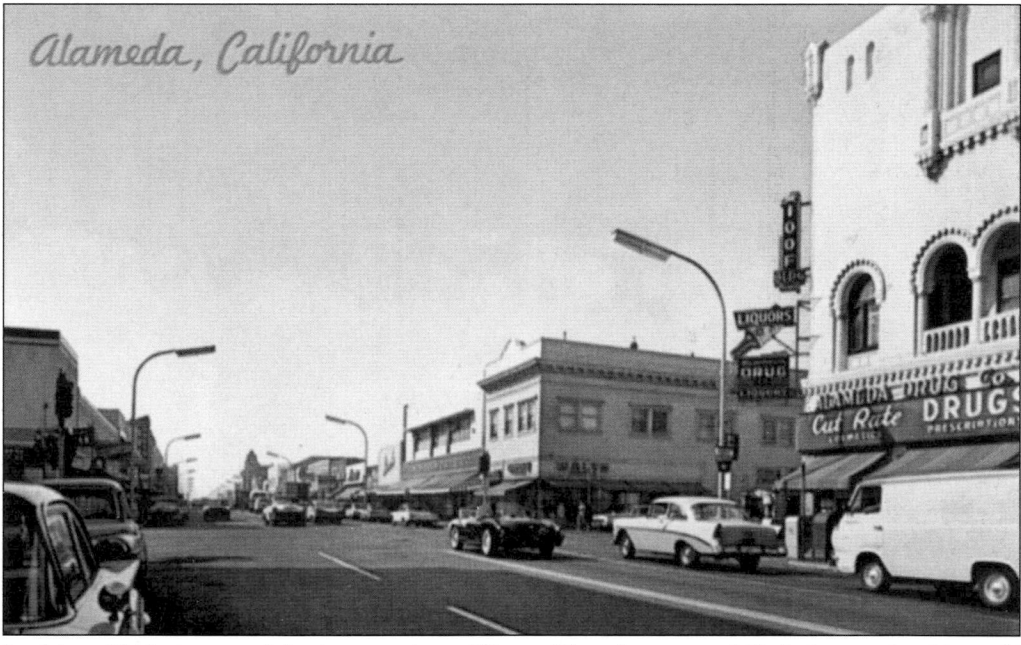

In this *c.* 1963 picture of the intersection of Santa Clara Avenue and Park Street, the Alameda Drug Company can be seen at the right. Notice the wonderful neon signs attached to the corner of the building. Sadly they are now long gone. Just beyond, at 1435–1437 Park Street, is one of the oldest surviving commercial buildings in Alameda, constructed in 1876 and remodeled in 1909. Originally owned by Adolph Schroeder, who dealt in hay, grain, and coal, it first housed a grocery and hardware store and a public meeting hall upstairs. After the 1909 changes, the upper floor was used for medical offices. (Published by Smith News Company, San Francisco.)

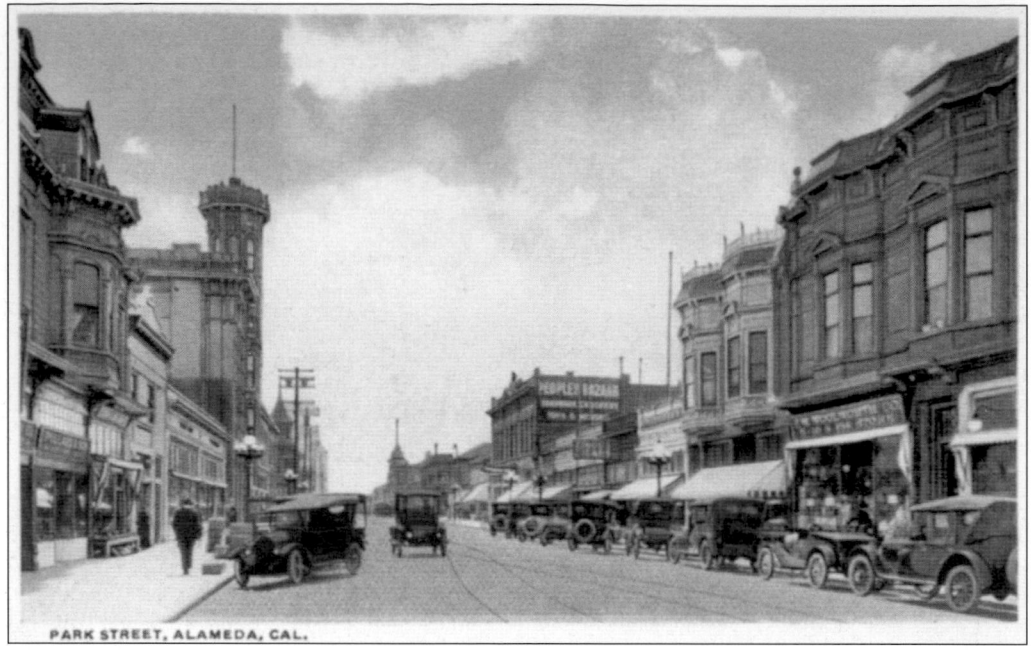

PARK STREET, ALAMEDA, CAL.

This *c.* 1922 view shows numerous autos on the 1400 block of Park Street between Santa Clara Avenue and Central Avenue. Woolworth's, the People's Bazaar, Pollard and Sons, Zingg's Cigars, and others served local residents' shopping needs. The tall building on the left with the tower is the Artesian Water Works. (Published by C. T. American Art.)

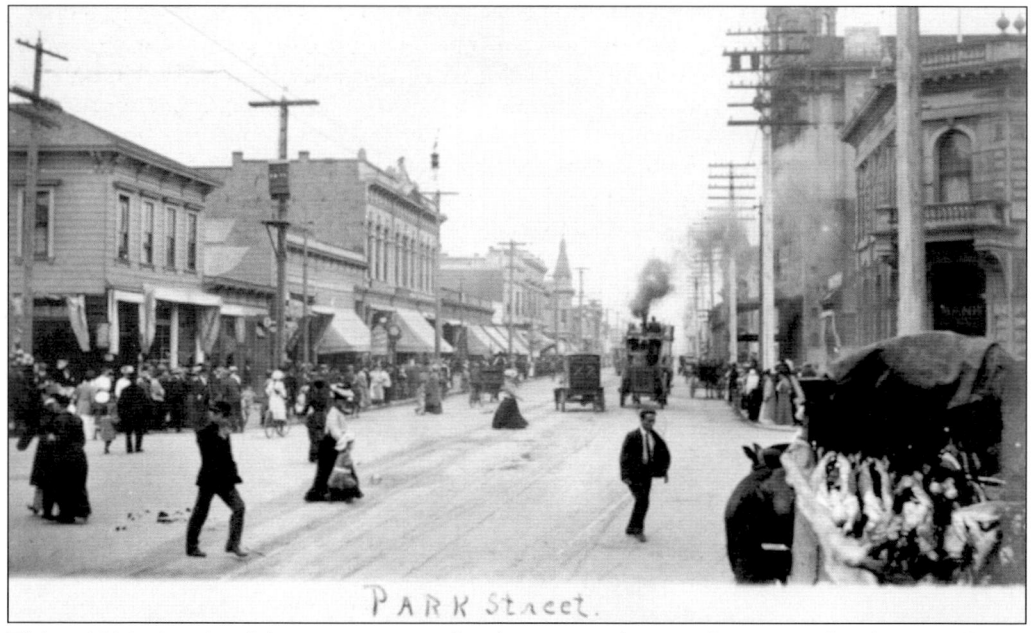

PARK Street.

This *c.* 1906 view is of the intersection of Park Street and Central Avenue, heading northeast. On the right is the First National Bank, designed by San Francisco architect and Alameda resident William Patton, and built in 1887, with the second story being added in 1902. This photographic postcard shows a busy commercial district, with various forms of transportation, including horse-drawn wagons and buggies, early automobiles, and bicycles.

18

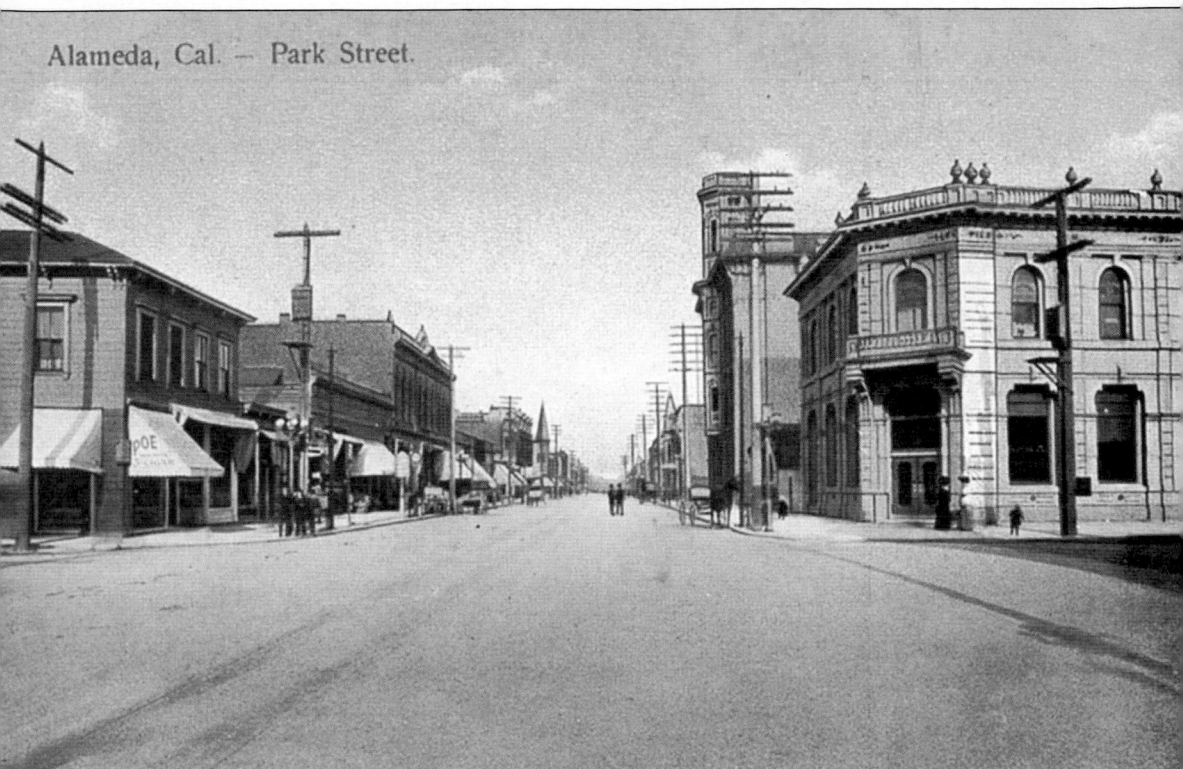

Alameda, Cal. — Park Street.

Postmarked in 1911, this view is of the expansive intersection of Central Avenue and Park Street. On the right is the First National Bank building, which was designed by William Patton and constructed in 1887, with a B. E. Remmel-designed second level added in 1902. The building underwent further reconstruction in 1910–1911. On the left is an Italianate structure at 1401 Park Street, built in 1875 for Fritz Boehmer, a local merchant and developer. Both of these buildings are still standing, but with major cosmetic changes to the exteriors. (Published by Pacific Novelty Company, San Francisco.)

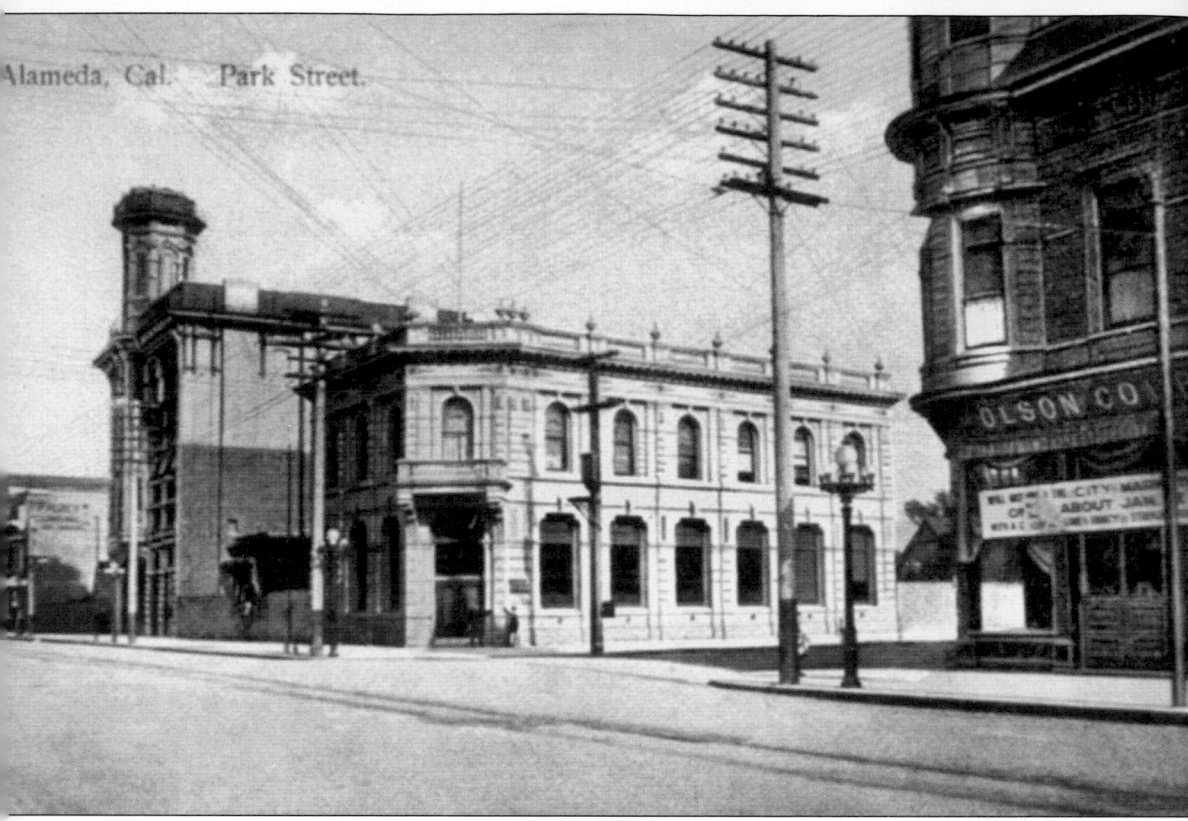

Alameda, Cal. Park Street.

Pictured on the right is the First National Bank building at Park Street and Central Avenue, and next to it on the left is the Artesian Water Works building. Designed by William Patton and completed in 1881, it housed the water works's offices, while on the top floor, a massive reservoir held water for dousing any fires in the immediate area. When it was demolished in 1955, a copper box was discovered sealed in the cornerstone. Among the artifacts within were a *San Francisco Chronicle* newspaper dated July 3, 1880, various fraternal lodge books and member lists from 1877–1879, a copy of the Declaration of Independence, copies of Alameda newspapers (the *Argus* and *Encinal*), 11 coins, and a few grains of wheat. The Queen Anne building on the far right was also designed by William Patton and built in 1890. Owner Fritz Boehmer, a German immigrant, developed the property, which was Alameda's main post office until 1900 and was referred to as the Post Office Block. Also occupying space in the block was the office of noted builder and developer Joseph A. Leonard. In 1894, the structure was purchased by Elma C. Farnham; subsequently, the name was changed to the Farnham Block. F. N. Delanoy's Commercial National Bank moved into the building in 1922 and commissioned a remodeling. In 1938, the building underwent a dramatic makeover designed by architect William E. Schirmer and was reborn as the Streamline Moderne beauty that remains to this day. (Published by Pacific Novelty Company, San Francisco.)

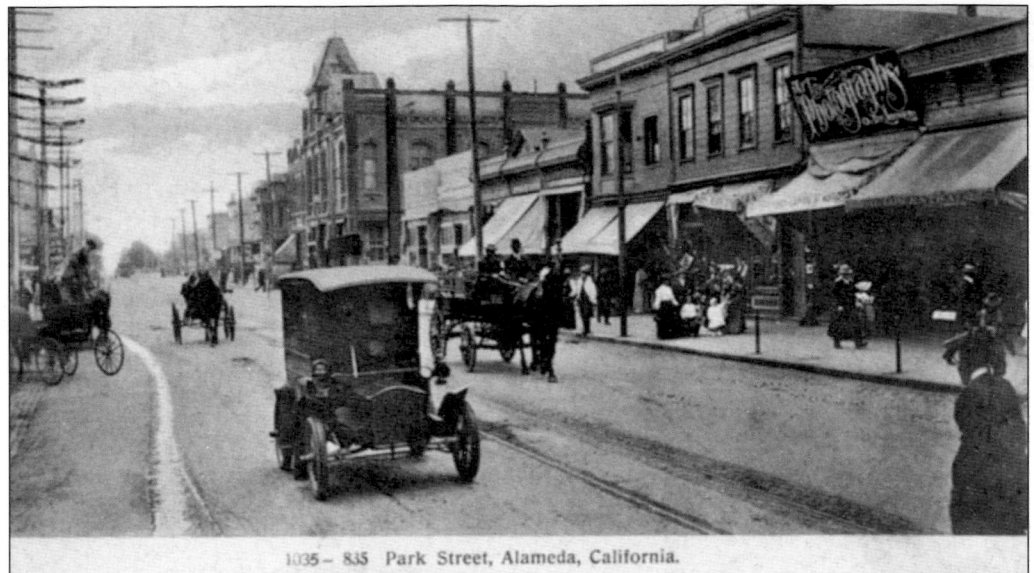

1035 – 835 Park Street, Alameda, California.

An automobile shares the street with horses and buggies in this *c.* 1906 image of Park Street, taken from Central Avenue. On the right is O. DeJoiner Art Photographs, located at 1351 Park Street and owned by Oscar DeJoiner. The awning over his storefront advertises "Postcards and Novelties," and it is possible that he made some of the photographic postcards in this book. (Published by the Cardinell-Vincent Company, Oakland.)

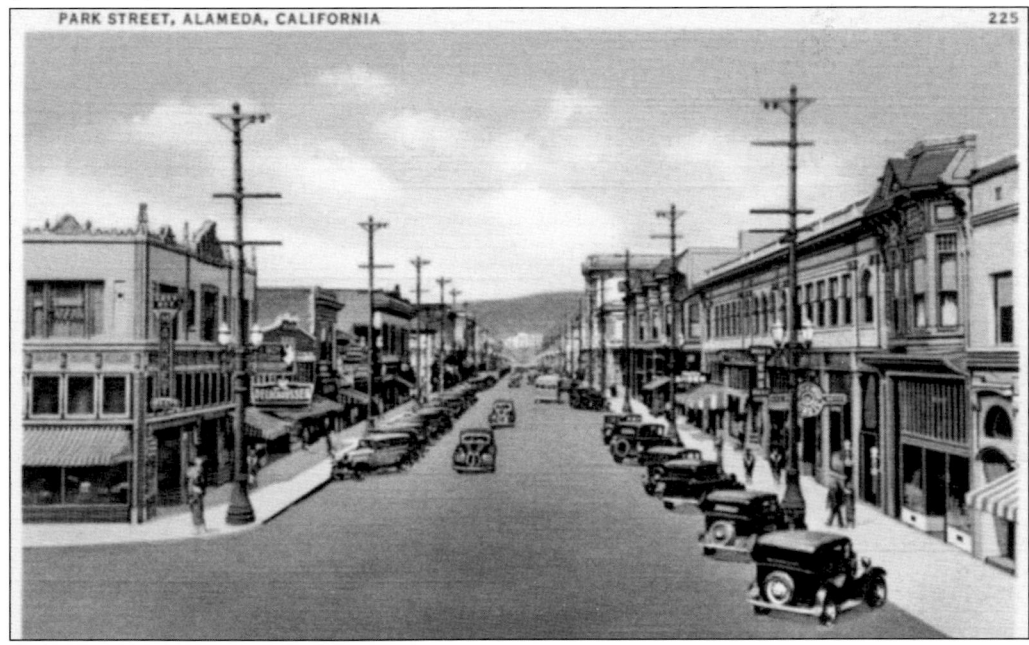

PARK STREET, ALAMEDA, CALIFORNIA   225

This 1935 chamber of commerce postcard shows the intersection of Alameda Avenue on the left and Park Street. The Busy Bee Market on the left was operated by James Fong, Chester Look, and Louie Wong and was located in the Kaliski Building, which still stands today. Also known as the Beverly Apartments or Marti-Rae Apartments, this gorgeous combination of residential and retail space was designed by Alexander A. Cantin and built by Conrad Roth in 1925. (Published by Stanley A. Piltz Company, San Francisco.)

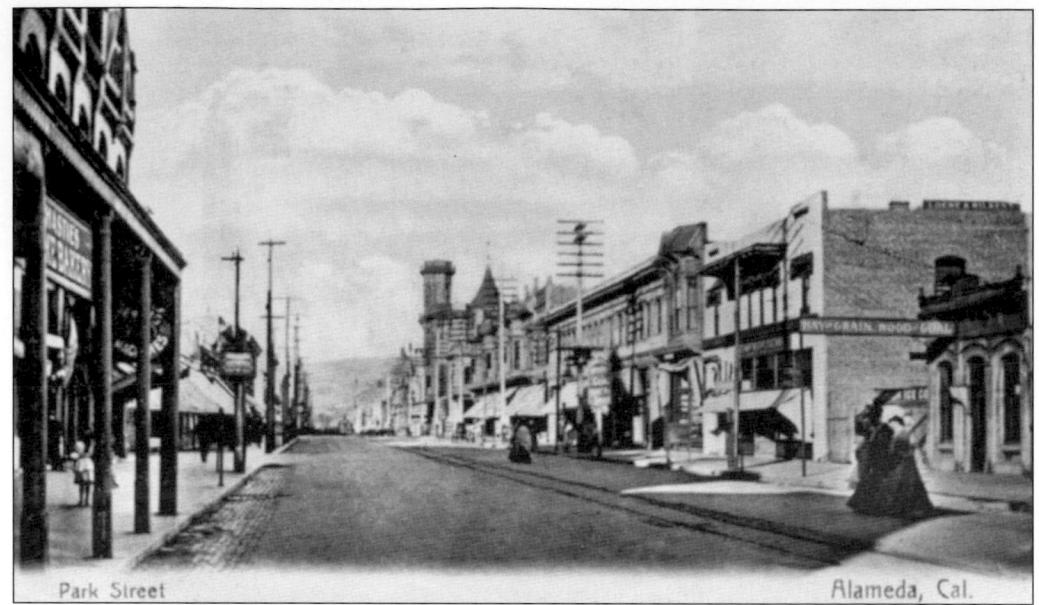

Park Street · Alameda, Cal.

The Oakland hills are visible in the background of this *c.* 1908 image of the 1300 block of Park Street, facing northeast. Businesses on this block included a bakery, an ice company, a hay and grain store, and a sewing machine store. The second store on the right at 1330 Park was designed by architects Cunningham and Politeo for original owner Arnold Postel in 1905. (Published by Cook and Cook, Oakland.)

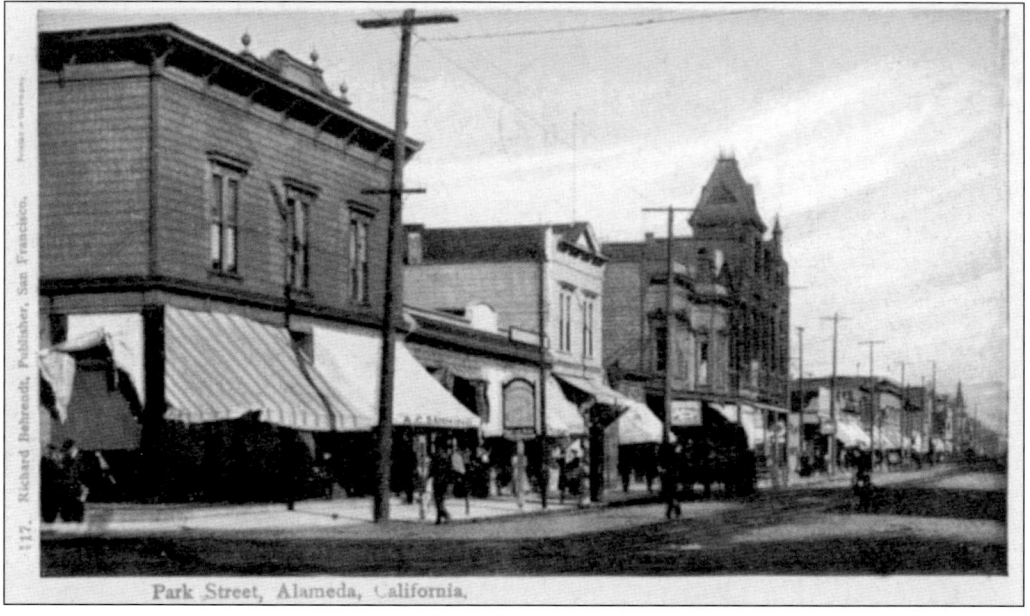

Park Street, Alameda, California.

A view of Park Street, taken from Encinal Avenue, looks toward the intersection of Alameda Avenue on the left. The tallest building visible is the Masonic temple, designed by architect Charles Mau of Oakland, which was completed in 1891. It is still standing today, as is the Italianate structure on the immediate left, which was built in 1877 as Hans Nelson's saloon. To date, it continues to operate as a popular bar, albeit under different ownership. (Published by Richard Behrendt, San Francisco.)

22

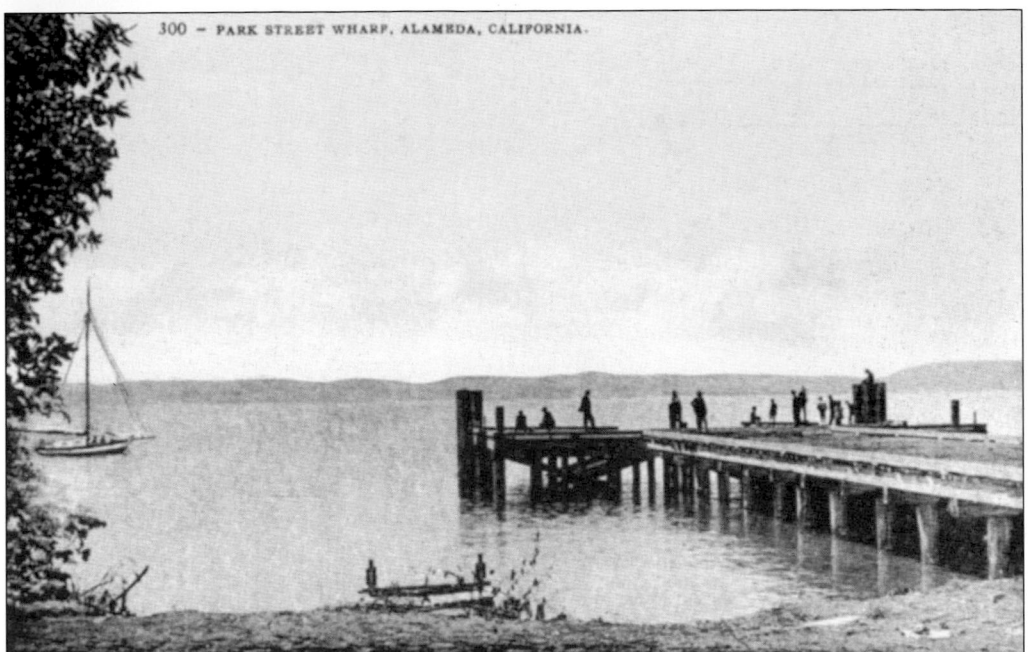

In 1874, Park Street was widened and sidewalks were added from Central Avenue to the bay shore. The Park Street wharf was most likely built in the 1880s to coincide with the construction of the Municipal Electric Light Plant, located at the end of Park Street. (Published by Edward H. Mitchell, San Francisco.)

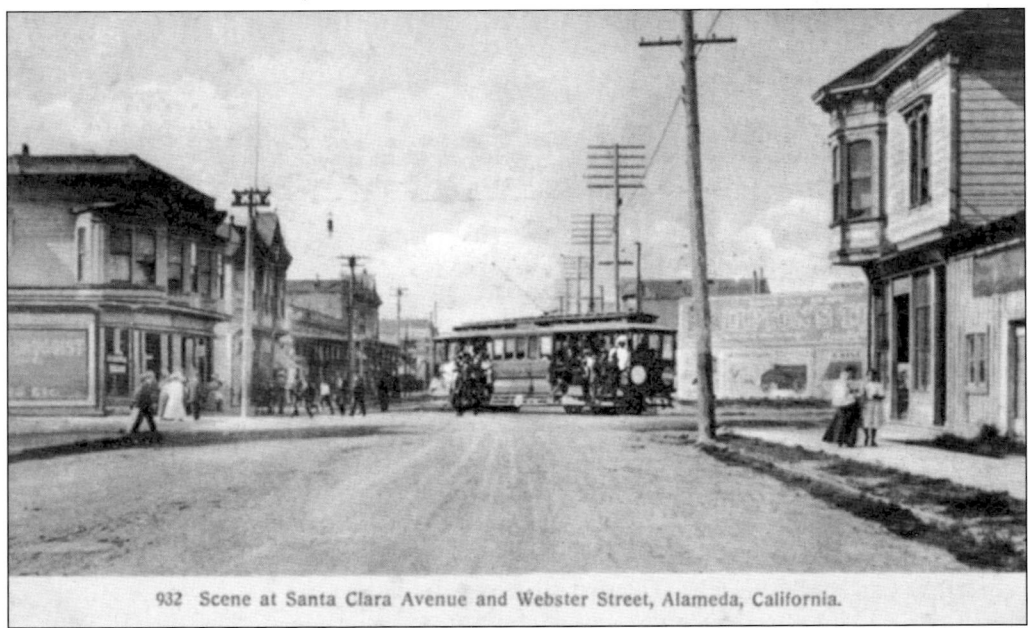

Webster Street was first paved in 1872. This postcard shows the intersection of Webster Street and Santa Clara Avenue, facing Oakland. Postmarked in February 1908, and sent to Honolulu, Hawaii, the young writer says in reference to the trolley, "This is the car we take to go to Oakland. It's cold up here, but we like it." The buildings pictured on the corners no longer exist. (Published by the Cardinell-Vincent Company, Oakland.)

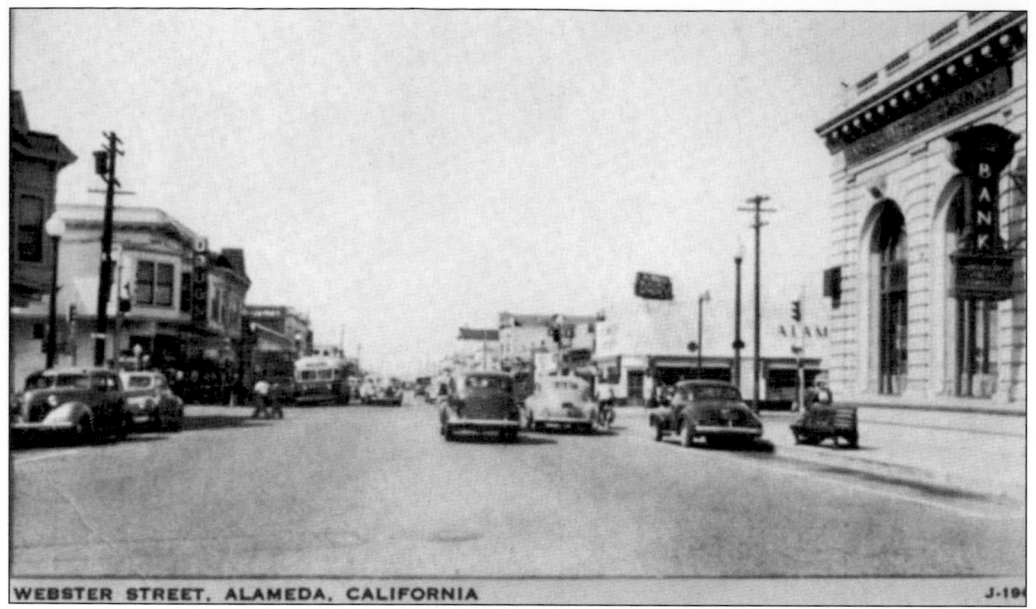

WEBSTER STREET, ALAMEDA, CALIFORNIA   J-19

This is the intersection of Webster Street and Santa Clara Avenue, with the Oakland hills in the distance, *c.* 1946. The American Trust Company on the right was built as the Alameda Savings Bank in 1917 and was designed by Edward T. Foulkes. The Alameda Dairy on the corner was originally a retail store that processed and sold milk and Better-Maid brand ice cream. Built in 1916 and designed by leading local architect A. W. Pattiani, the building was remodeled in the Streamline Moderne style by the Bay Area architectural firm of Bliss and Fairweather in 1940. Since 1970, it has been occupied by Tillie's Diner. (Published by Wayne Paper Box and Printing Corporation, Fort Wayne, Indiana.)

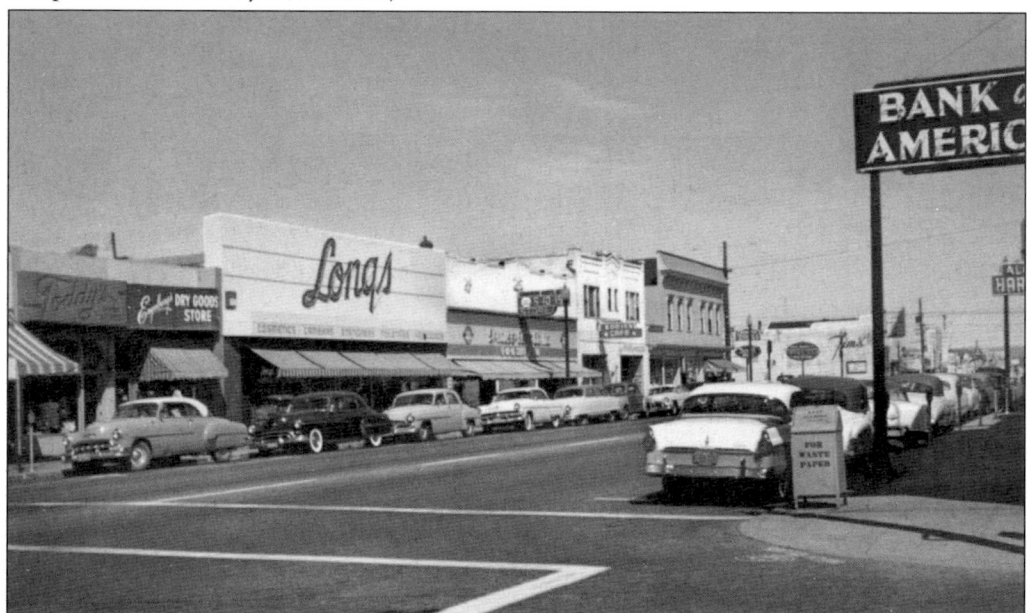

This 1950s postcard view of Webster Street was taken from the corner of Haight Avenue and Webster, heading toward Oakland. A Longs drugstore, 5-10-15¢ store, and Eddie's Cafe decorate the area with colorful neon signs. (Published by E. F. Clements, San Francisco.)

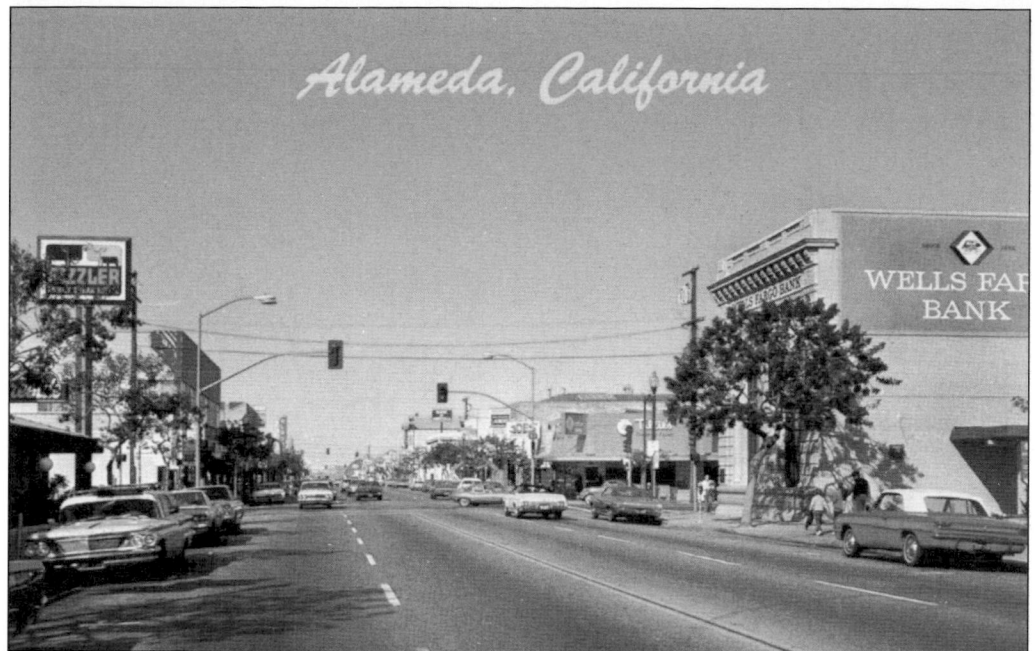

The intersection of Webster Street and Santa Clara Avenue, with the Oakland hills in the distance, is shown here in the early 1970s. The 1917 Edward T. Foulkes-designed bank on the right is one of the many structures he created in the area, including Alameda Hospital and the *Oakland Tribune* building. Tillie's Diner, just beyond, continues its tradition of friendly service and good food. (Published by R. and C. Hakanson, San Pablo.)

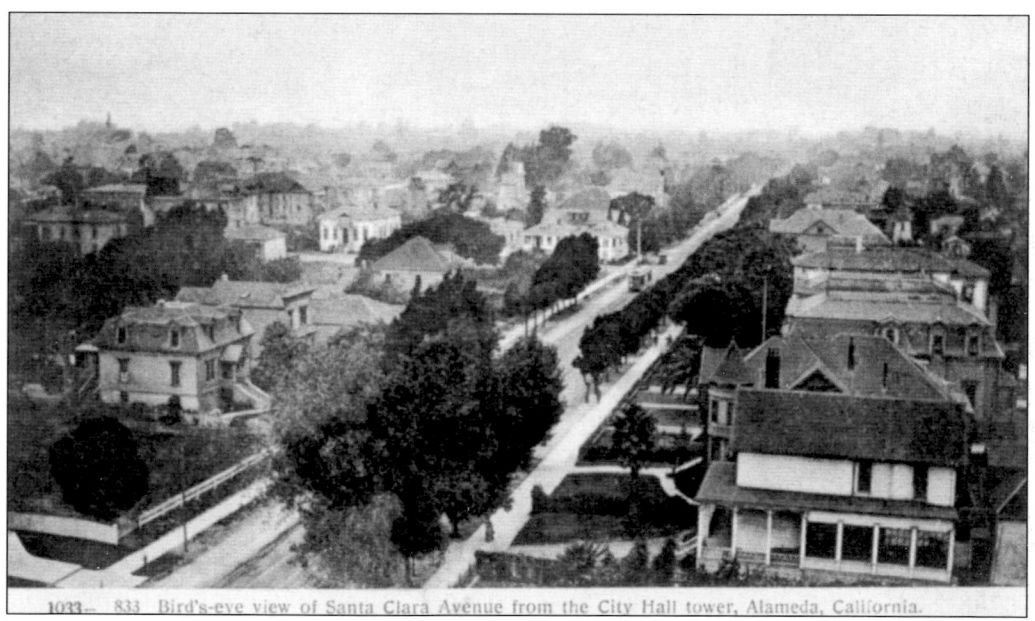

This *c.* 1907 view looks down Santa Clara Avenue to a residential district toward Grand Street. Note the trolley heading southeast toward Park Street. (Published by Cardinell-Vincent Company, Oakland.)

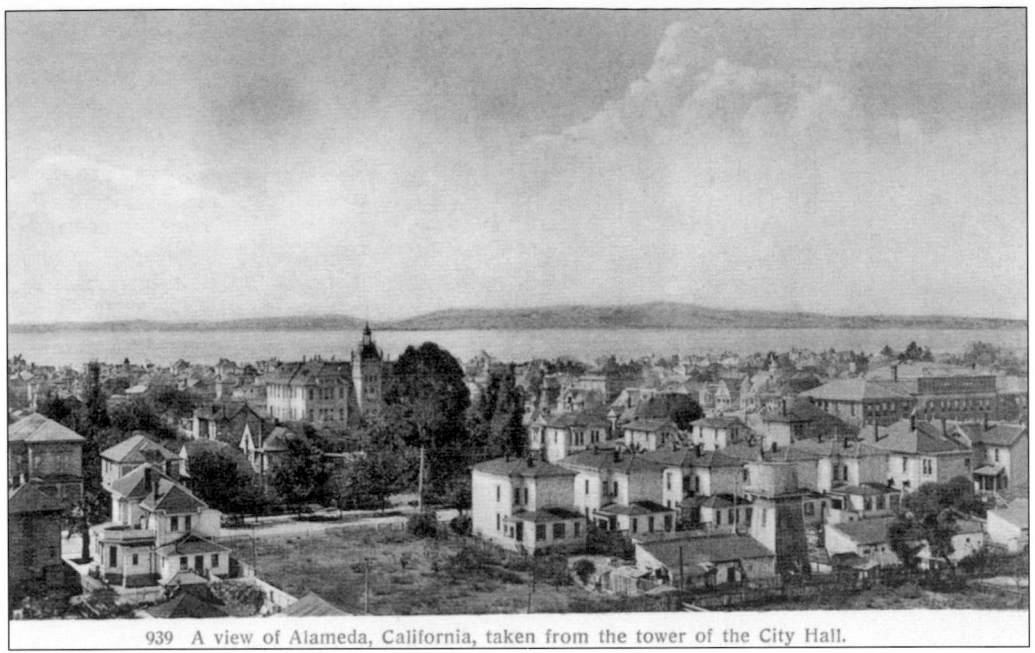

939 A view of Alameda, California, taken from the tower of the City Hall.

This bird's-eye view looks over Central Avenue northwest toward the peninsula beyond the bay. (Published by the Cardinell-Vincent Company, Oakland.)

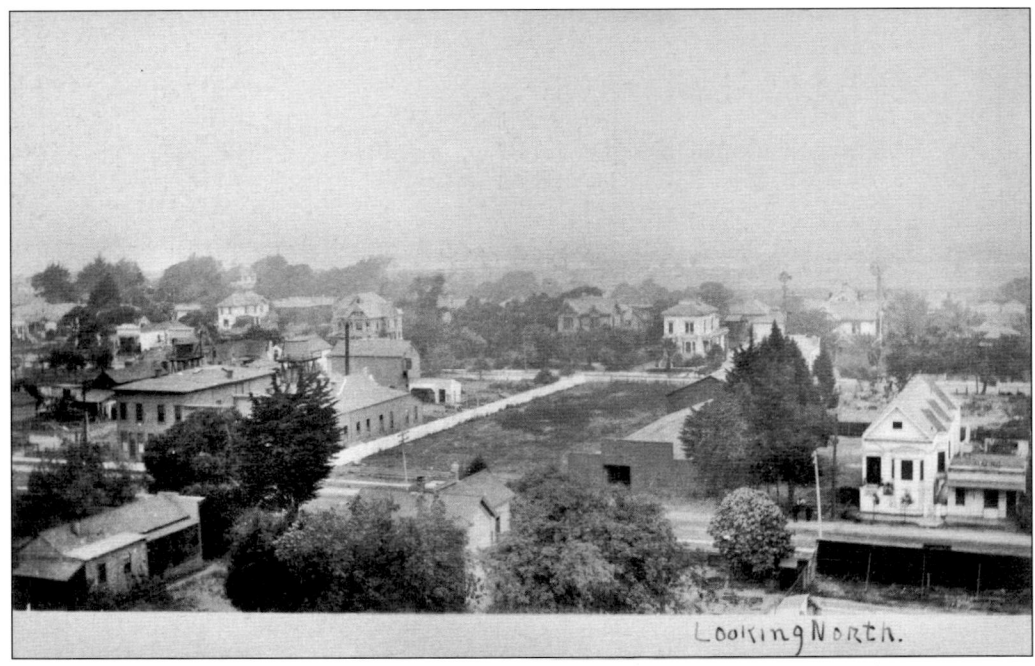

Looking North.

Here is a *c.* 1906 image taken from city hall, looking over Lincoln Avenue near the intersection of Oak Street. The house in the lower right corner is 2261 Lincoln, built in 1905 and designed by architects Martin and Coffey. The house still stands, although the glazing shop next to it is now gone.

Three

PUBLIC BUILDINGS

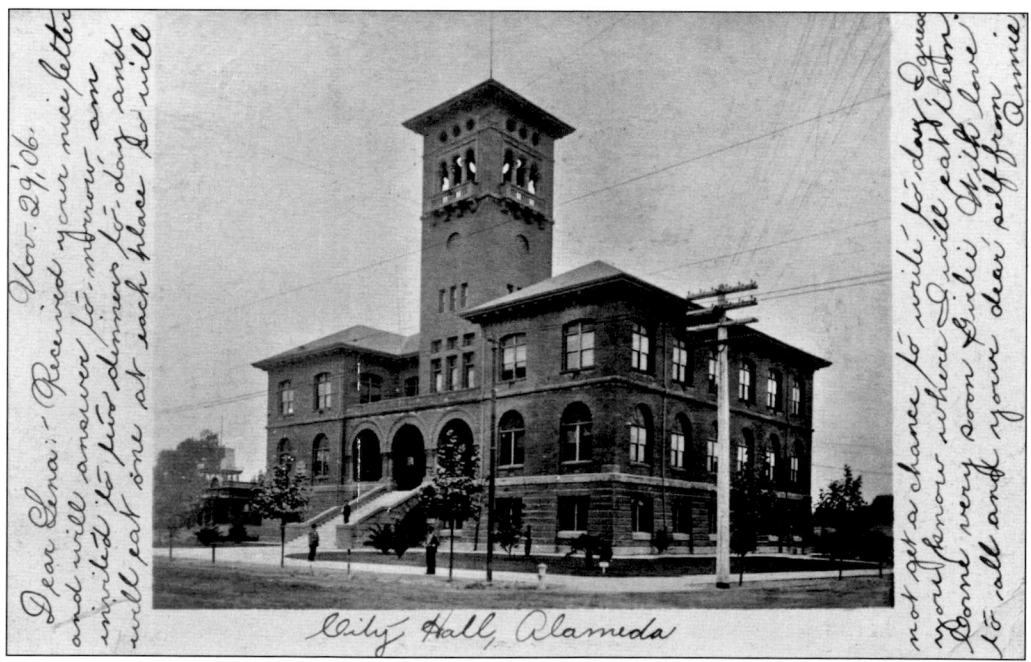

Alameda City Hall, located at Santa Clara Avenue and Oak Street, was designed in the Italian Villa style by Percy and Hamilton and built by Thomas Day and Sons in 1895. In this photographic postcard from 1906, the majestic red brick structure is framed by young trees, as well as the sender's written plans for Thanksgiving.

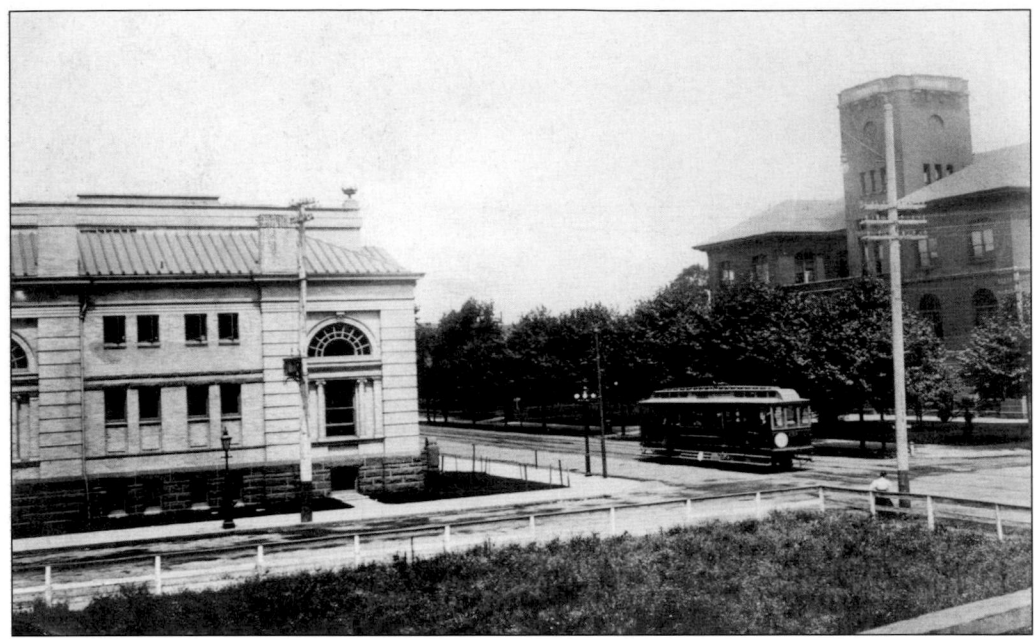

The Carnegie Library is on the left and city hall is on the right at this intersection of Santa Clara and Oak Street. Mailed in 1907, this photographic postcard shows that the tower of the city hall has been shortened due to damage from the 1906 earthquake. The fenced field in the foreground is now a drugstore parking lot.

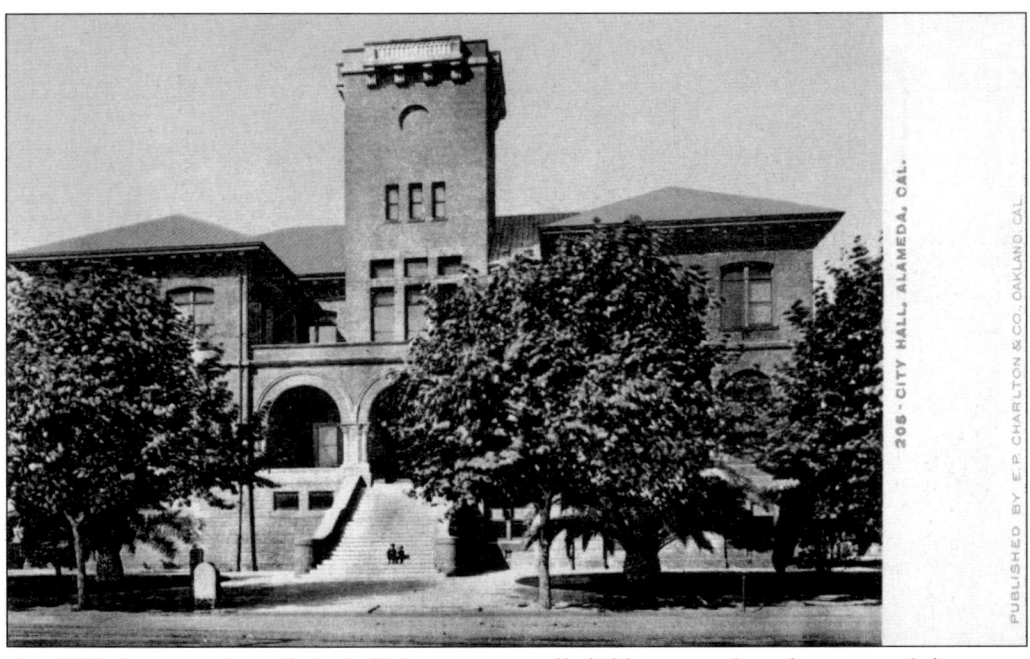

A *c.* 1908 close-up view of city hall shows two small children seated on the steps and the once-small trees flourishing. (Published by E. P. Charleton and Company, Oakland.)

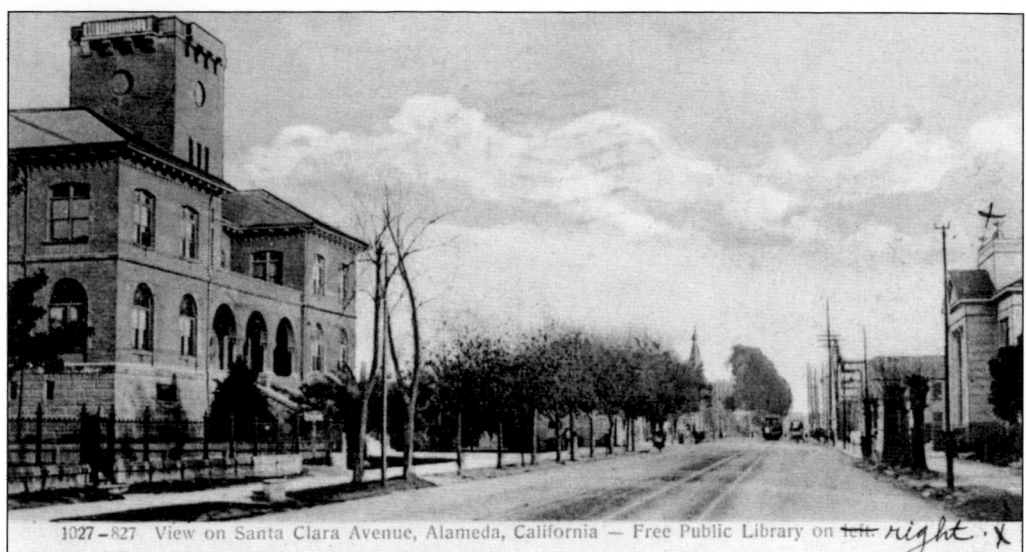

1027—827 View on Santa Clara Avenue, Alameda, California — Free Public Library on ~~left~~ *right* · ✗

This view, looking southeast on Santa Clara Avenue toward Oak Street, shows Park Street beyond. On the left is city hall, and on the right (despite what is printed on the card, which was corrected by the sender) is the Carnegie Library. In the distance on the left is the steeple of the Odd Fellows hall and post office. (Published by the Cardinell-Vincent Company, Oakland.)

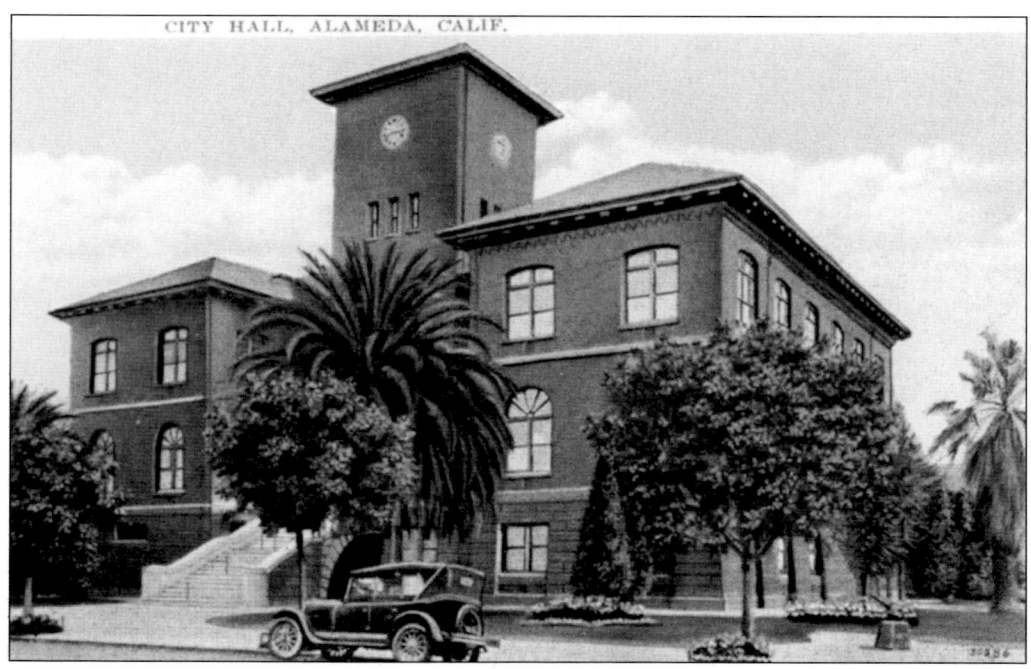

CITY HALL, ALAMEDA, CALIF.

A 1920s view of city hall shows more alterations to the tower, including the addition of a clock. (Published by the Western Notion and Novelty Company, Oakland.)

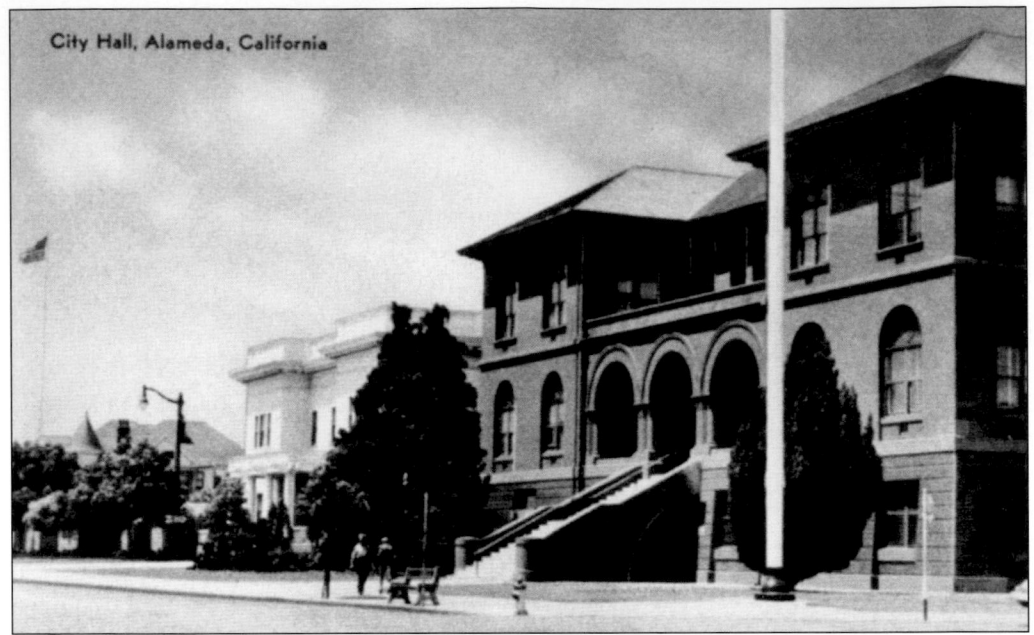

City Hall, Alameda, California

The city hall tower was finally removed in 1937 because of instability. This 1940s chamber of commerce postcard shows city hall without the tower and with the addition of a flagpole. The Elks Lodge can be seen to the left, with Victorian residences beyond.

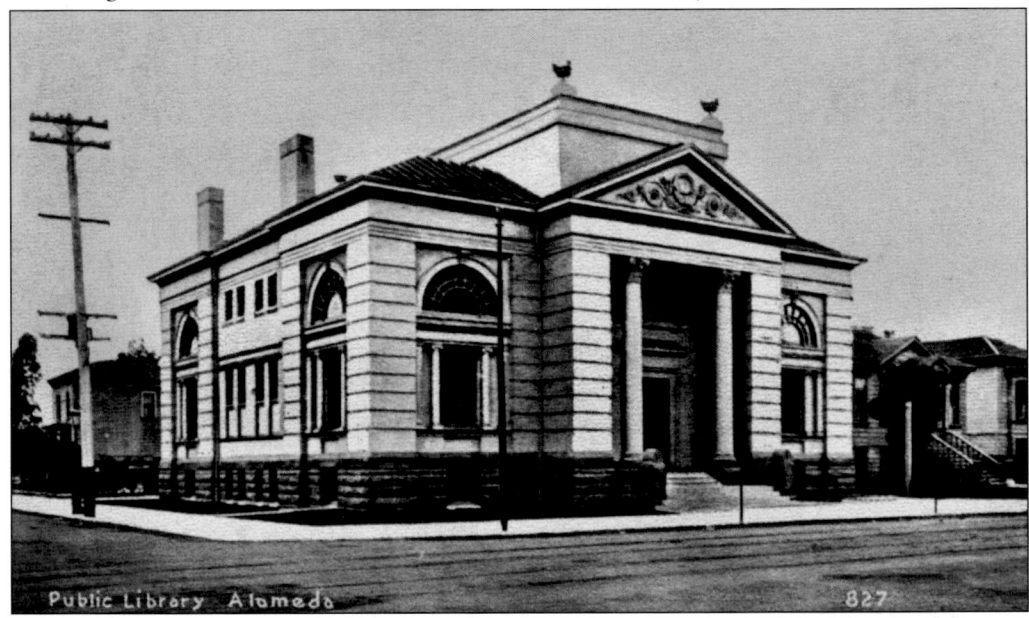

Public Library Alameda   827

In 1901, philanthropist Andrew Carnegie pledged $35,000 to the residents of Alameda for a new library, with the condition that the city spend $3,500 per year on maintenance and upkeep of the structure. Upon acceptance of this generous offer, groundbreaking ceremonies were conducted on May 6, 1902, on the corner of Santa Clara Avenue and Oak Street, across from city hall. On July 12 of that year, the cornerstone was laid. Designed in the neoclassical style by Willcox and Curtis, the library was built by C. H. Foster and Son for a cost of $29,992. This postcard was mailed in 1911. (Published by Edward H. Mitchell, San Francisco.)

30

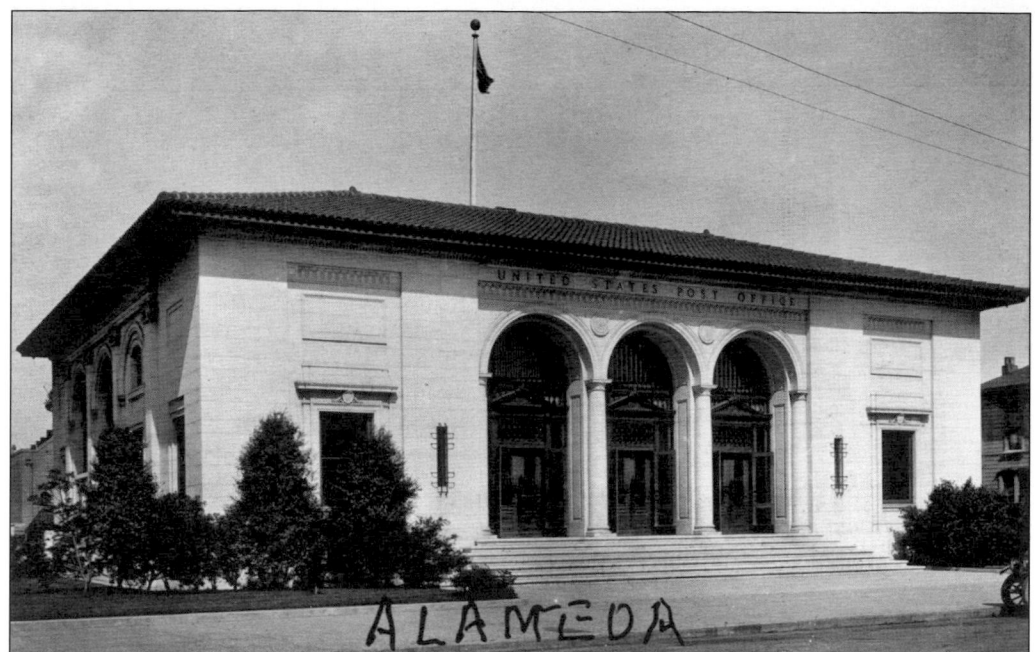

In 1890, free delivery of mail began. This 1920s photographic postcard shows the Spanish Colonial Revival post office on Central Avenue designed by William A. Newman. Completed in 1914 and enlarged in 1932, it was used briefly as a municipal court and offices in the 1970s and designated an Alameda Historical Monument in 1978. It now serves as a medical facility.

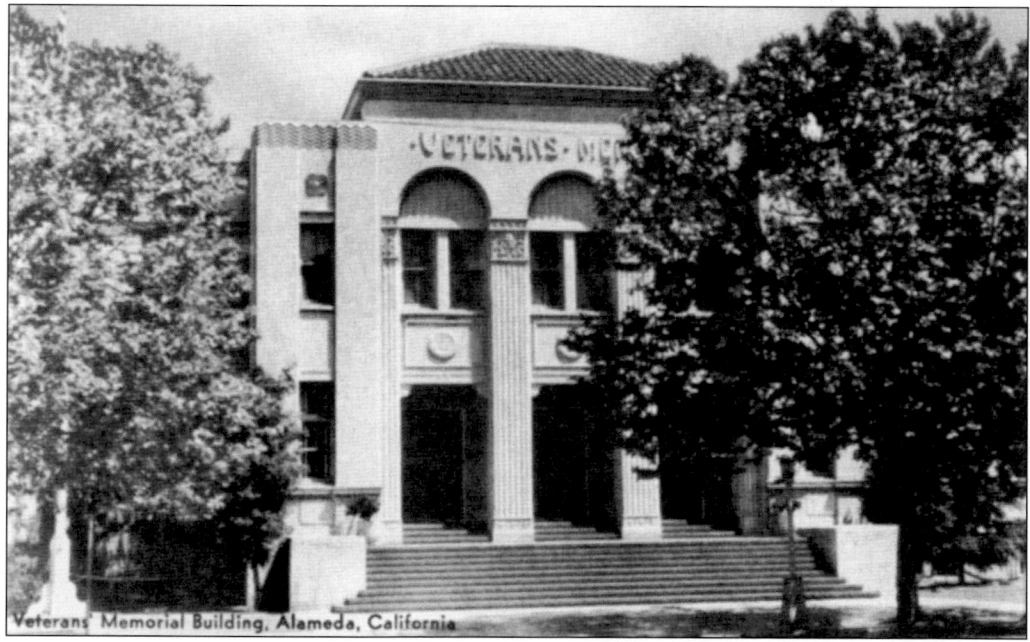

Designed by Henry H. Meyers in the art deco style and constructed in 1929, the Veterans' Memorial at 2203 Central Avenue was the ninth and final veterans building this noted architect produced in Alameda County. It was designated an historical landmark in 1982. (Lithograph by Greenwood Printers Limited, Oakland.)

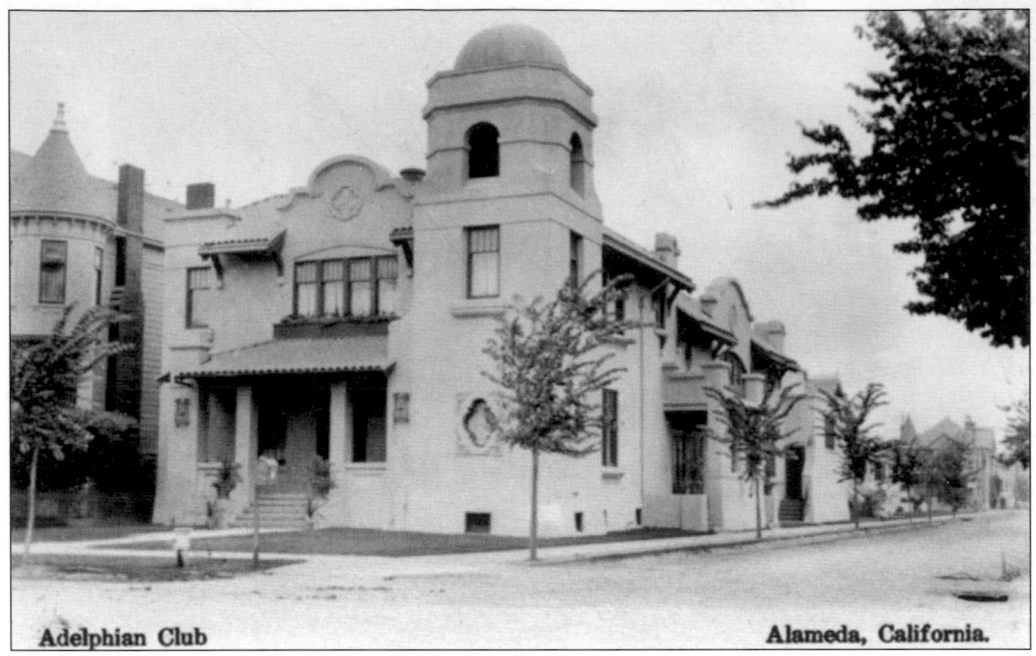

Adelphian Club   Alameda, California.

This *c.* 1909 photographic image shows the Mission Revival-style Adelphian Club at Central Avenue and Walnut Street. Designed by architect W. H. Willcox and completed in 1908, it is an official Alameda City Monument and the meeting place for Alameda's oldest ladies' club, The Adelphians, organized in 1897. During the flu epidemic of 1918, it served as a medical facility; later, at the onset of World War II, it was a USO center.

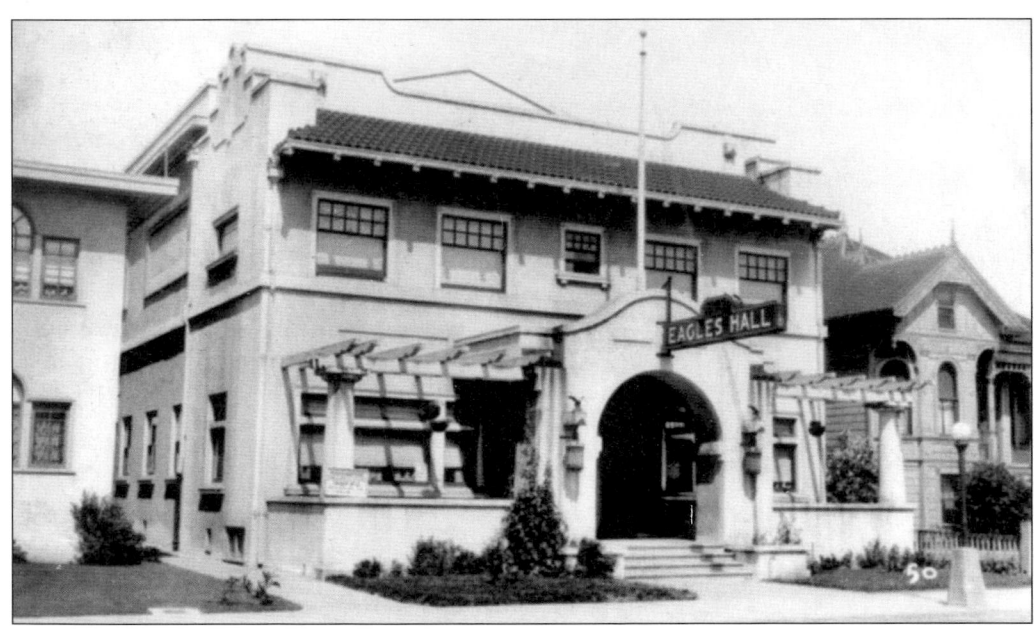

Aerie No. 1076 was organized in 1905. Eagles Hall, designed by local architect William DuFour, was constructed in 1914. A more elaborate neon sign was added later and still lights up the evening sky to this day. This photographic postcard dates from around 1930.

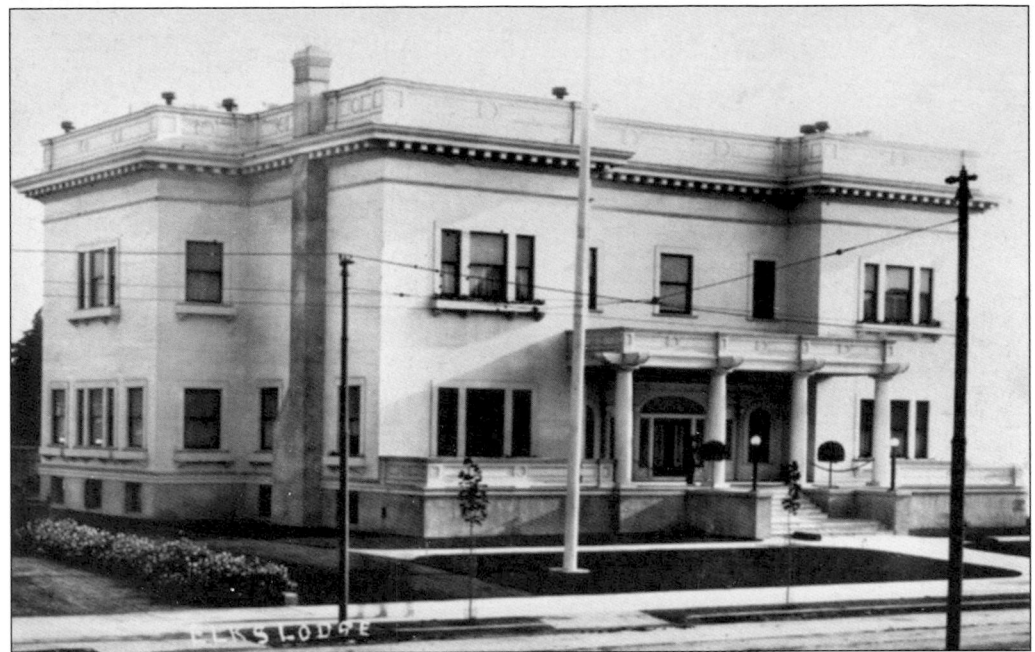

Lodge No. 1015, BPOE (the Benevolent and Protective Order of the Elks) was founded in March 1906, with its first meetings held at Woodmen's Hall at Park Street and Alameda Avenue. Another small building was constructed and used briefly until this structure was built in 1909. This photographic postcard was mailed in 1911.

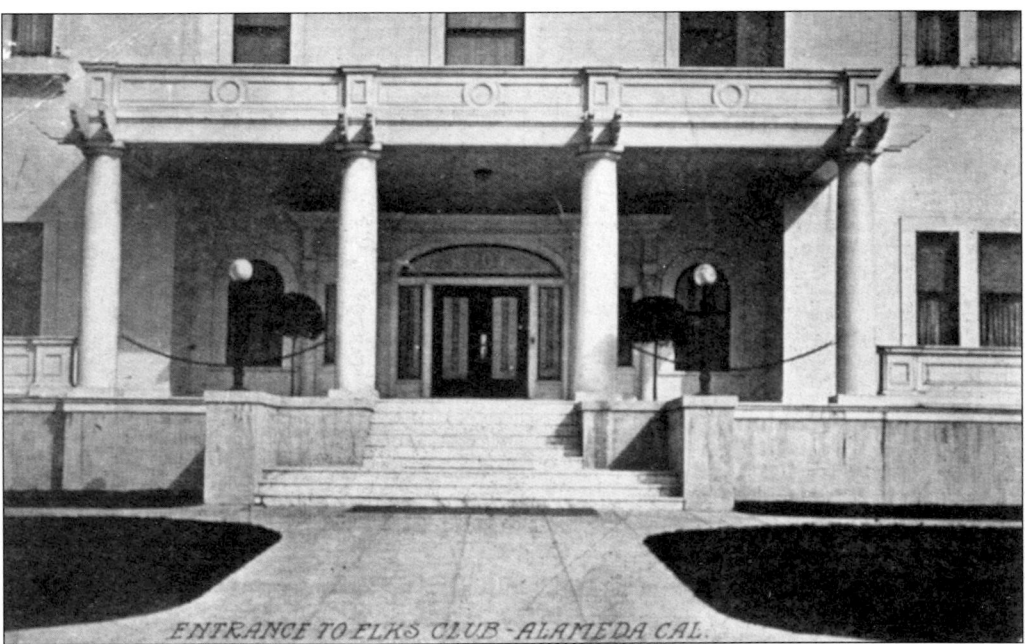

Situated next door to city hall, the Elks Club was designed by architect J. E. Freeman in the neoclassical style. This c. 1910 postcard shows the grand entrance on Santa Clara Avenue. (Published by the Cardinell-Vincent Company, San Francisco.)

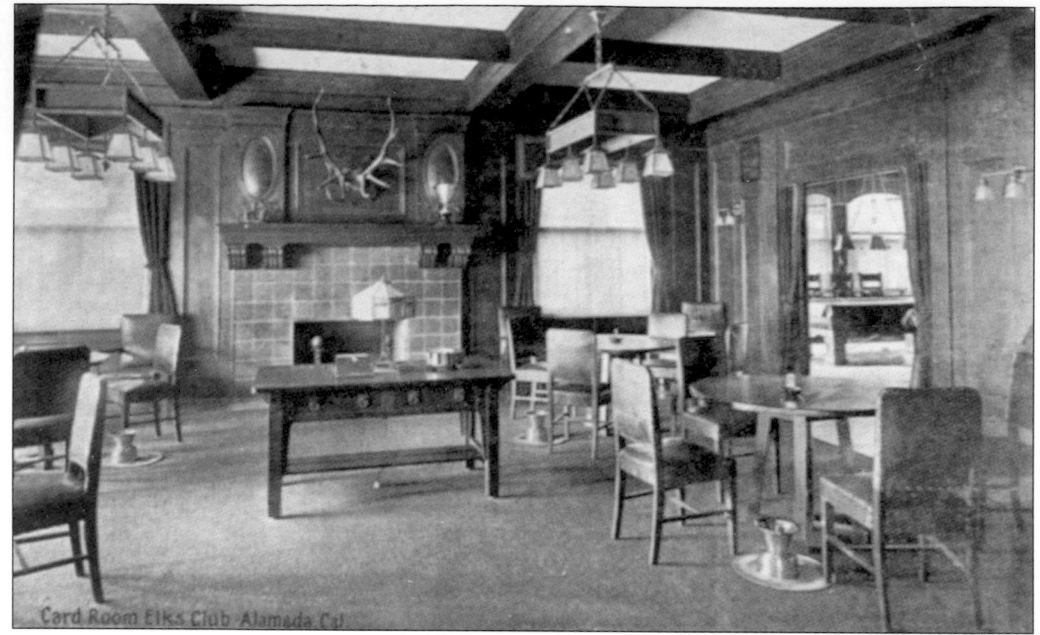

Shown here is the card room in the Elks Club. Note the spittoons beneath each table. A billiards room can be seen through the doorway. (Published by the Cardinell-Vincent Company, San Francisco, *c.* 1910.)

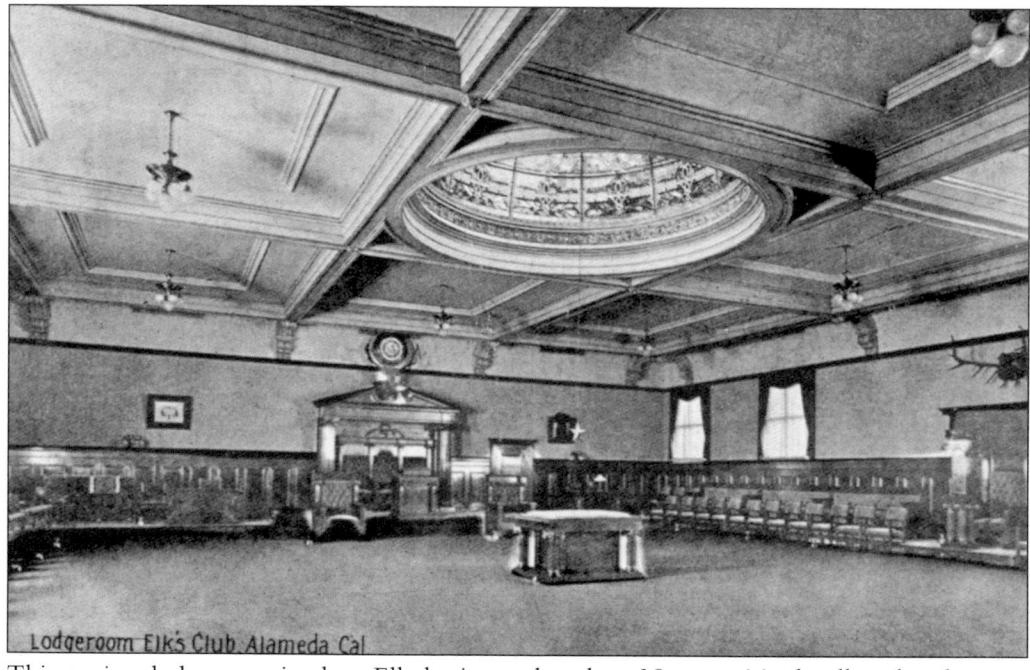

This spacious lodge room is where Elks business takes place. Not surprisingly, elk antlers decorate the room. (Published by the Cardinell-Vincent Company, San Francisco, *c.* 1910.)

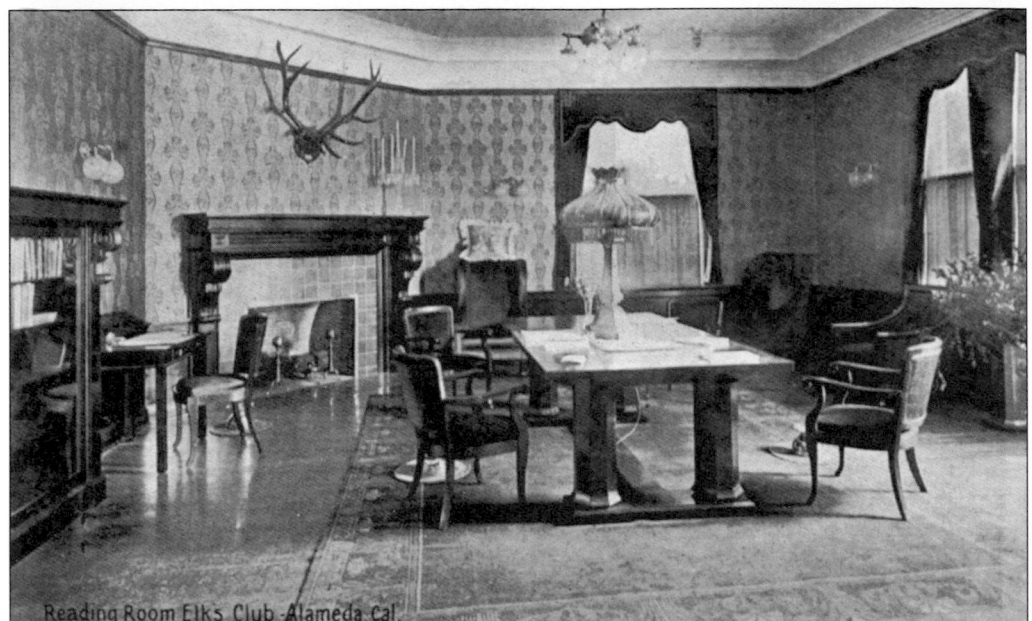

Reading Room Elks Club - Alameda, Cal.

This postcard shows the reading room, with more elk antlers over the fireplace. Like the two previous cards, this one was published by the Cardinell-Vincent Company of San Francisco around 1910. At that time, the Elks Club had over 400 members.

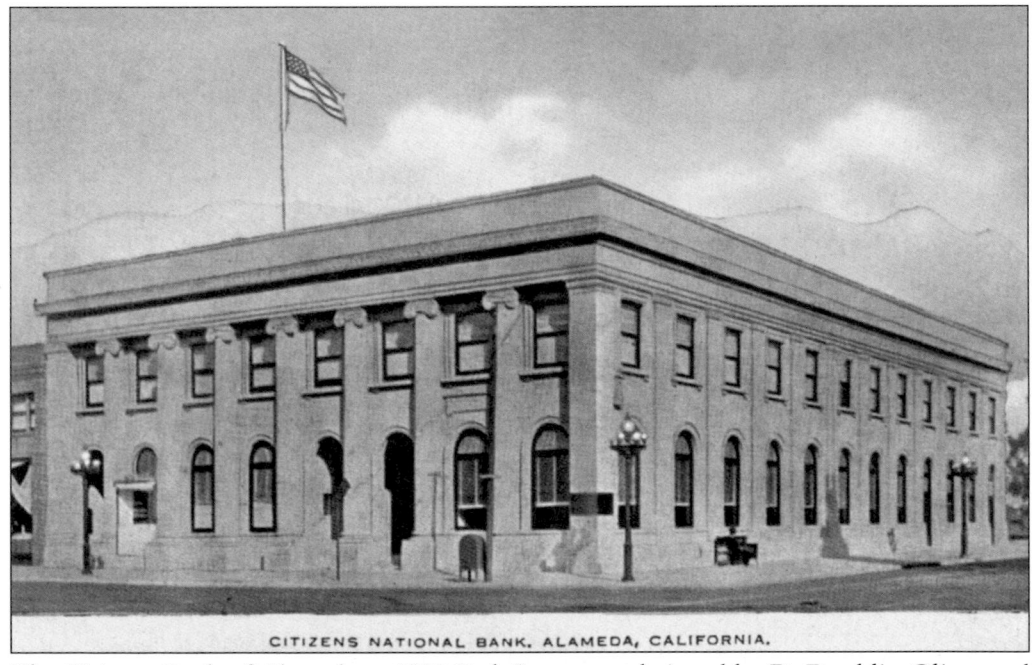

CITIZENS NATIONAL BANK, ALAMEDA, CALIFORNIA.

The Citizens Bank of Alameda at 1500 Park Street was designed by D. Franklin Oliver and Edward T. Foulkes and built by Frank B. Gulbreth and Company in 1906 in the neoclassical style. In the 1920s, it became the Bank of Italy and then the Bank of America in 1930. An addition was constructed in 1924. (Published by Pacific Novelty Company, San Francisco.)

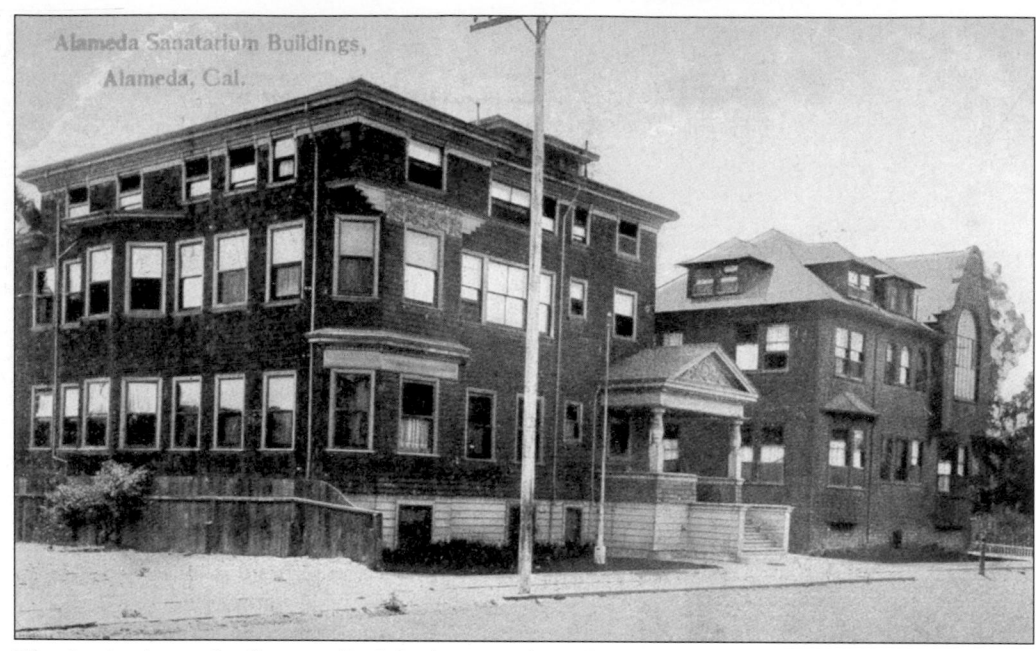

The Sanitarium, the first medical facility in Alameda, was founded by registered nurse Kate Creedon, who received her medical training at St. Luke's Hospital in San Francisco. In 1894, assisted by her sisters Mae and Margaret, she opened the island facility in a small house, which soon expanded in 1901 and again in 1903. This *c.* 1910 postcard shows the front entrance on Clinton Avenue near Willow Street. (Published by Newman Postcard Company, San Francisco.)

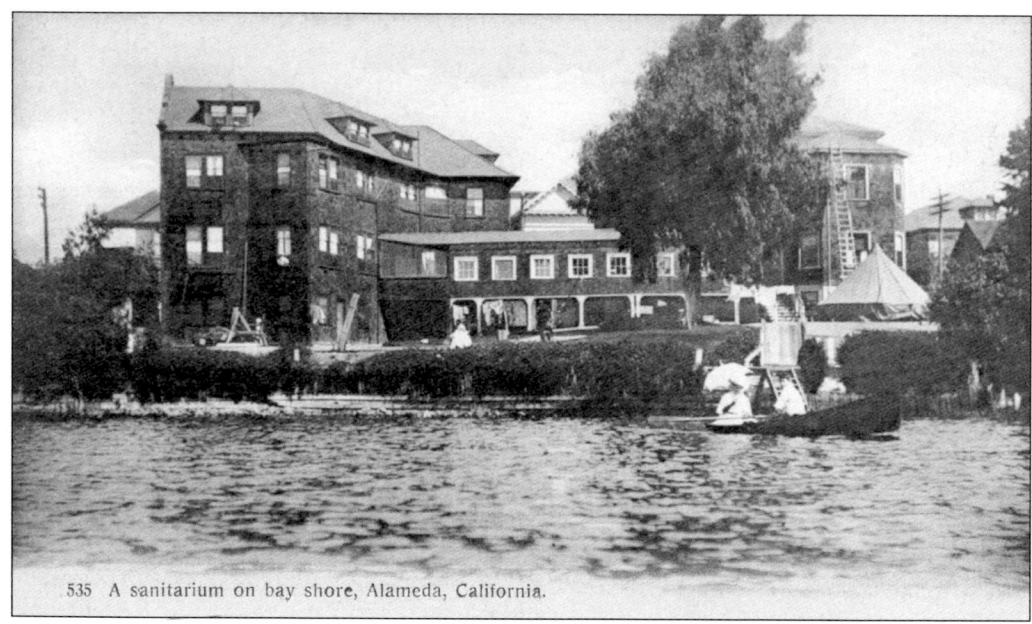

A couple in a canoe passes by the rear of the Alameda Sanitarium at the edge of the bay. After expansion of the small, original structure, the resulting three-story building also housed a nursing school, which had its first graduation ceremony on January 18, 1905, for a class of five women. (Published by the Cardinell-Vincent Company, Oakland, *c.* 1907.)

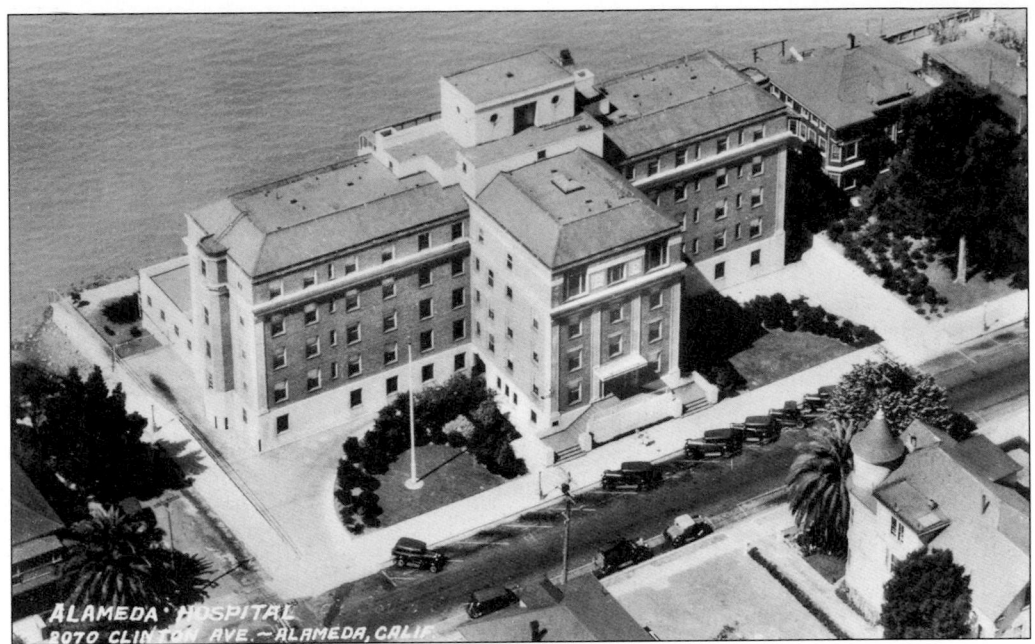

ALAMEDA HOSPITAL
2070 CLINTON AVE. — ALAMEDA, CALIF.

This *c.* 1935 photographic postcard shows the 110-room Alameda Hospital at Clinton Avenue and Willow Street. Located on the former site of the Alameda Sanitarium, it was built in 1924 and opened in 1925, with sanitarium founder Kate Creedon directing activities until her death in May 1927. At the time of this photograph, the hospital sat directly at the edge of the bay.

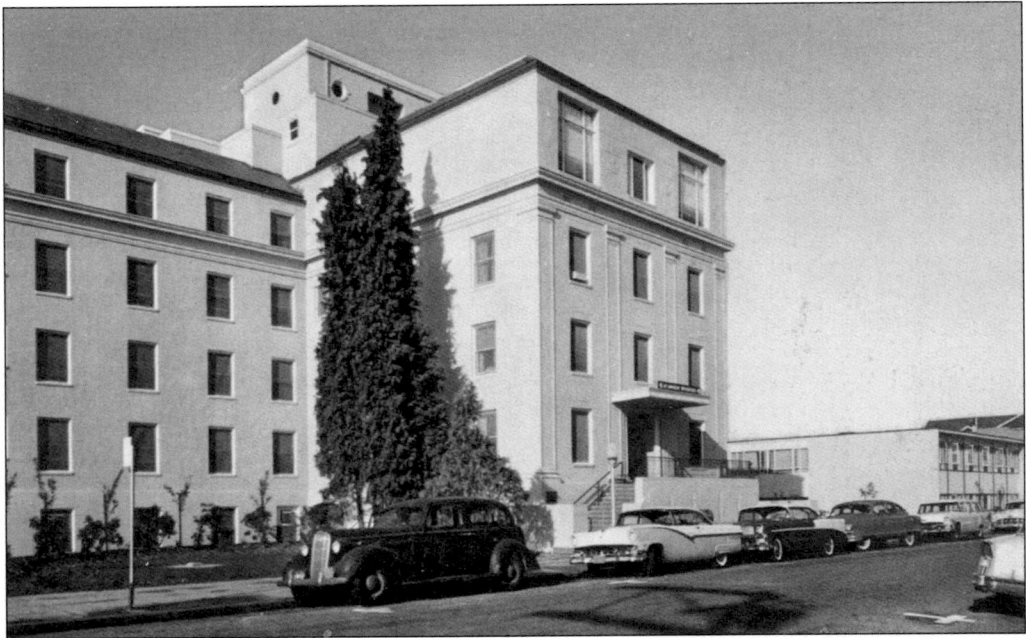

The Alameda Hospital was designed by architect Edward T. Foulkes and built by Vogt and Davidson. Originally made of brick, it was stuccoed in the 1950s and was notable for being the first West Coast hospital to be wired for electricity. In this *c.* 1957 view, the new Stevens Wing can be seen on the right, which increased the bed count to 135. (Published by Mike Roberts, Berkeley.)

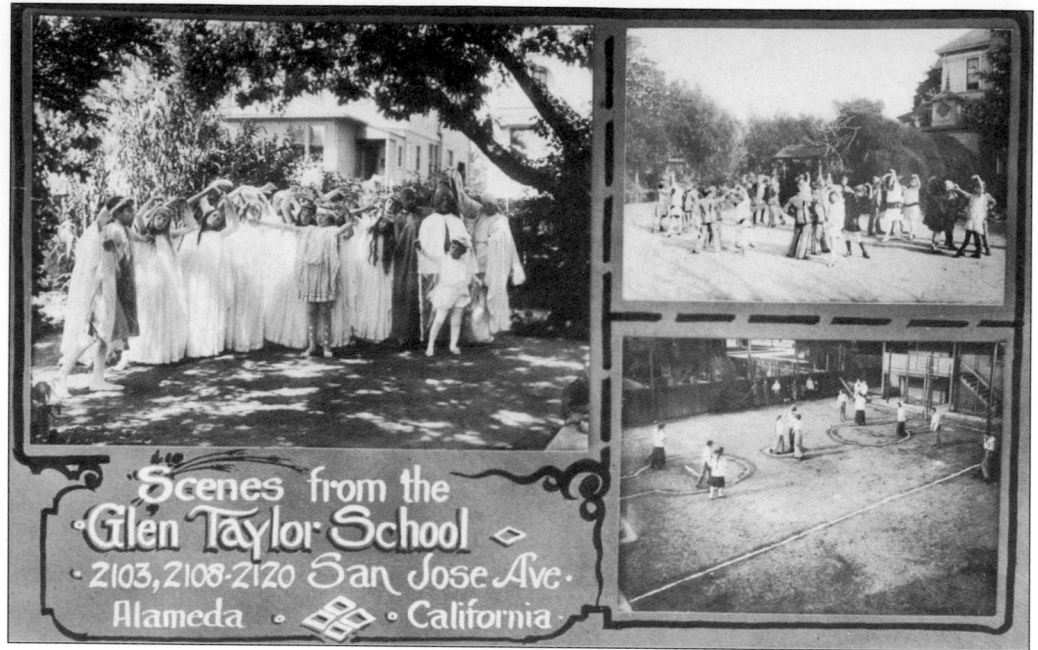

This *c.* 1915 photographic postcard advertises the dramatics and sports programs at the Glen Taylor School, which was started in 1902 at 2103–2120 San Jose Avenue. This private school soon outgrew its limited space and in 1936, was moved to a 12-acre farm in Walnut Creek.

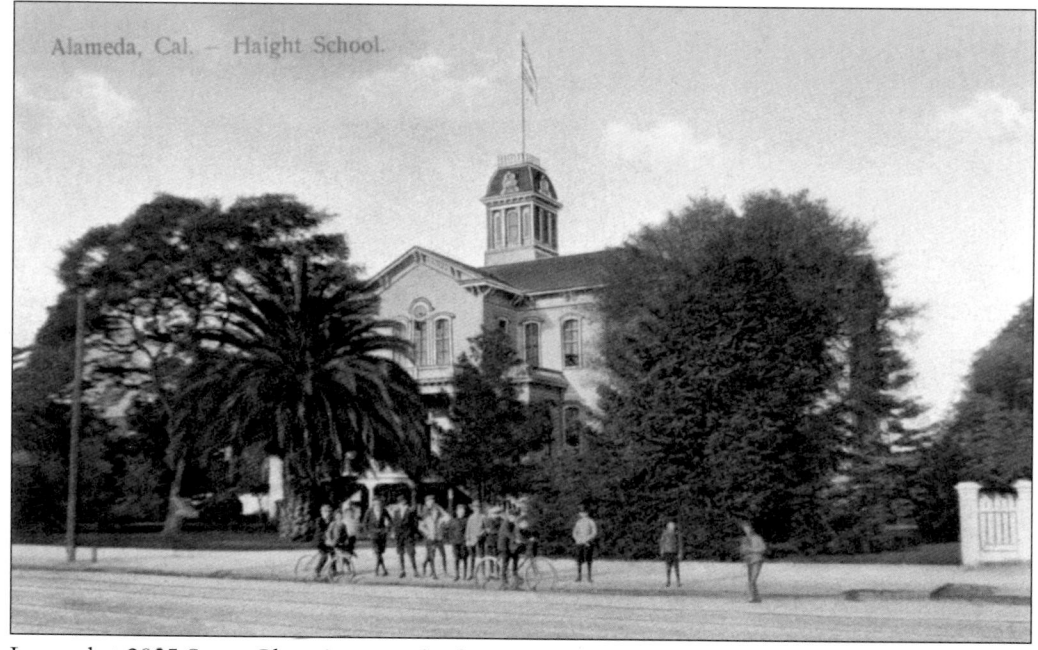

Located at 2025 Santa Clara Avenue, the first Haight School was built in 1875 and named after former governor Henry Huntley Haight. After an increase in population following the 1906 earthquake, the old Italianate structure was torn down in the summer of 1910 to prepare for a new, larger facility. (Published by the Pacific Novelty Company, San Francisco, *c.* 1908.)

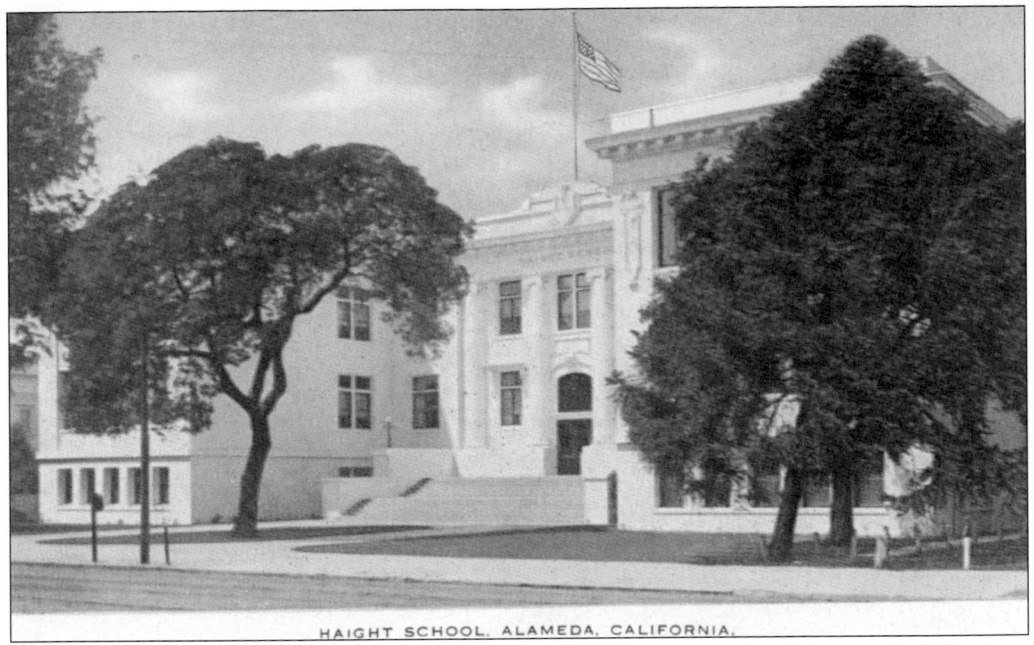

HAIGHT SCHOOL, ALAMEDA, CALIFORNIA.

The cornerstone for the Haight School was laid on October 14, 1910, and the new building was dedicated on September 1, 1911. Designed by Cunningham and Politeo and built by the Powell brothers, the two-story school contained a library, auditorium, offices, and classrooms. After it was deemed to be unsafe in the event of an earthquake, the school was destroyed in the summer of 1973. (Published by the Pacific Novelty Company, San Francisco, *c.* 1925.)

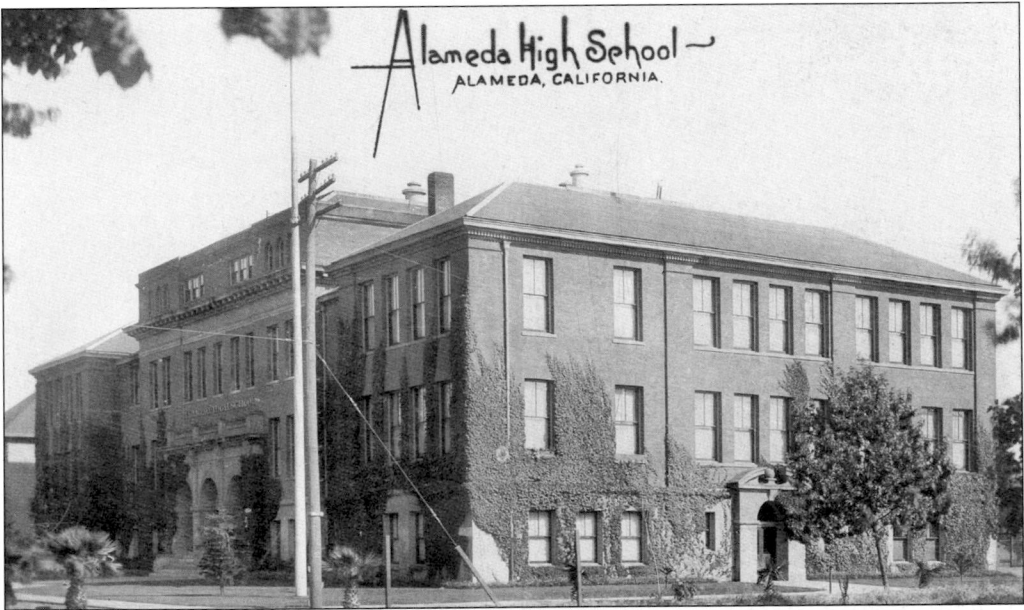

Alameda High School — ALAMEDA, CALIFORNIA.

Alameda High School was dedicated on May 23, 1903, at Walnut Street and Central Avenue. The three-story brick structure was built for a student body of 300, but by 1925, it had surpassed 500. That year, when the new high school was built, this structure was remodeled and used as the west wing. It was torn down in 1956 and replaced by a new west wing. (Published by American Industrial Photo Company, San Francisco.)

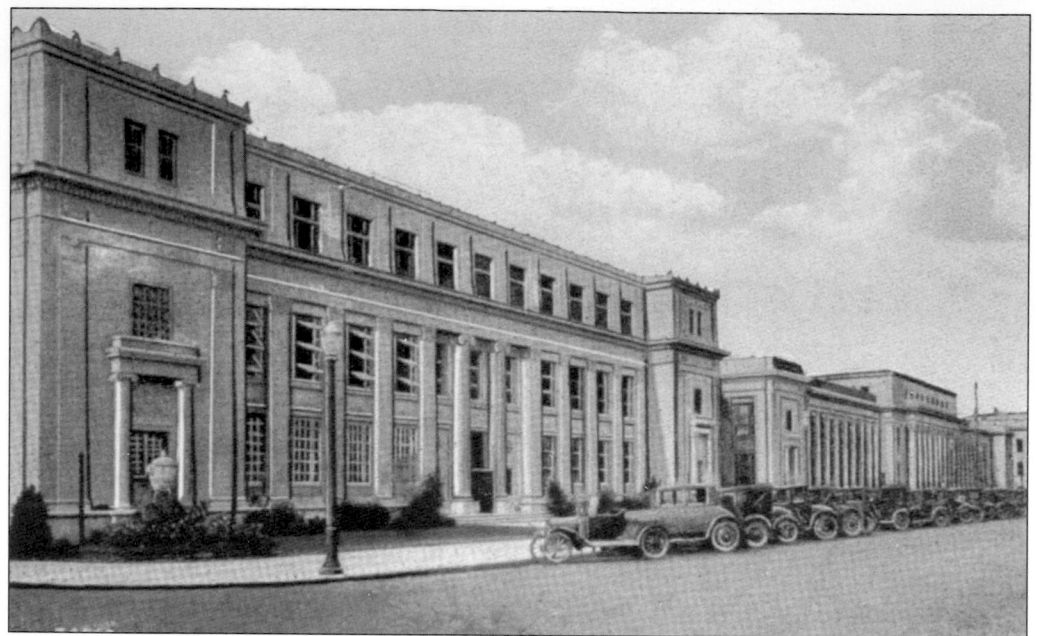

Designed by architect Carl Werner, Alameda High School was dedicated on August 18, 1926. This majestic structure on Central Avenue between Oak and Walnut Streets is still in use as the Alameda Free Library, an adult school, and school district offices. (Published by Western Notion and Novelty Company, Oakland.)

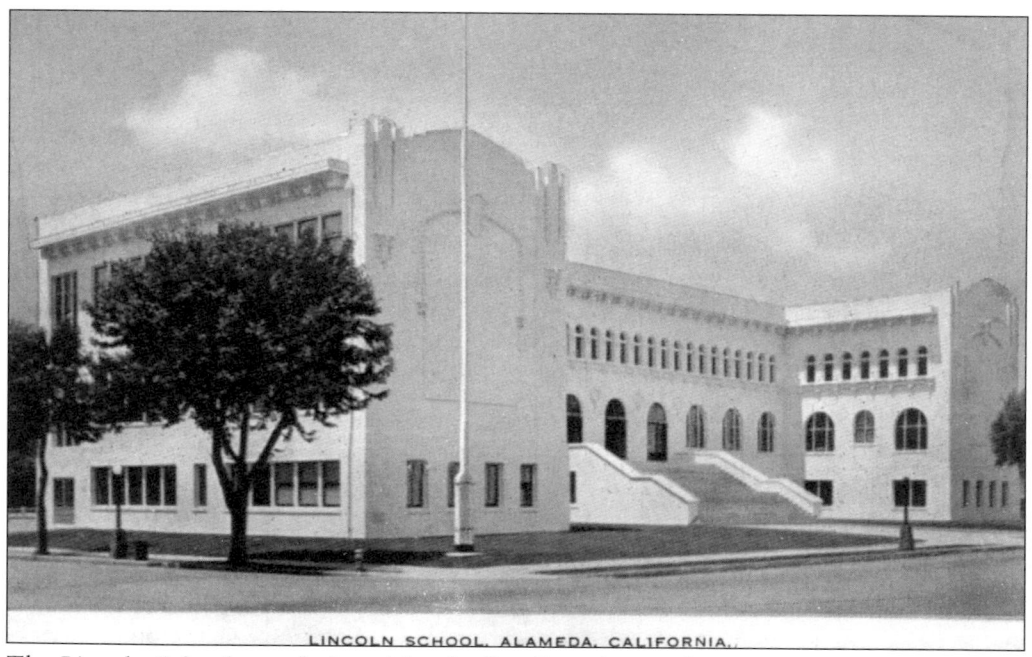

The Lincoln School was designed by the San Francisco architectural firm of Politeo and Cunningham in 1917 as a replacement for the 1892 Victorian-era Wilson School building. It was destroyed by fire in 1923. (Published by Pacific Novelty Company, San Francisco.)

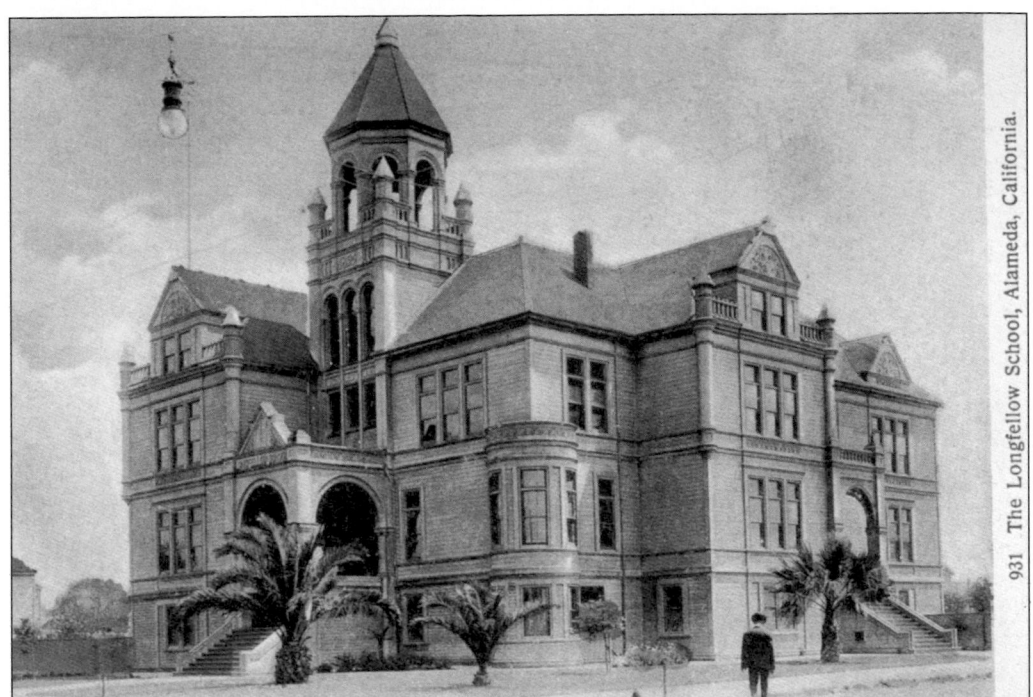

931 The Longfellow School, Alameda, California.

Named after America's first poet, the Longfellow School opened at Pacific Avenue and Fifth on August 12, 1895. Designed by William Armitage, it was called "the pride of the residents of West Alameda." Sadly this Victorian Romanesque beauty was torn down in the 1950s and replaced by a more subdued structure. (Published by the Cardinell-Vincent Company, Oakland.)

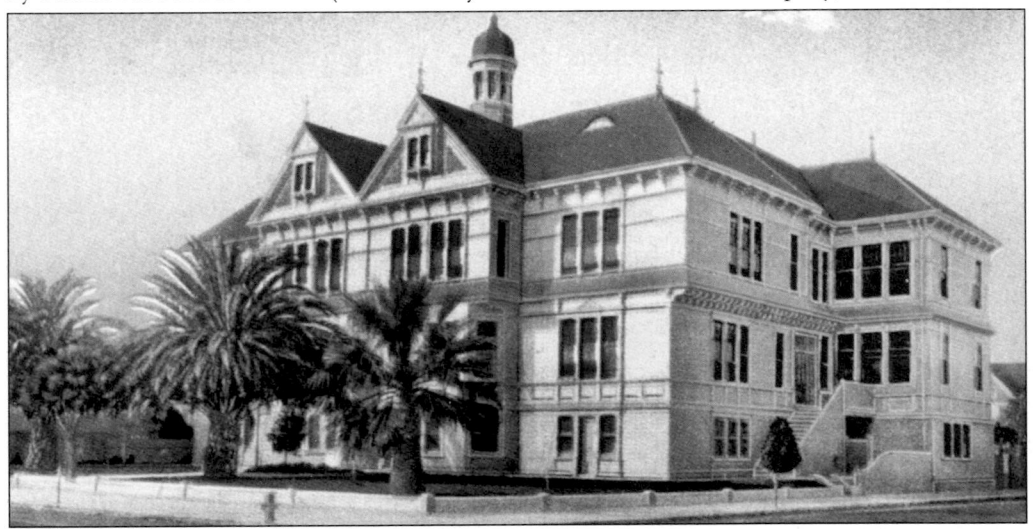

The Encinal School was opened in March 1891, between Bay Street and St. Charles Street on Santa Clara Avenue. On June 18, 1901, the school was renamed Mastick School in honor of Edwin B. Mastick, an Alameda visionary known as Alameda's First Citizen. Mastick pushed for many Alameda improvements, including the paving of streets, organization of the electric light plant, and the creation of a sewer system. The original Mastick School was demolished and rebuilt on the same site in the Moderne style by Alameda architect Andrew Haas in 1939. (Published by Edward H. Mitchell, San Francisco, *c.* 1939.)

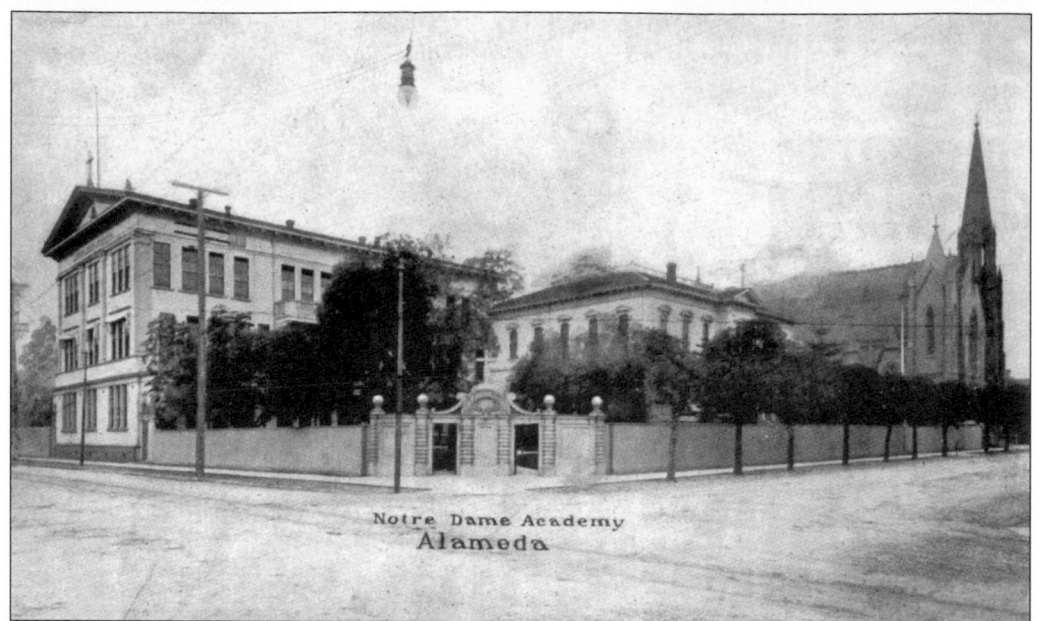

Notre Dame Academy
Alameda

This printed photographic postcard shows the Notre Dame Academy at Chestnut Street and San Jose Avenue south of the Chestnut train station. On the right is St. Joseph's Church, built in 1894. The sender of the card is Sister M. of the academy who thanks the addressee "for the lovely Carnations. The sanctuary is a mass of beautiful blooms presented to me by kind hearts and therefore very cordially appreciated." Although no publisher is given, the card may have been produced by the academy for advertising and correspondence purposes.

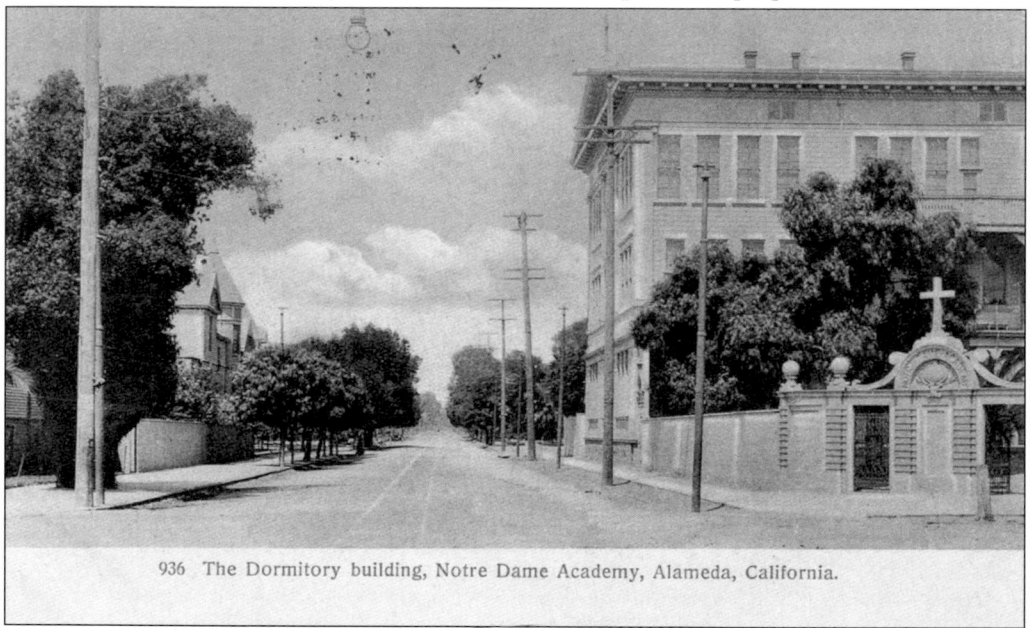

936 The Dormitory building, Notre Dame Academy, Alameda, California.

This *c.* 1906 postcard shows the Notre Dame Academy dormitory. Conducted by the Sisters of Notre Dame, the academy was opened in the spring of 1881 as a private Catholic girls' school. The dormitory structure on the right was an addition, most likely built after the turn of the century. (Published by the Cardinell–Vincent Company, Oakland.)

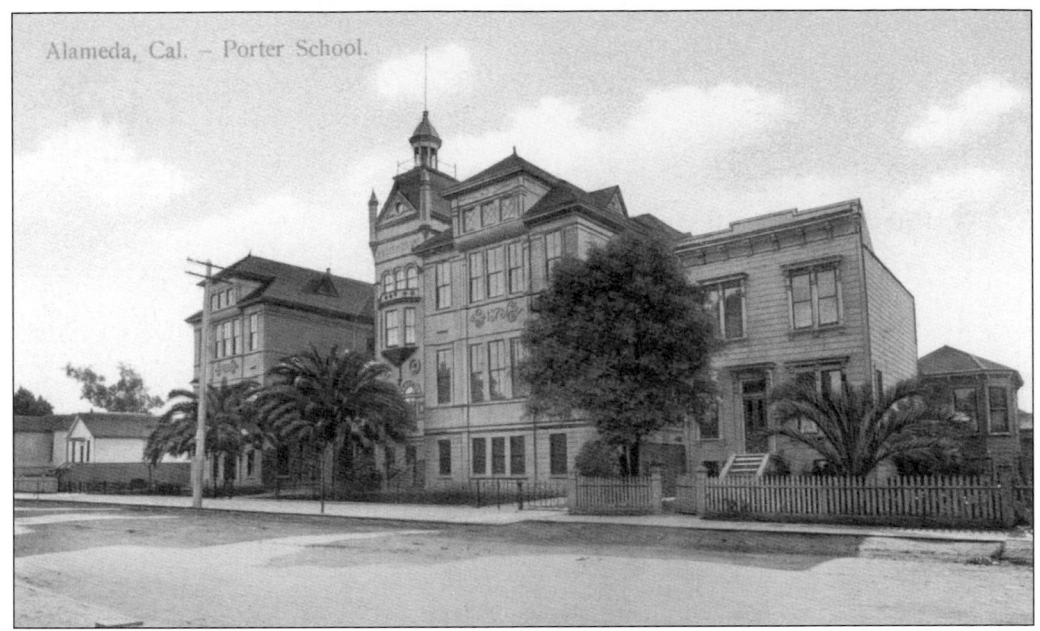

Located between Walnut and Oak Streets at 2230 Alameda Avenue, Porter School opened in July 1879 and was named in memory of Nathan Porter, a state senator and member of the board of education who died while in office. (Published by the Pacific Novelty Company, San Francisco, *c.* 1910.)

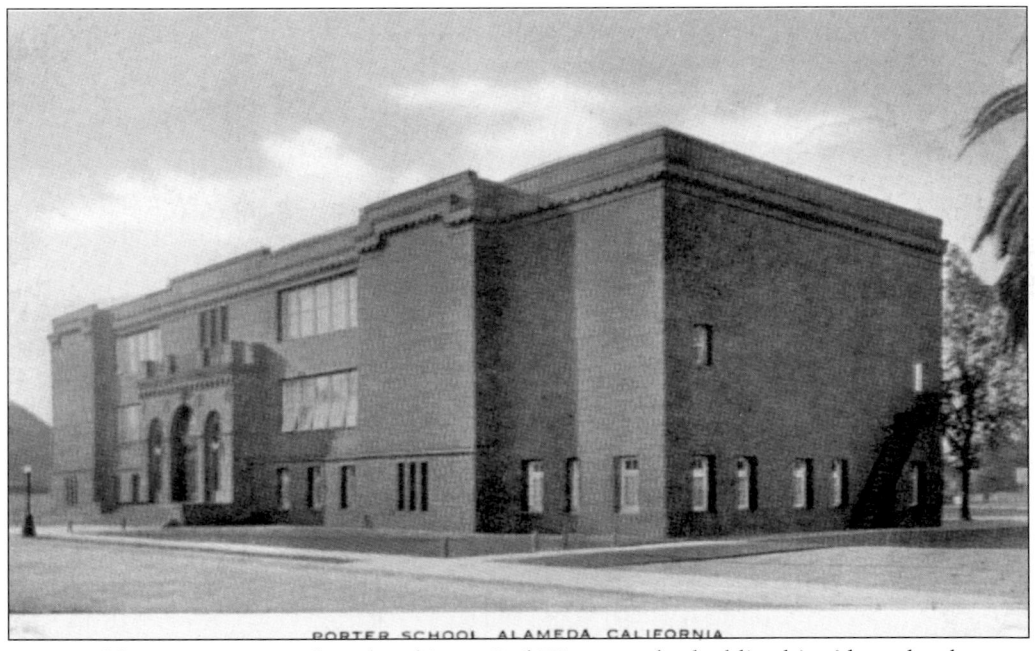

Designed by San Francisco–based architect Carl Werner, who had lived in Alameda, the new Porter School was built in 1916 on the site of the 1879 structure. It burned down in 1973. The property on which it stood is now part of the present Alameda High School campus. (Published by the Pacific Novelty Company, San Francisco, *c.* 1925.)

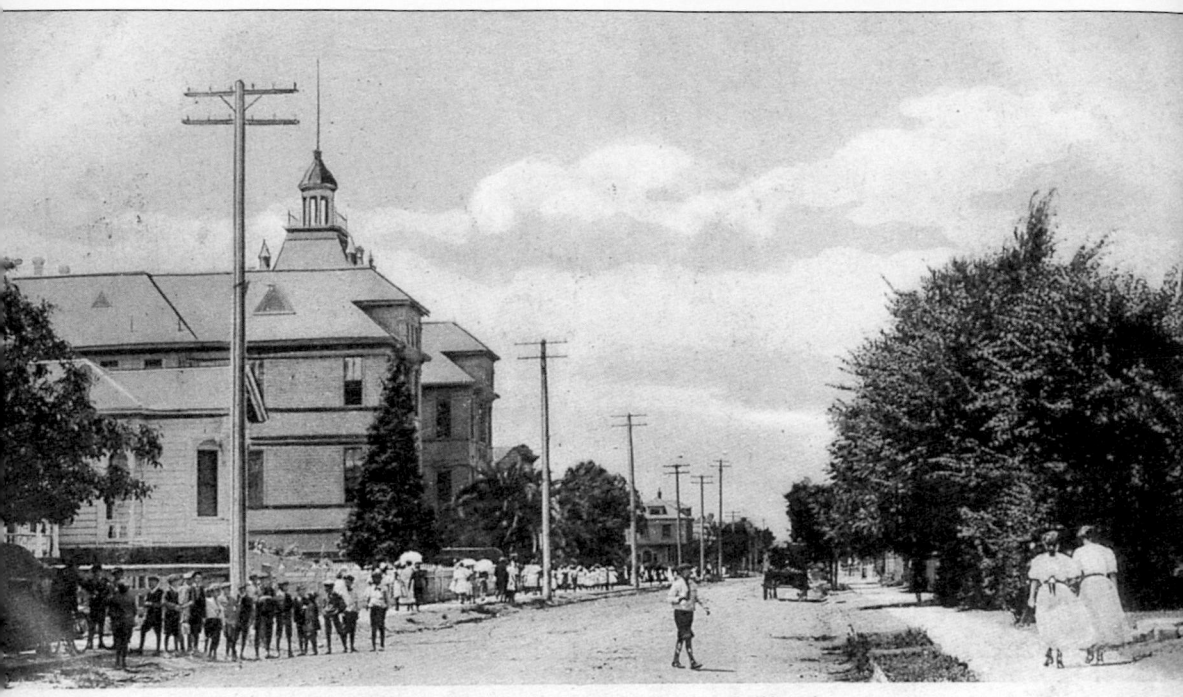

1038— 838 The Wilson Public School, Alameda, California.

The Wilson School opened at Van Buren and Mound Street in January 1892 and was named for a former board of education president. After additions were built to deal with overcrowding, the name was changed to Lincoln School on February 13, 1911. Eight more classrooms were added, along with offices and an auditorium. (Published by the Cardinell-Vincent Company, Oakland.)

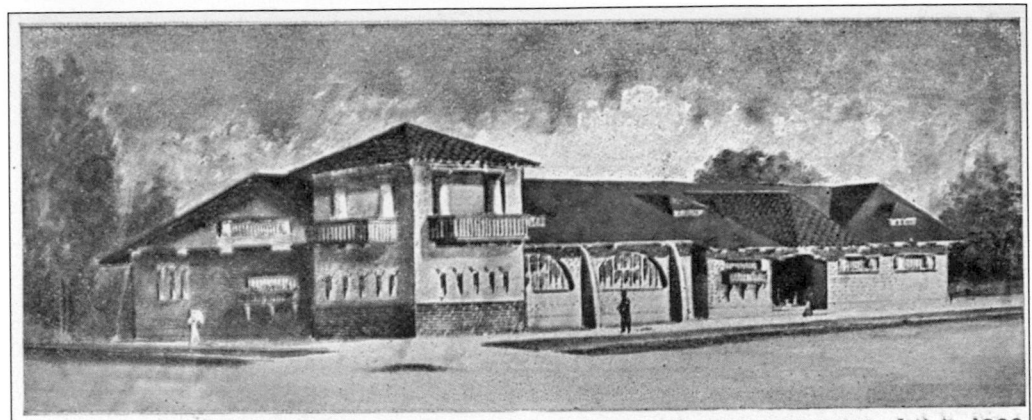

THE FIRST CHRISTIAN CHURCH OF ALAMEDA, CALIFORNIA, NOW BUILDING—JULY, 1906.

This postcard advertises the First Christian Church, built in July 1906 and completed in 1907, at the corner of San Jose Avenue and Park Street. Delanoy and Randlett built this church for a cost of $15,000 in a Craftsman version of Mission Revival; major remodeling in 1956 changed its exterior.

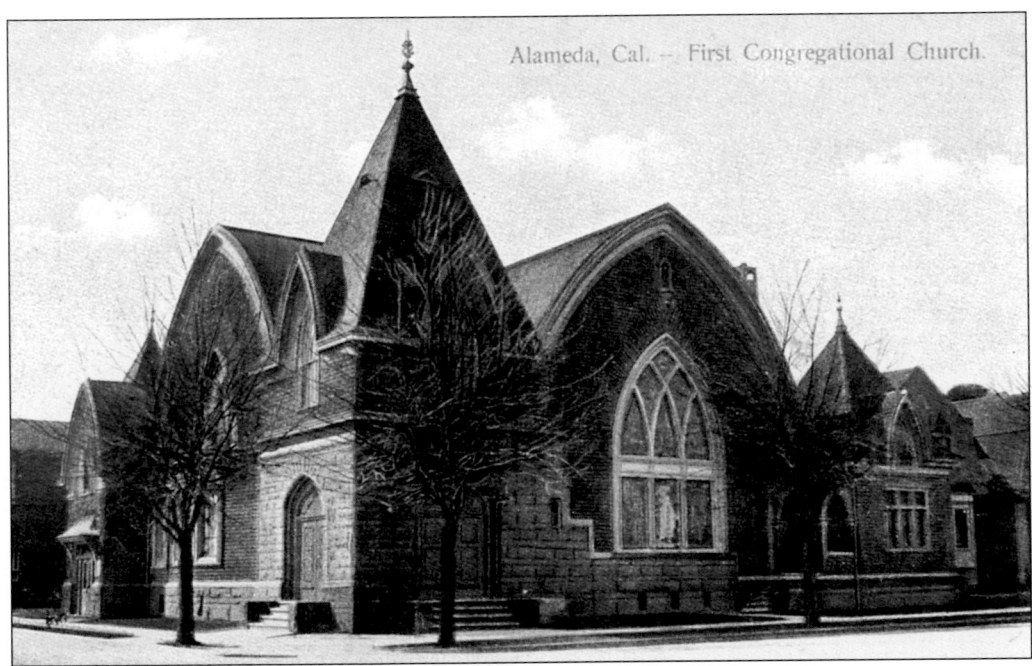

The First Congregational Church, designed by D. Franklin Oliver and constructed in 1904 for $26,100, was built by Delanoy and Randlett. This Shingle-style church still stands at Chestnut Street and Central Avenue. (Published by Pacific Novelty Company, San Francisco.)

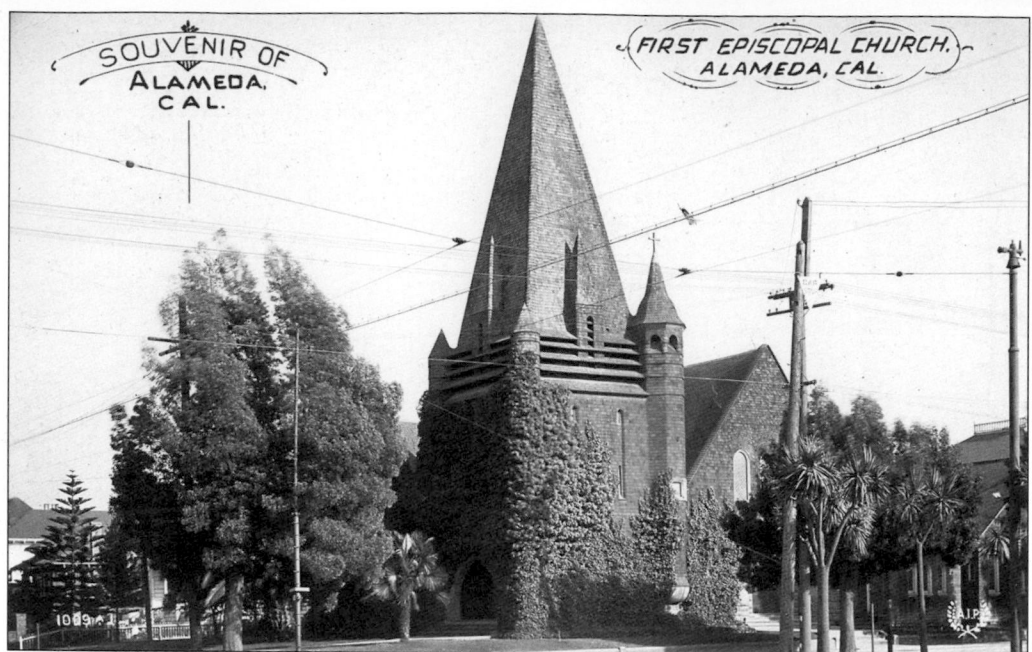

This photographic postcard of the Christ Episcopal Church and a souvenir of Alameda, California, was postmarked in 1912. (Published by American Industrial Photo Company, San Francisco.)

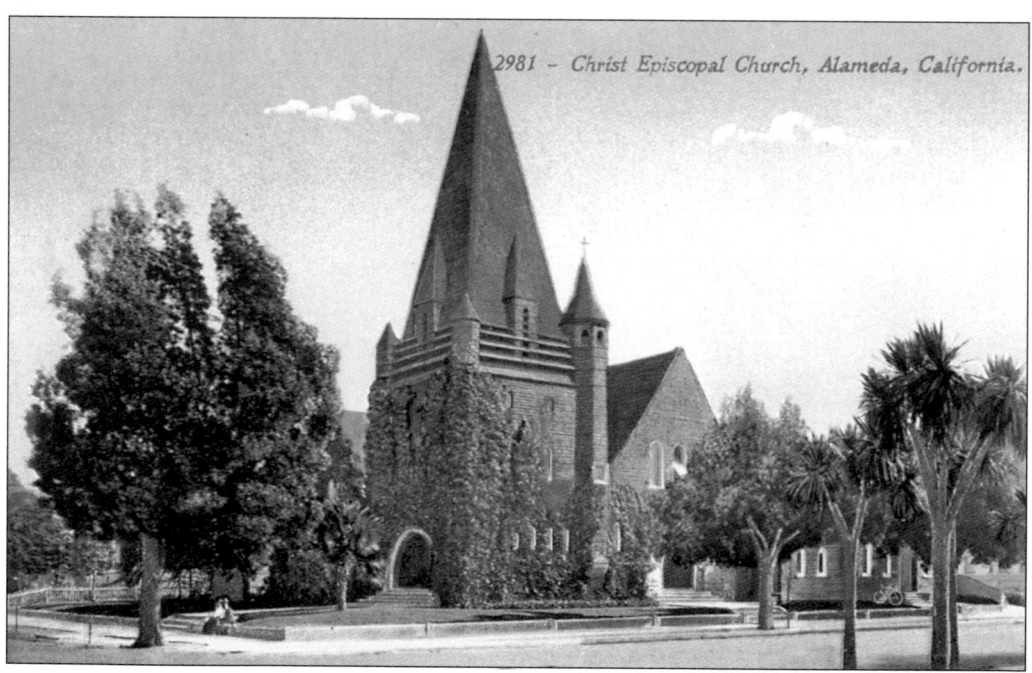

The Christ Church building, shown in this *c.* 1910 postcard, was constructed at the corner of Santa Clara Avenue and Grand Street in 1891. It was destroyed by arson fire in December 1960. The building that now stands on this lot was built and completed in 1962. (Published by Edward H. Mitchell, San Francisco.)

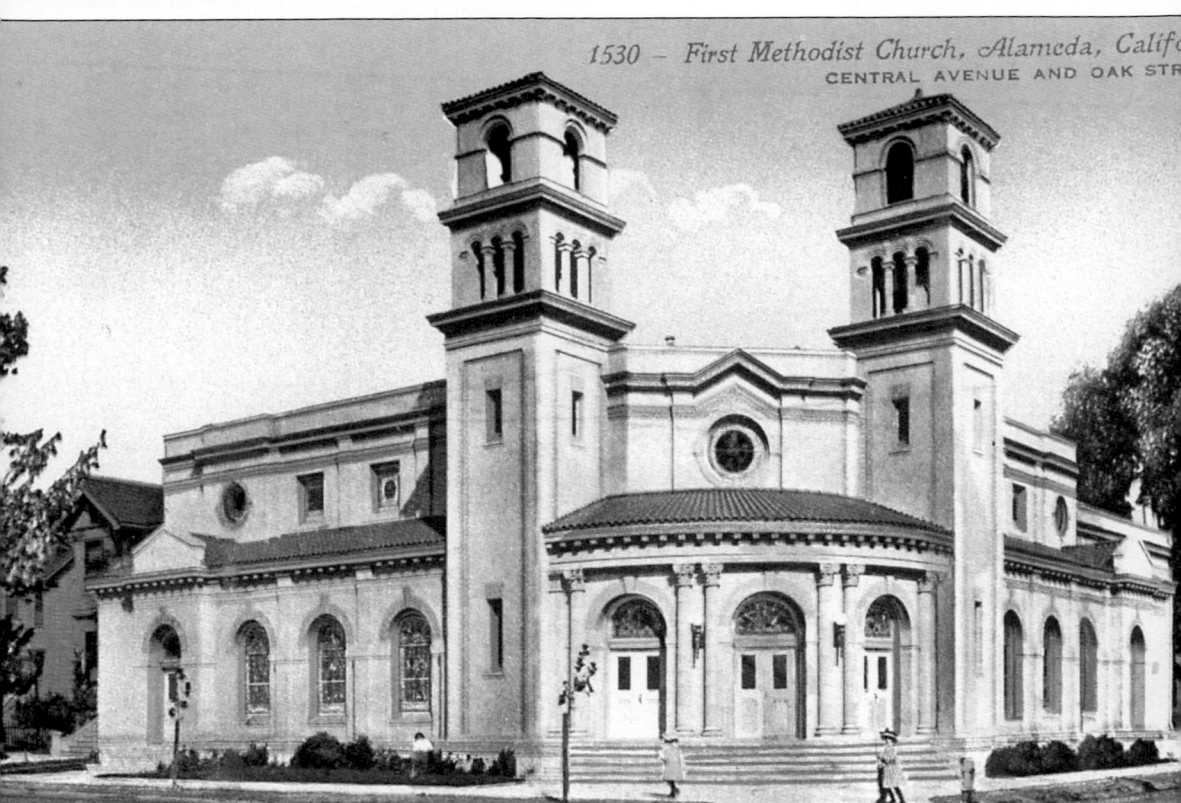

Founded in 1853, the First Methodist Church, the oldest congregation in Alameda, was first located at Jackson and Mound Streets. In 1875, it was moved to the southwest corner of Park Street and Central Avenue. The congregation's location became permanent at Central Avenue and Oak Street in a church designed by the San Francisco architectural firm of Henry Meyers and Clarence Ward and built by John Peacock. Construction on the Spanish Colonial Revival structure began in 1908, and the church was dedicated on October 31, 1909. The church is known for its unique twin towers at the front entrance and the carillons that are played daily at 12:00 p.m. and 6:00 p.m. (Published by Edward H. Mitchell, San Francisco.)

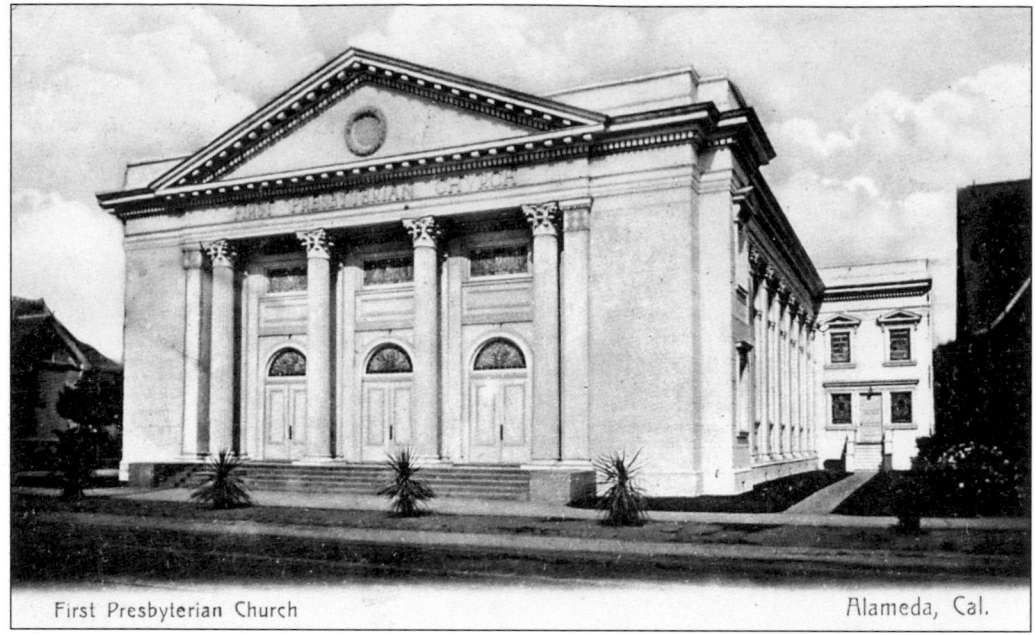

First Presbyterian Church   Alameda, Cal.

Henry Haight Meyers, a prominent local architect and congregation member, designed this neoclassical church. Built in 1903 for a cost of $22,000, it was dedicated on Easter Sunday, April 3, 1904. In 1977, it was declared an Alameda Historical Monument. (Published by Cook and Cook, Oakland, *c.* 1907.)

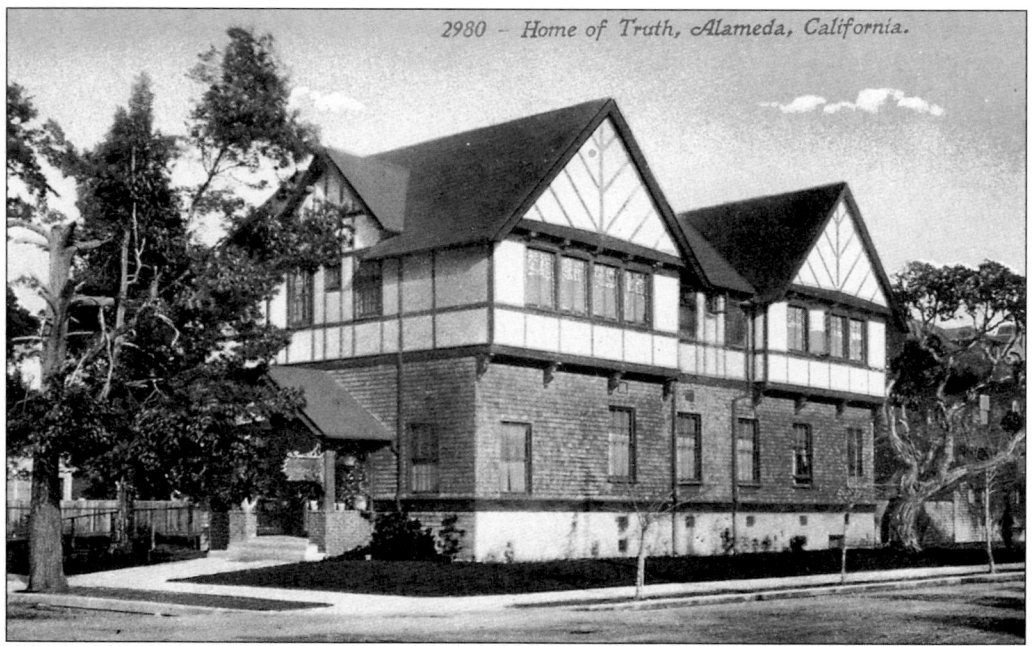

2980 – Home of Truth, Alameda, California.

The Home of Truth, a church and spiritual center based on the religious tradition of New Thought, still stands at Grand Street and Alameda Avenue. It was built in 1905 by sisters Annie Rix Militz and Harriet Hale Rix and designed by architect Burt E. Remmel, who also resided in Alameda. The center was originally owned by Alice Rix, who lived next door at 1709 Alameda Avenue. (Published by Edward H. Mitchell, San Francisco.)

A message on the back of this card says, "Dear Sister: We are now living in Cal in California style, wish you could see, it is certainly fine." This Gothic Revival church at San Antonio Avenue and Chestnut Street was dedicated in 1894. After remodeling in 1919, it burned down and was replaced by a Mission Revival structure, shown below, in 1921. (Published by Souvenir Publishing Company, San Francisco.)

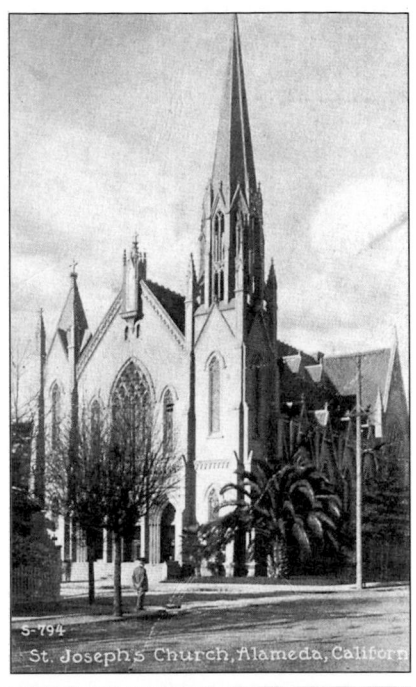

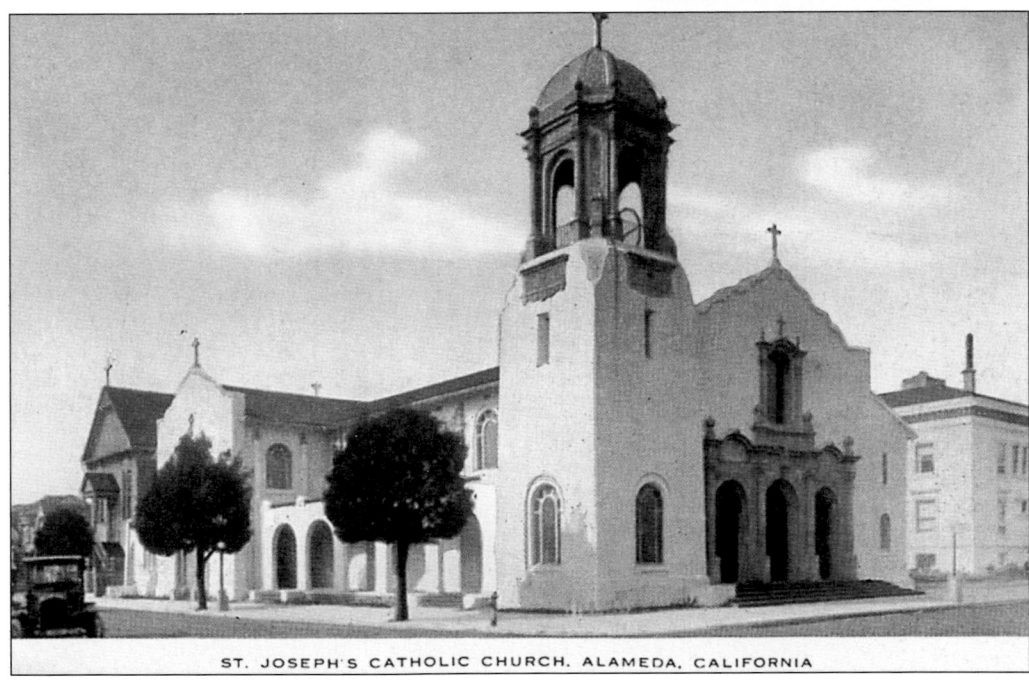

ST. JOSEPH'S CATHOLIC CHURCH. ALAMEDA, CALIFORNIA

This 1920s postcard shows the St. Joseph's Catholic Church and Basilica, still located at San Antonio Avenue and Chestnut Street. Designed by architect H. A. Minton, it officially opened on Christmas Day, 1921. Originally from Massachusetts, Minton was sent by the mayor of Boston with a group of architects to help rebuild San Francisco after the 1906 earthquake. Minton settled in Alameda in 1921, where he raised seven children. The church became an Alameda Historical Monument in 1977 and was placed on the National Register of Historic Places in 1978. (Published by Pacific Novelty Company, San Francisco.)

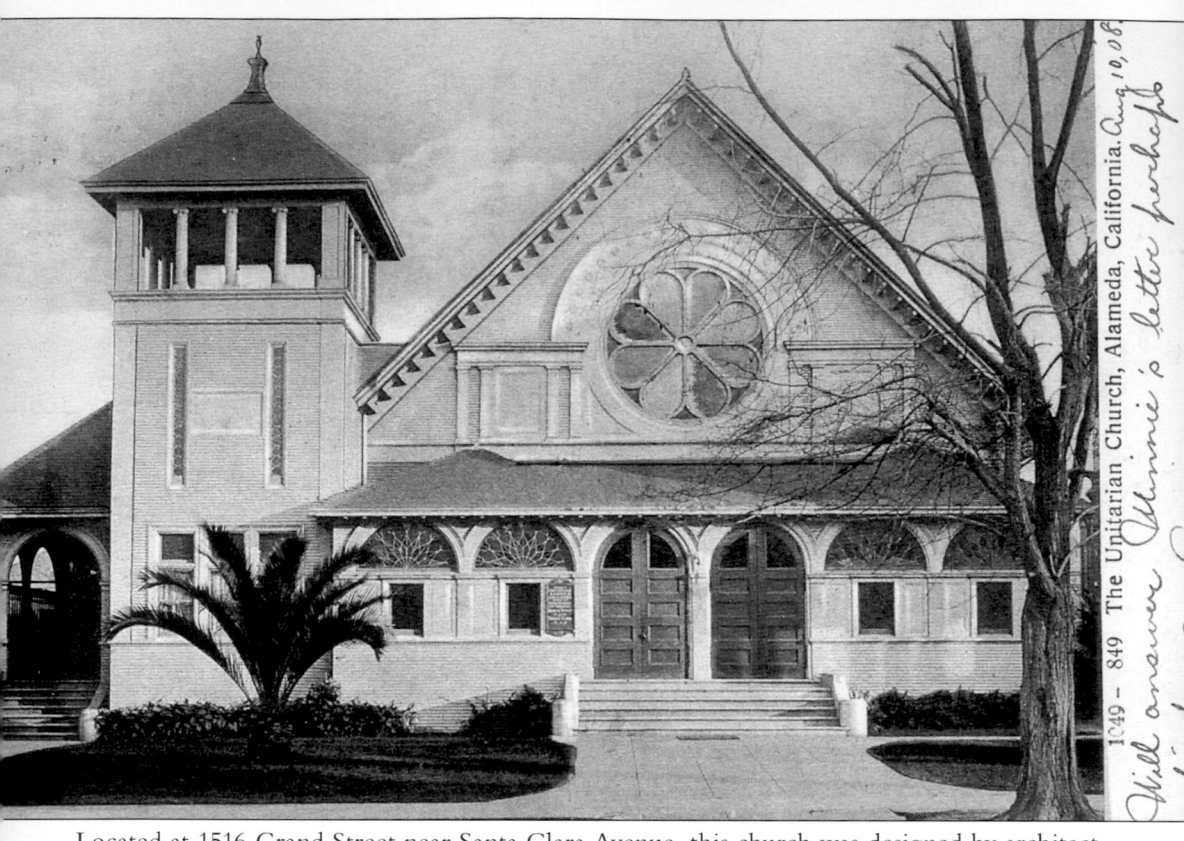

Located at 1516 Grand Street near Santa Clara Avenue, this church was designed by architect W. J. Mathews and built by Herbert E. Jones for the Unitarian Society of Alameda in 1893 for a cost of $8,430. (Published by the Cardinell–Vincent Company, Oakland, *c.* 1908.)

Four

PARKS AND PLAYGROUNDS

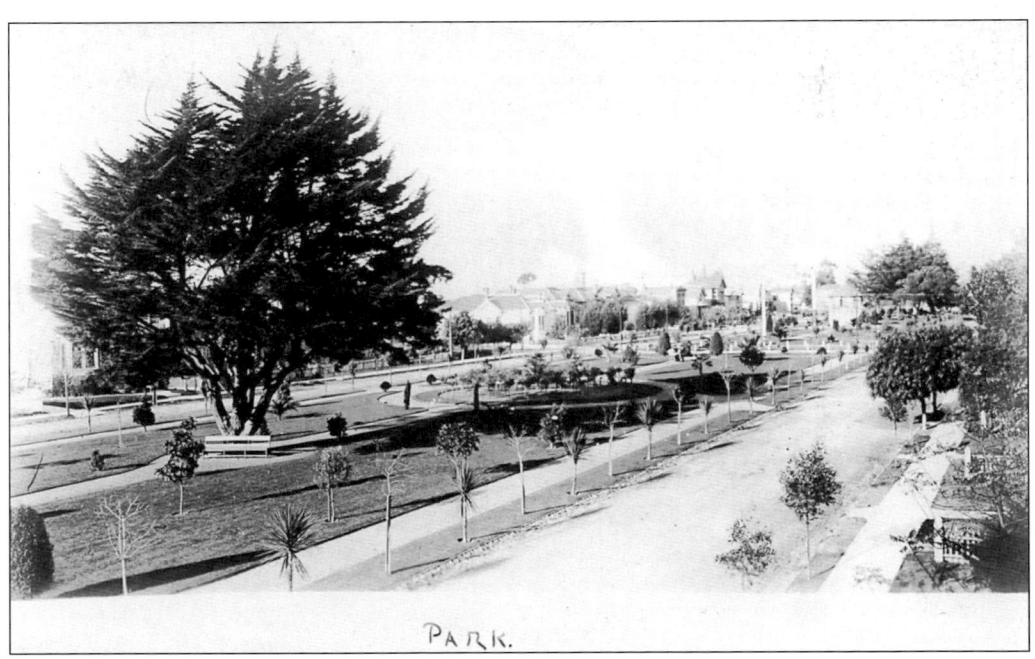

PARK.

Jackson Park at Encinal Avenue and Park Avenue, the subject of this *c.* 1906 postcard, is the oldest park in Alameda, officially opened in 1894. The pattern of trees, paths, and lawns were designed by a local florist, and the bandstand, built in 1890 for only $200, is the oldest municipally-owned structure on the island. The area was originally subdivided in 1867 as the Park Station land tract. The Victorian houses around what would later become Jackson Park were built on speculation; others were intended as rental properties and middle-class family residences.

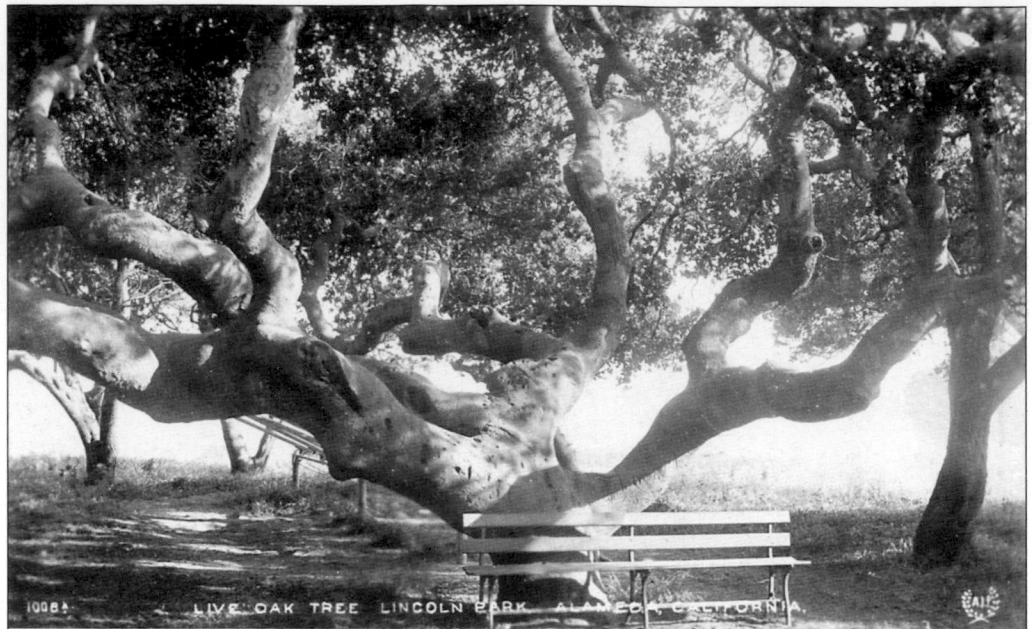

In 1887, Capt. R. Thompson built a three-story mansion on a large piece of land on High Street, but the home, which had never been occupied, burned down shortly after completion. The property was then abandoned until 1908, when the city bought it from Thompson for $40,000. This postcard was mailed in 1912. (Published by the American Industrial Photo Company, San Francisco.)

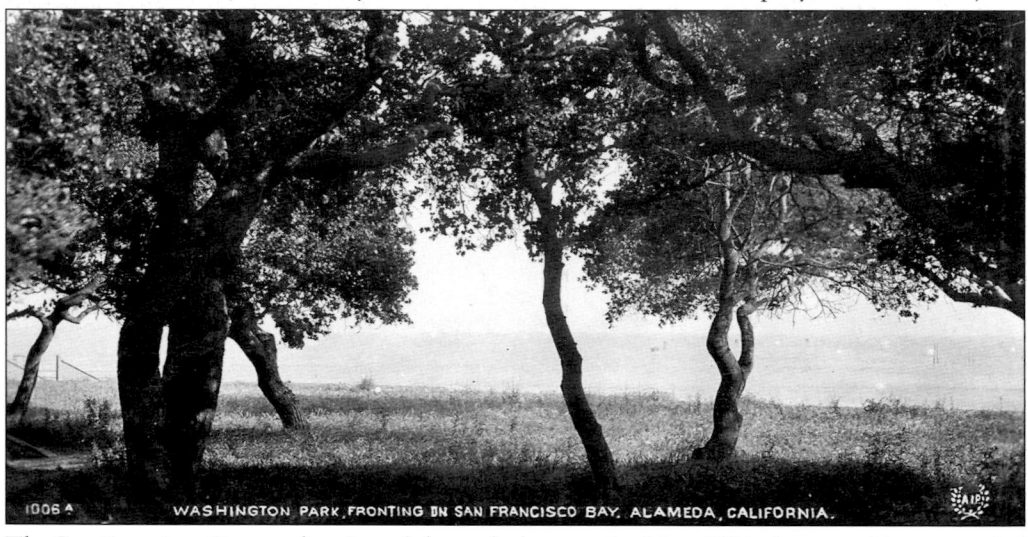

The San Francisco Bay can be viewed through the trees in this *c.* 1914 photographic postcard of Washington Park, located at Central Avenue and Eighth Street. Originally part of the Taylor Tract, the land was purchased by the city in 1908 and dedicated to the public in 1912. The baseball field was once the Hayes Estate, and after the Hayes family left, the home was occupied by Madam Young, a renowned spiritualist. A windmill on the park grounds pumped salt water from the bay, which was used to keep dust down on Alameda streets. In 1958, a retired Southern Pacific Railroad switch engine from 1915 (No. 1227) was added to the park's features. Renovations in the 1970s and 1980s enlarged the park to its present size. (Published by the American Industrial Photo Company, San Francisco.)

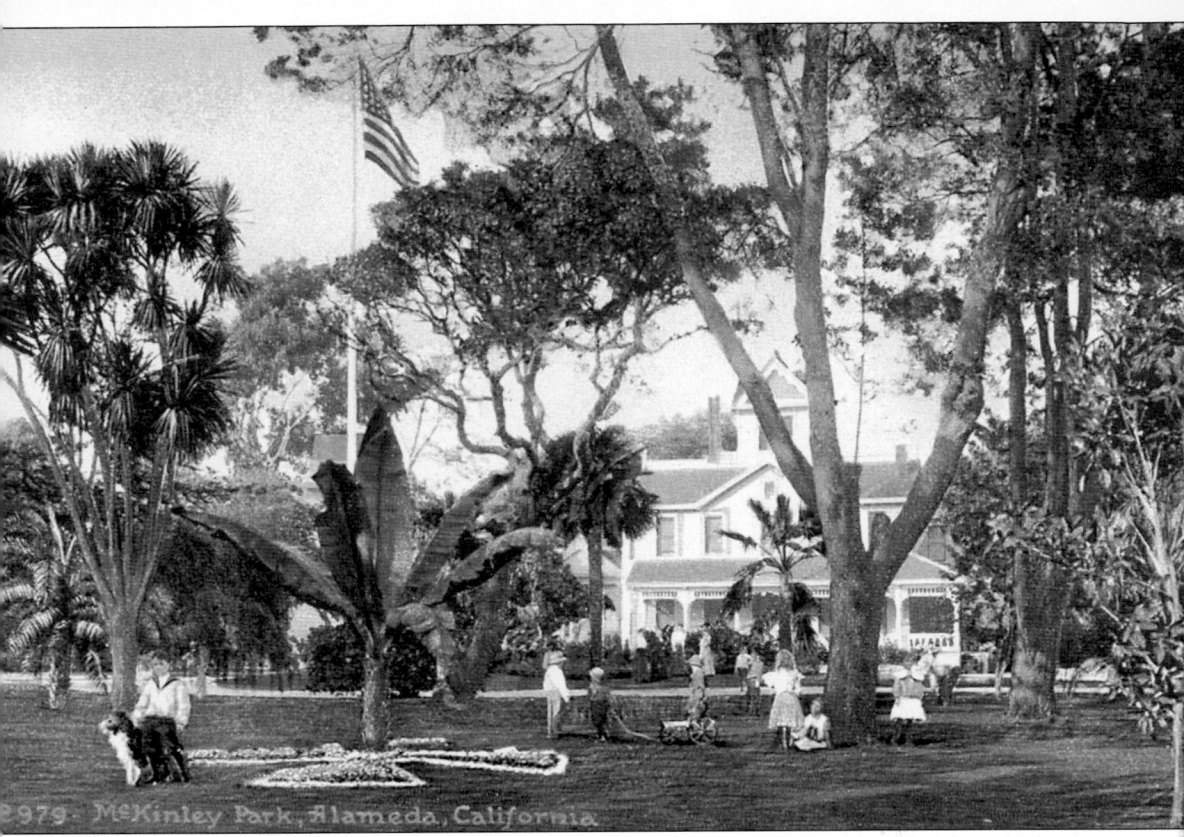

2979 McKinley Park, Alameda, California

In 1885, San Francisco attorney James A. Waymire built a spectacular 12-room home at Buena Vista Avenue and Walnut Street. Besides a ballroom with parquet floors, there was also a hot house to provide flowers for the lavish gardens. The grounds were outfitted with tennis and croquet courts, statuary, an aviary filled with exotic and domestic birds, a variety of trees, and a windmill and tank house to supply water. Sadly this paradise did not last. Due to debts and the loss of his law practice, Waymire was forced to sell the property in 1909 to the city for $24,000. The mansion, seen in this *c.* 1912 postcard, was demolished in the late 1930s to make room for a football field for Alameda High, and eventually the park was reduced in size from the original estate's three and one-half acres to one acre. Some of Waymire's improvements to the land still exist in the streets that were laid out and graded by him in what was originally a "cow pasture." (Published by Edward H. Mitchell, San Francisco.)

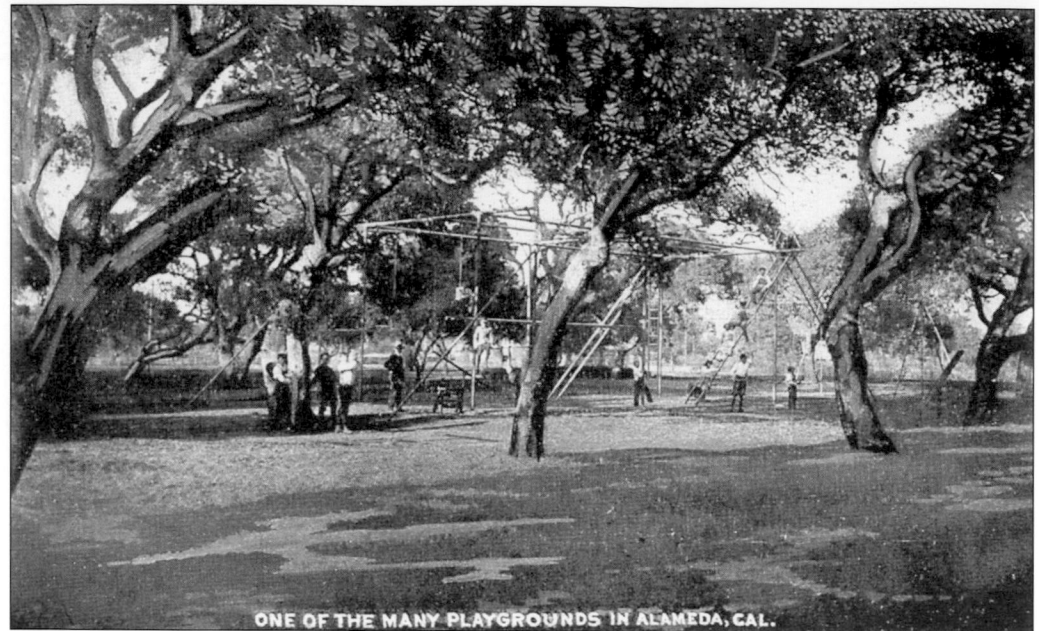

ONE OF THE MANY PLAYGROUNDS IN ALAMEDA, CAL.

One of the three new parks of 1909 (Lincoln, Washington, or McKinley) is seen on this *c.* 1910 postcard that shows boys enjoying the early playground equipment. (Published by Newman Postcard Company, San Francisco.)

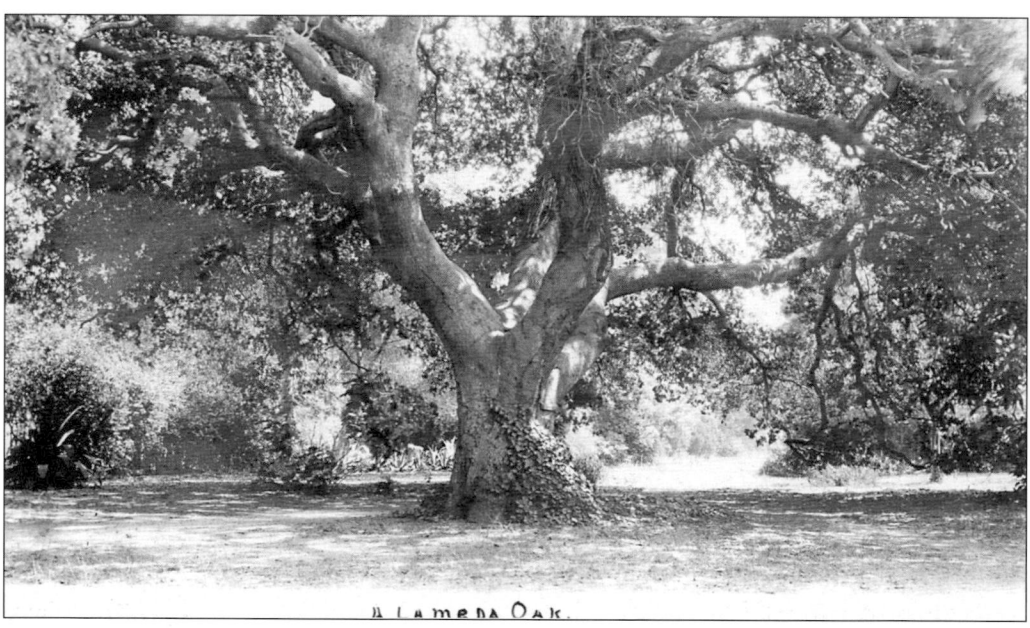

A l a m e n a Oak.

Before it was settled, Alameda was nearly completely covered in oak groves. Most of the trees were lumbered over a 20-year period, and it is said that no trees standing today indicate the size they once were. As the oak tree population dwindled in the early 1900s, Alameda residents became more appreciative and protective of them (that being evident in their appearance on postcards). This *c.* 1906 image offers a glimpse of such a tree, whose whereabouts or wellbeing cannot be attested to.

Five

RESIDENTIAL AREAS

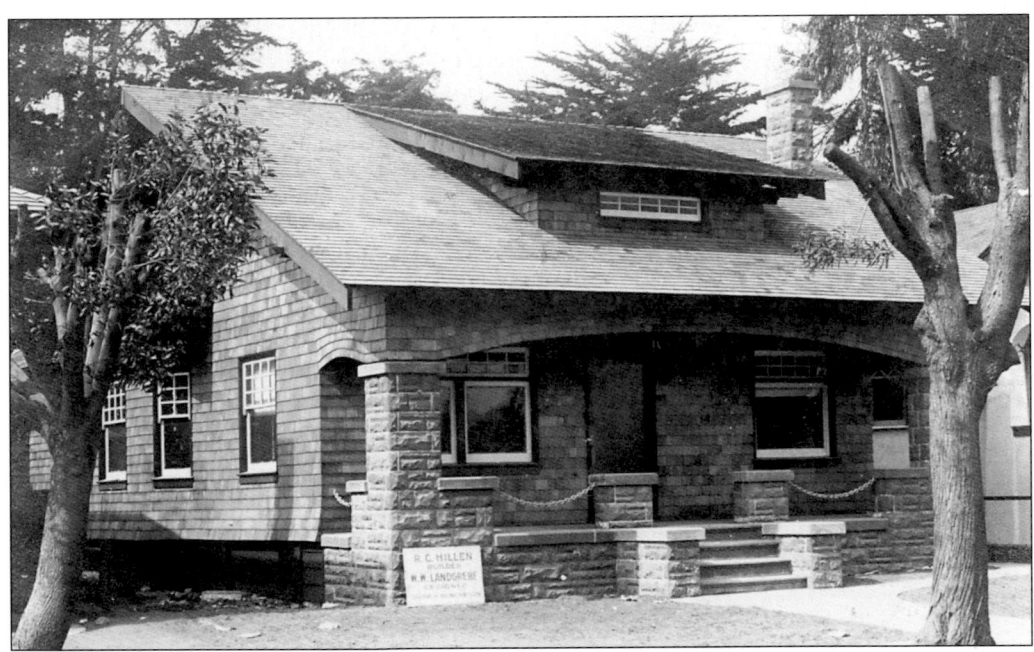

Mailed in April 1912, this Robert C. Hillen advertising postcard shows a brown–shingled, bungalow-style home at 3218 Liberty Avenue, designed by W. W. Landgrebe, who also worked with Hillen on several houses on Court Street. The house still stands, with few exterior changes.

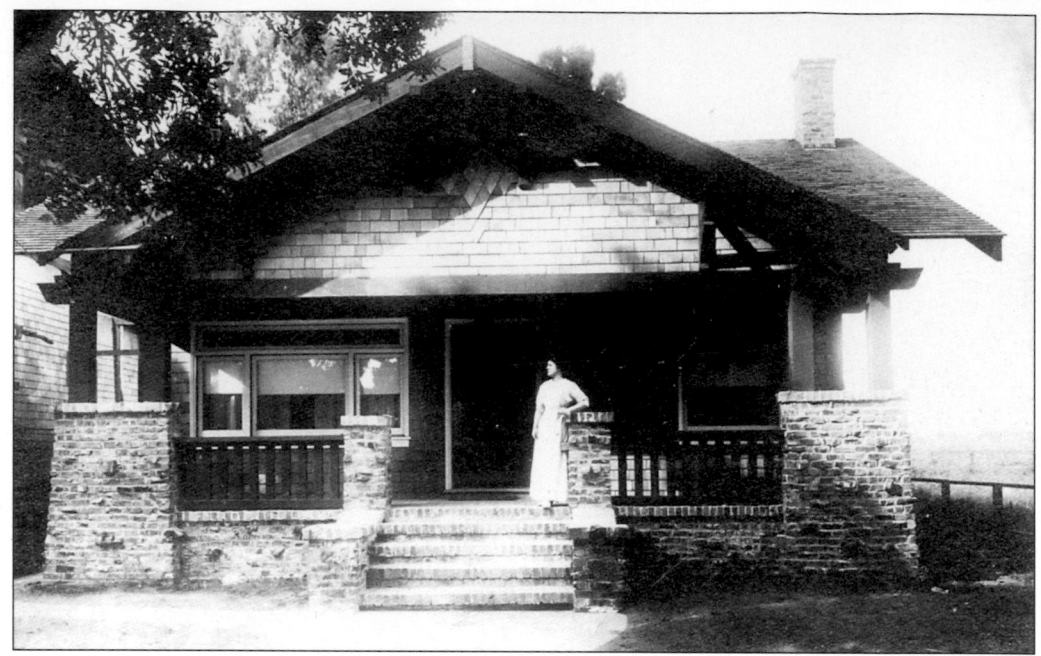

This advertising postcard, postmarked in November 1911, shows a recently completed home with Craftsman elements at 3225 Liberty Avenue, built by Robert C. Hillen. The house still stands, with minor outside changes. Hillen was a local contractor who had an office at 1505 Fernside Boulevard.

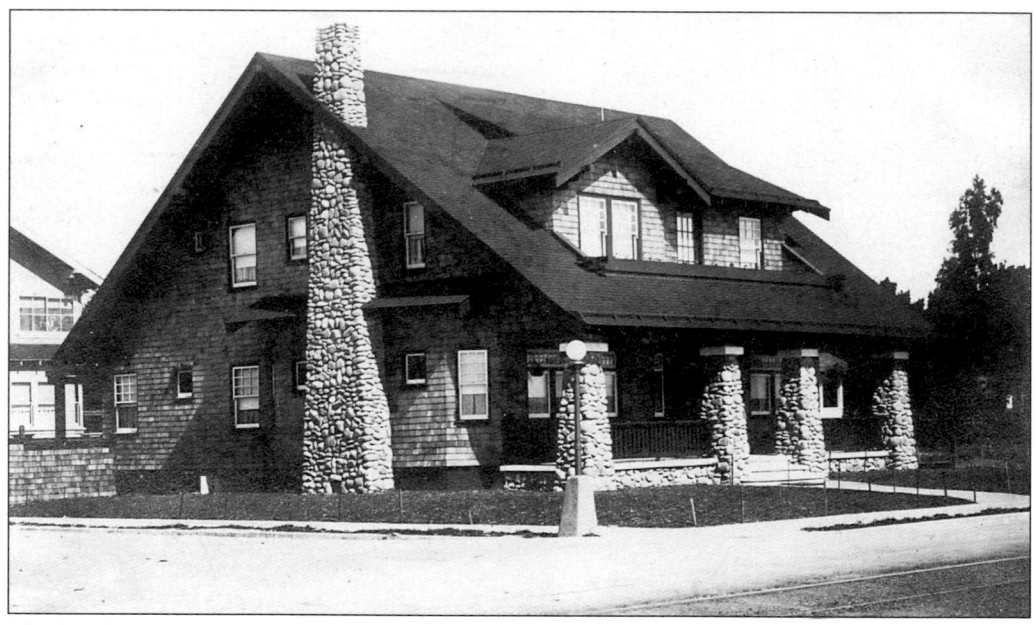

The handwritten message on the back of this April 1912 Robert C. Hillen advertising postcard says, "An elegant beach for boating or bathing is at the East end of Liberty Avenue, Lincoln Park playground, but a minute's walk; two blocks from the Lincoln School and handy to markets." This house is located at 1501 Fernside Boulevard at the corner of Liberty Avenue; the lovely stone pillars and chimney have since been replaced by wood and brick.

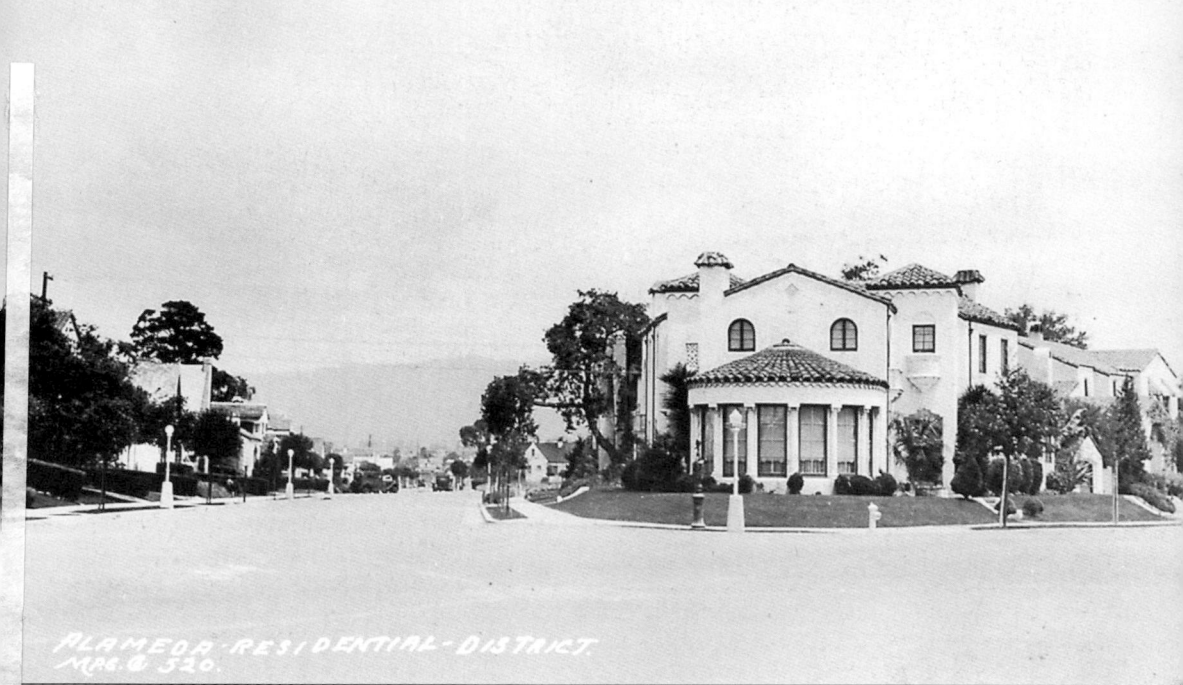

Alameda-Residential-District.
Mag @ 520.

This *c.* 1934 photographic postcard of the Fernside district, showing a Spanish Colonial–style house on the corner of Gibbons and Northwood Drives, illustrates a type of architecture common in this area. The Fernside neighborhood occupies land that was once the A. A. Cohen property, once the largest estate in Alameda. After marrying Emilie Gibbons in 1854, young attorney Alfred Andrew Cohen built his home, called Fernside, on 106 acres bounded by Central Avenue, High Street, and Versailles Street. He established a railroad company and eventually became an attorney for Central Pacific. In 1874, his success compelled him to construct a new, lavish home for his large family of seven children. The spectacular 50-room mansion that he built included servant's quarters, a library, a ballroom, a great hall, an atrium, and a five-story tower above it all. Other buildings on the estate contained a bowling alley and billiard hall, as well as a two-story carriage house and stables. Unfortunately Cohen's enjoyment of his paradise was brief; he died while traveling by train in November 1887. His wife and one of his sons continued to live quietly at Fernside after Cohen's death, but tragedy struck again in March 23, 1897, when the grand main house was destroyed by fire. After Emilie's death in 1924, the land south of Fernside Boulevard was sold by her children. The resulting model subdivision of Tudor, Mission, and other period revival homes still exists today.

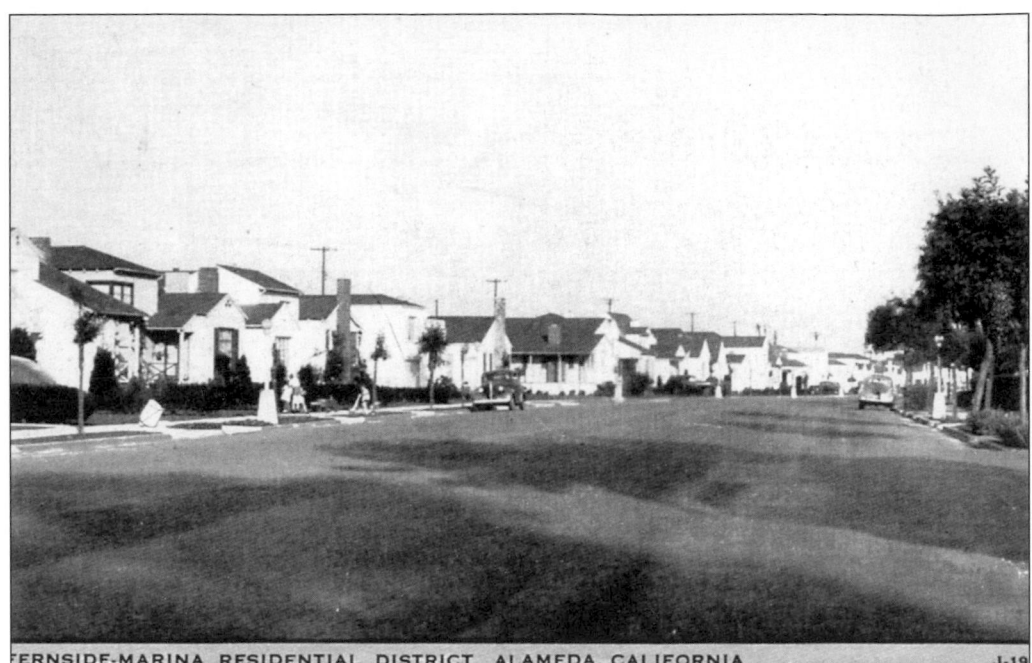

FERNSIDE-MARINA RESIDENTIAL DISTRICT, ALAMEDA, CALIFORNIA   J-19

A 1940s postcard of Fernside Boulevard, taken from Fremont Drive, shows Harvard Drive in the distance. (Manufactured by Wayne Paper Box and Printing Corporation, Fort Wayne, Indiana, *c.* 1942.)

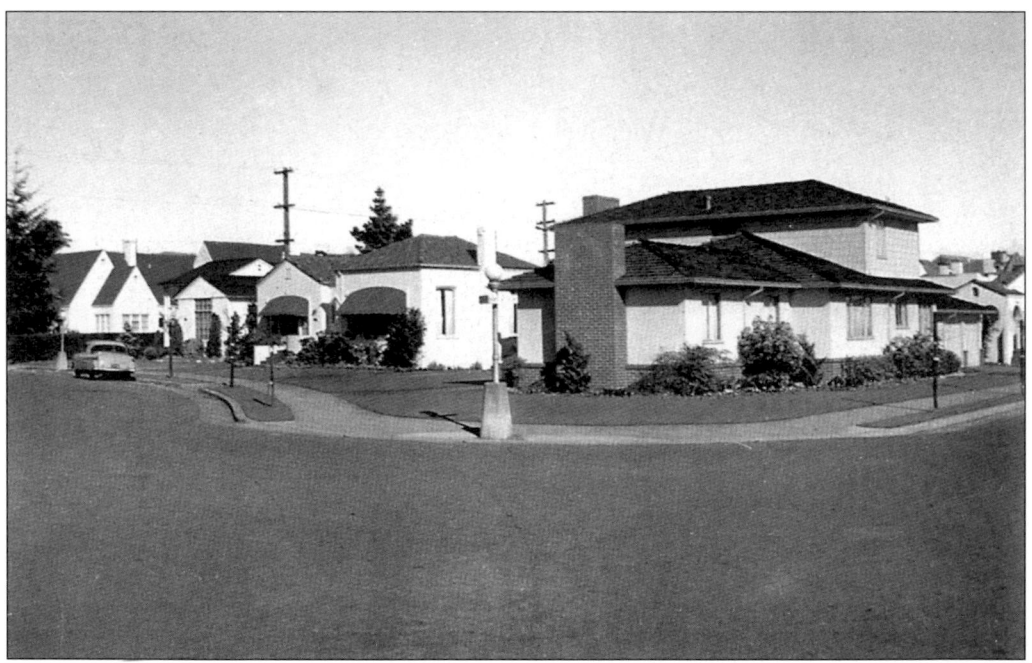

This 1950s postcard shows the intersection of Southwood Drive and Bayo Vista Avenue. The description on the back says this area of Alameda is "where you'll enjoy beautiful sun-flooded homes and gardens and comfortable weather the whole year around." Very little has changed since this picture was taken. (Published by the Alameda Chamber of Commerce.)

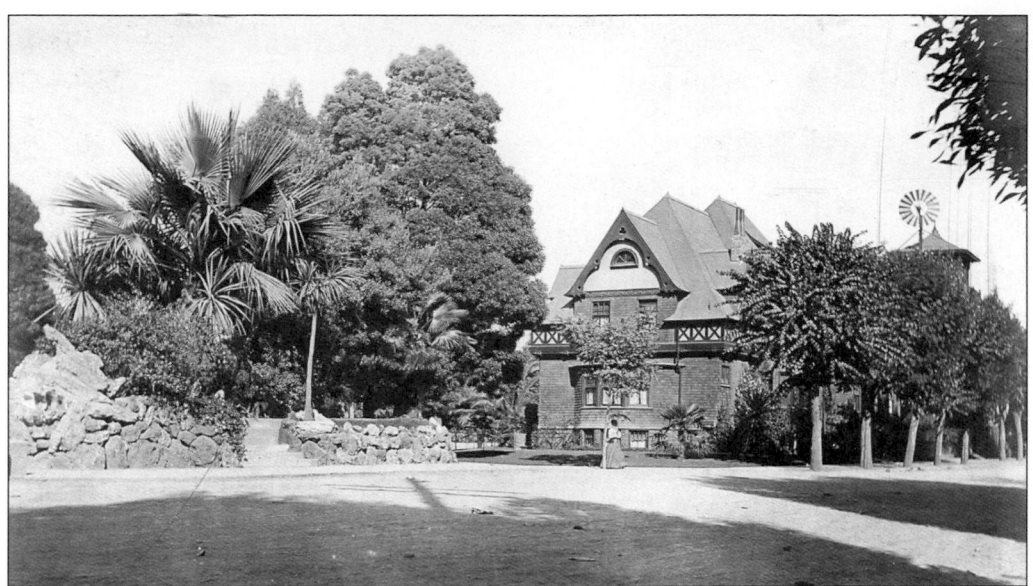

The beautiful home of local physician Dr. Pond is shown in this *c.* 1906 photographic postcard. The Pond home, located behind the monument known as the Rockery, was designed by A. W. Pattiani and built in 1901. Tragically, it was torn down in the early 1970s.

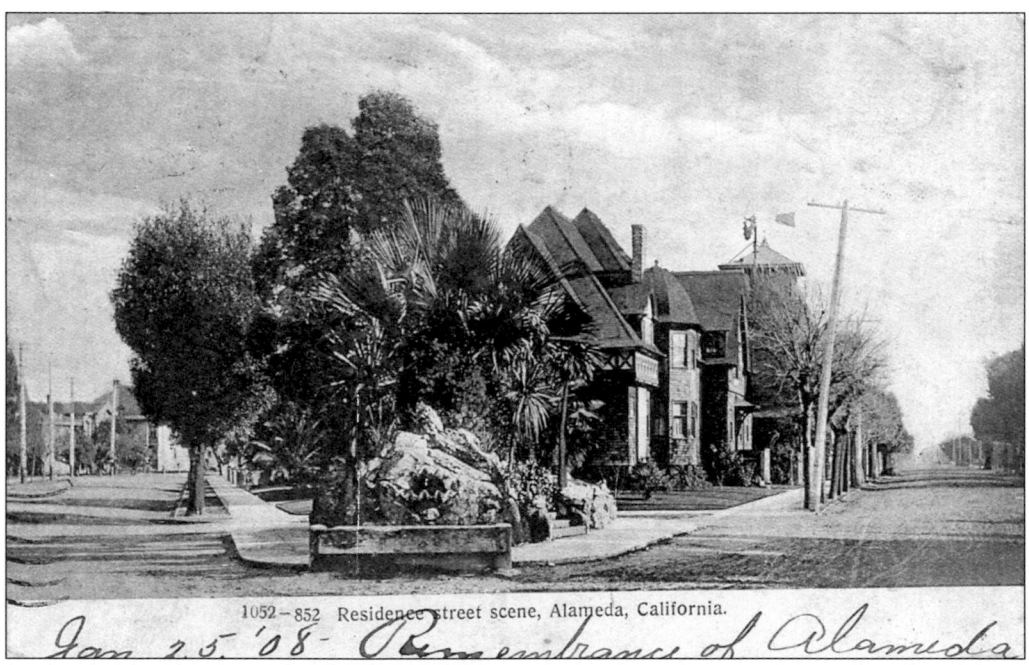

1052–852 Residence street scene, Alameda, California.

Mailed in January 1908, this postcard shows the Rockery at the intersection of Central and Alameda Avenues. Built around 1895, the Rockery was designed by the Joseph A. Leonard Company's head draftsman, George A. Dodge. Although damaged by vandals, the Rockery still exists. A plaque designates it as a memorial dedicated to Louise Maguire by the Women's Organizations of Alameda. (Published by the Cardinell-Vincent Company, Oakland.)

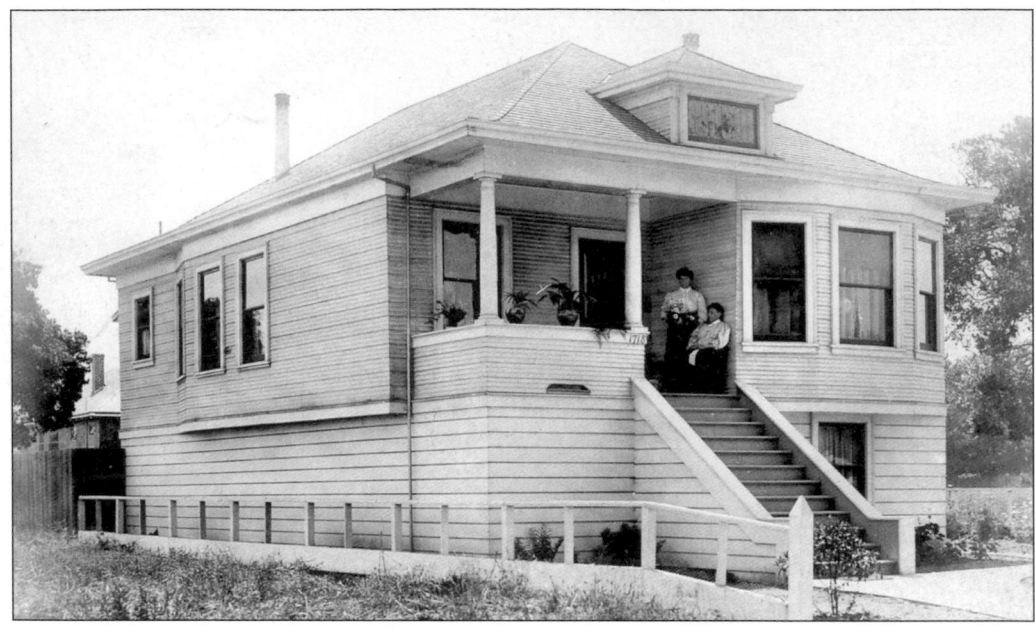

Although somewhat altered in appearance, this house is still present at 1718 Ninth Street. A 1920s bungalow occupies what was once the empty lot next door. Built in 1907, this Colonial Revival cottage was a single-family home when the postcard message, "Our new house," was written on the postcard on July 13, 1908. Owner W. R. Pease had a grocery store on Lincoln Avenue.

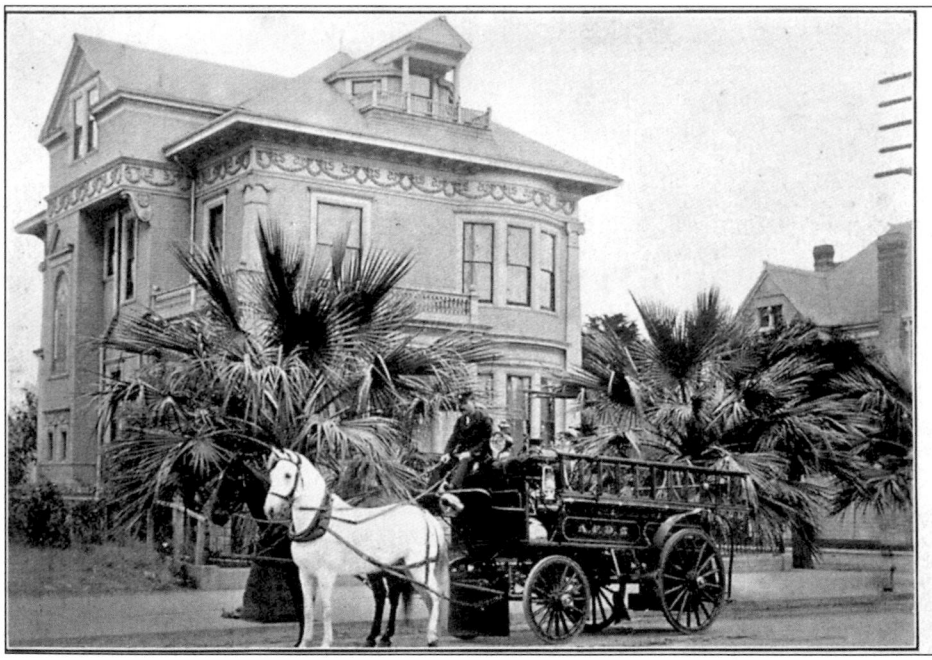

A Beautiful Home on Central Avenue Alameda California

Hartley Bros., Publishers Alameda California

This *c.* 1902 postcard shows the Alameda Fire Department's horse-drawn wagon in front of a large home on Central Avenue at the corner of Everett Street. Built in 1897, it was torn down before 1940, when the Lucky Store was built upon the site.

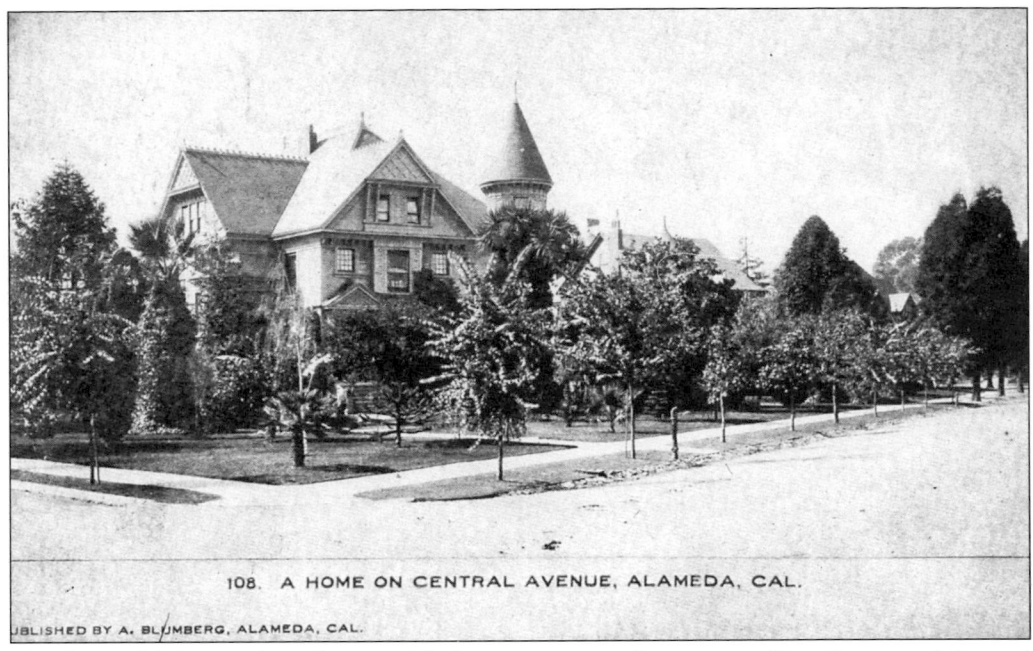

108. A HOME ON CENTRAL AVENUE, ALAMEDA, CAL.

PUBLISHED BY A. BLUMBERG, ALAMEDA, CAL.

This beautiful Queen Anne home with the turret was at the corner of Paru Street and Central Avenue. Built in 1889, this Gold Coast mansion was owned by Samuel Haslett, who ran a warehouse company in San Francisco. Sadly the home was demolished prior to World War II. (Published by A. Blumberg, Alameda, *c.* 1905.)

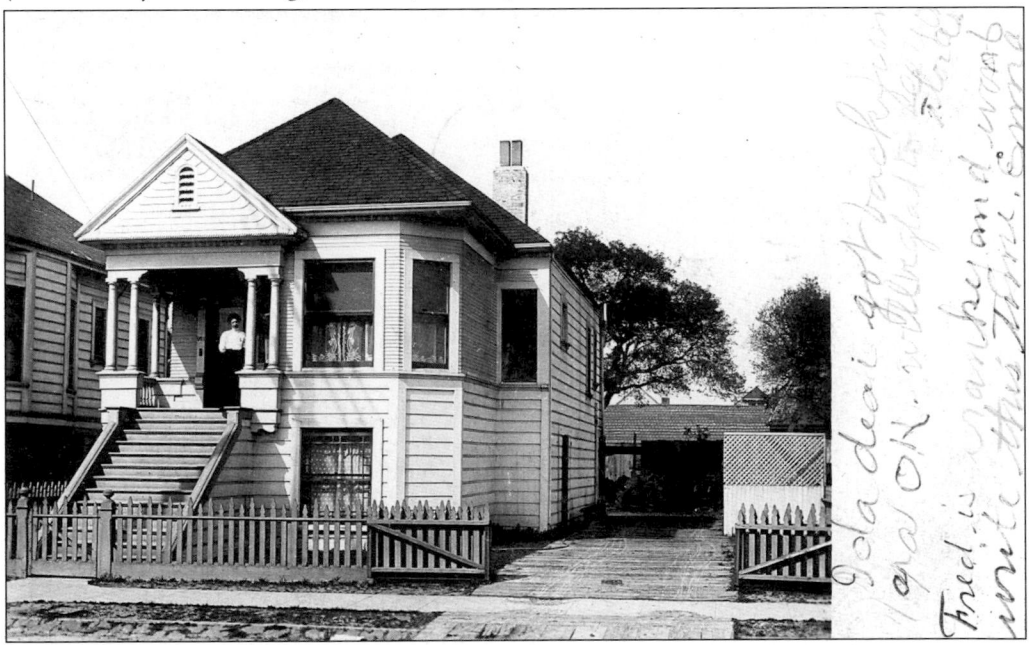

The sender of this postcard card, Emma, writes to Ida in San Francisco in May 1908 that this house is "where I hang out sometimes." She also mentions that "Fred is cranky and won't write this time." Located at 931 Central Avenue, this Queen Anne cottage was designed and built by Marcuse and Remmel in 1895. Over the years, changes and additions have drastically altered its exterior.

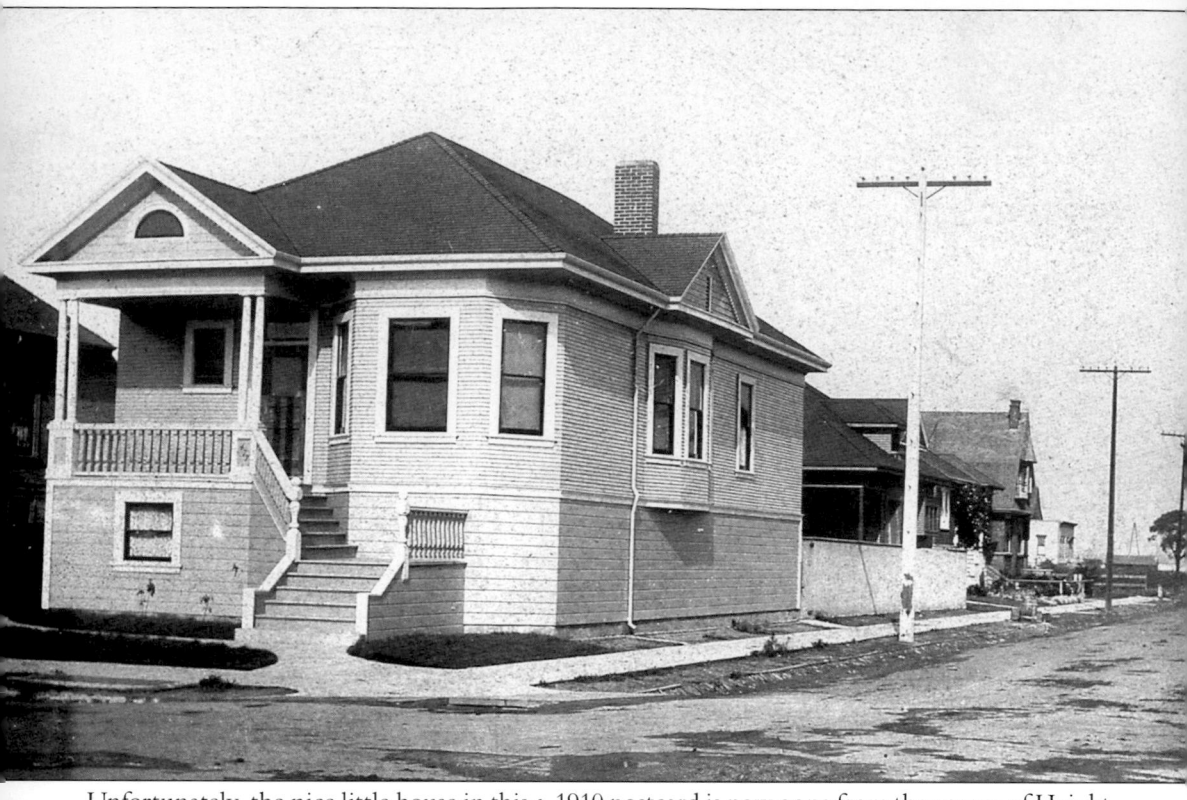

Unfortunately, the nice little house in this *c.* 1910 postcard is now gone from the corner of Haight Avenue and Fifth Street. Note the dirt streets and empty lots in the distance on the right.

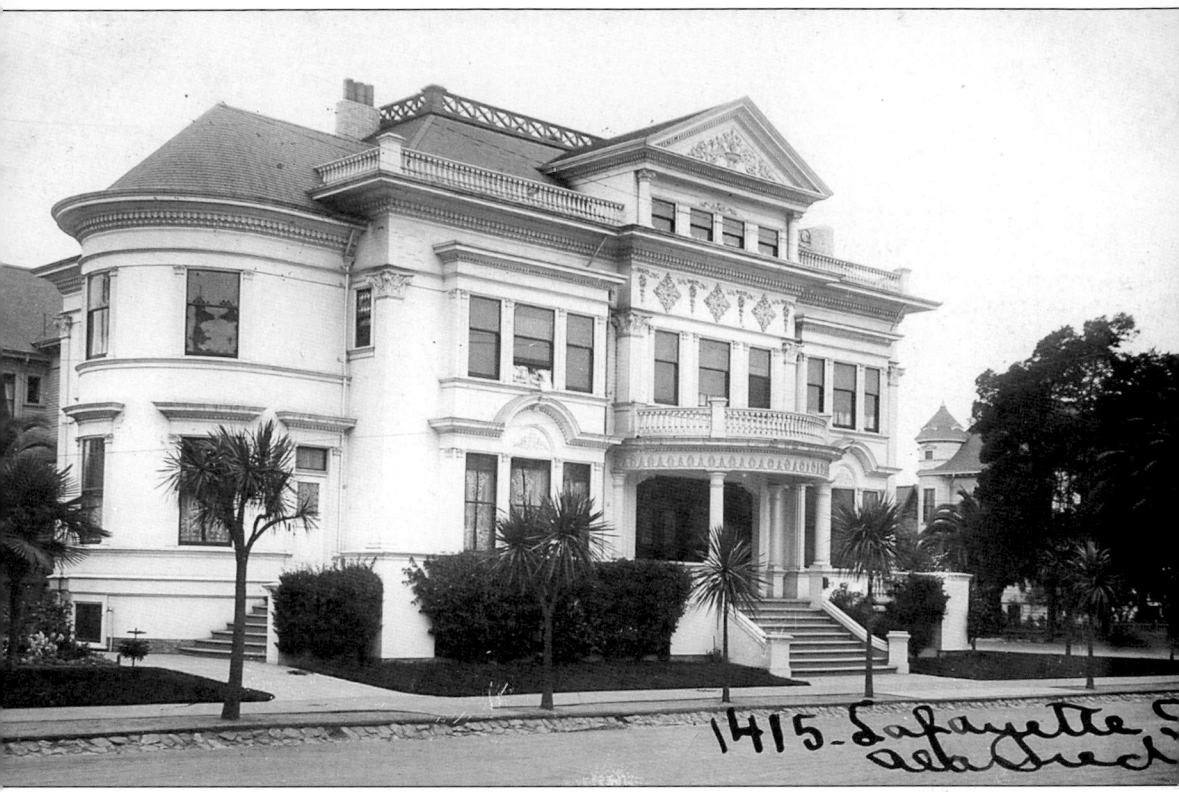

Built in 1901 for Mrs. M. J. Wall, the original cost of this stunning home was $16,000. Designed by architect T. D. Newsom and built by the Alameda Land Company, this Colonial Revival mansion still graces the intersection of Lafayette and Central Avenue to this day.

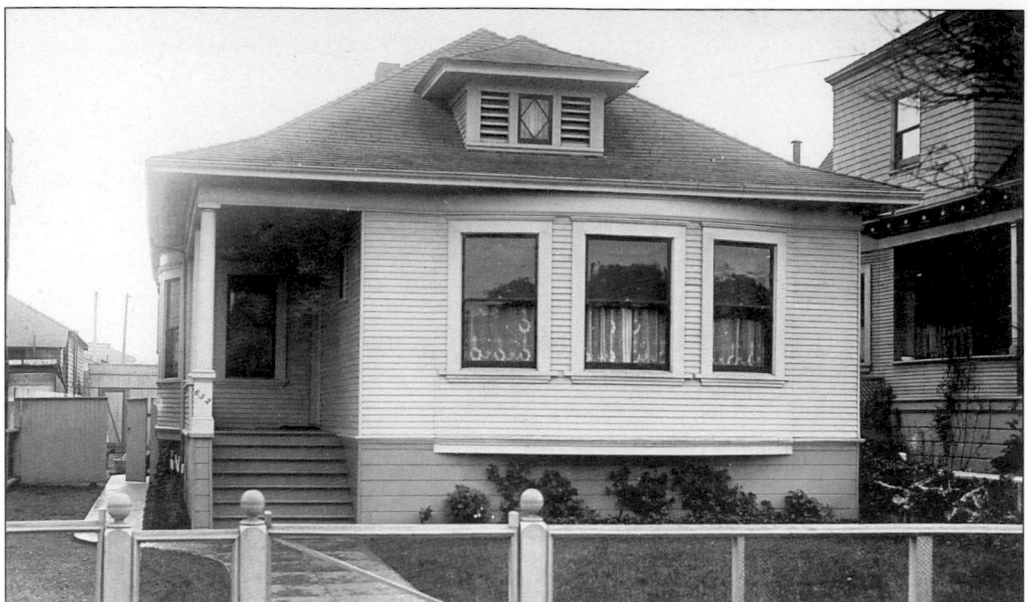

Another charming Colonial Revival home, this one was built in 1906 and still stands at 632 Lincoln Avenue. Mailed in 1908, the postcard message from Emma Brink states: "Dear Cousin Annie, this is our little cottage where we live."

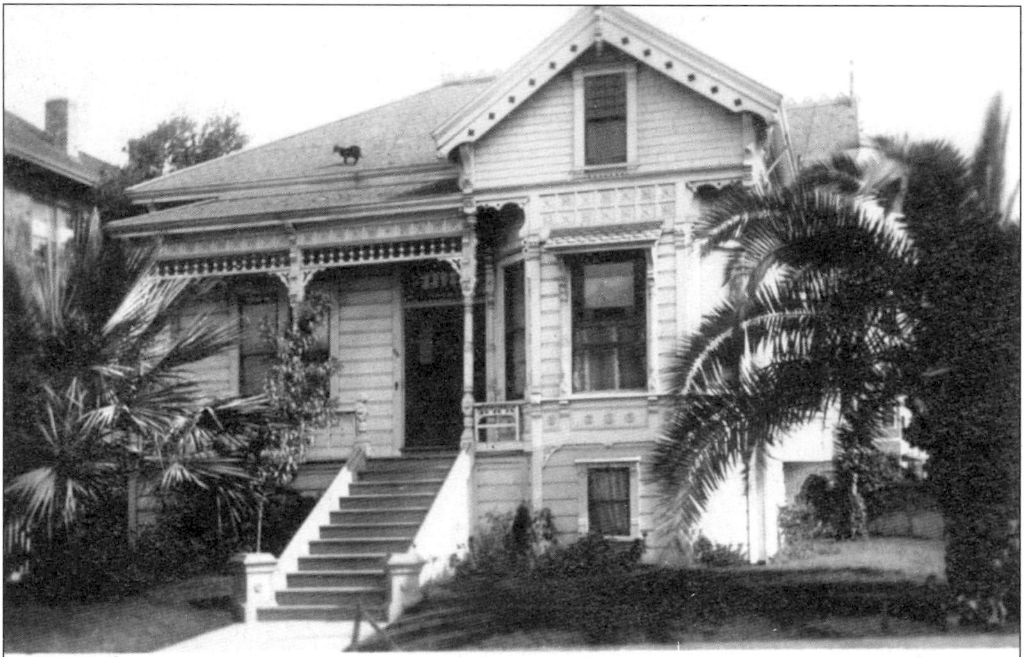

This postcard, mailed in 1910, has a message from Ethel, who writes, "Dear Sarah, we are not dead, but are living in the house pictured on this card. I had everything ready to write tonight, but had a pair of pants handed me ripped from stern to stern, consequently I must sew a little." This Queen Anne cottage, built in 1886, still stands at 2171 San Antonio Avenue, minus some of the front porch gingerbread and the cat on the roof.

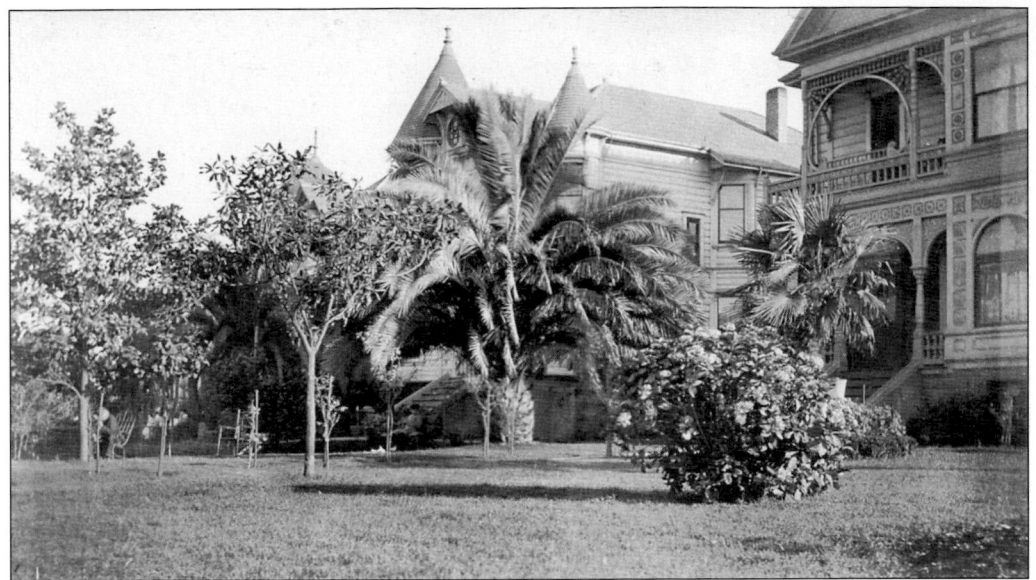

Palm trees, rosebushes, and young trees decorate the gardens of these elaborate Victorian homes on Santa Clara Avenue in this *c.* 1906 photographic postcard. The house on the left behind the palm, which is numbered 2112–2114, was built in 1892 and divided into flats in 1908. The original architect was Otto Collischonn, and the 1908 alteration was designed by A. W. Cornelius. The house on the right is now gone.

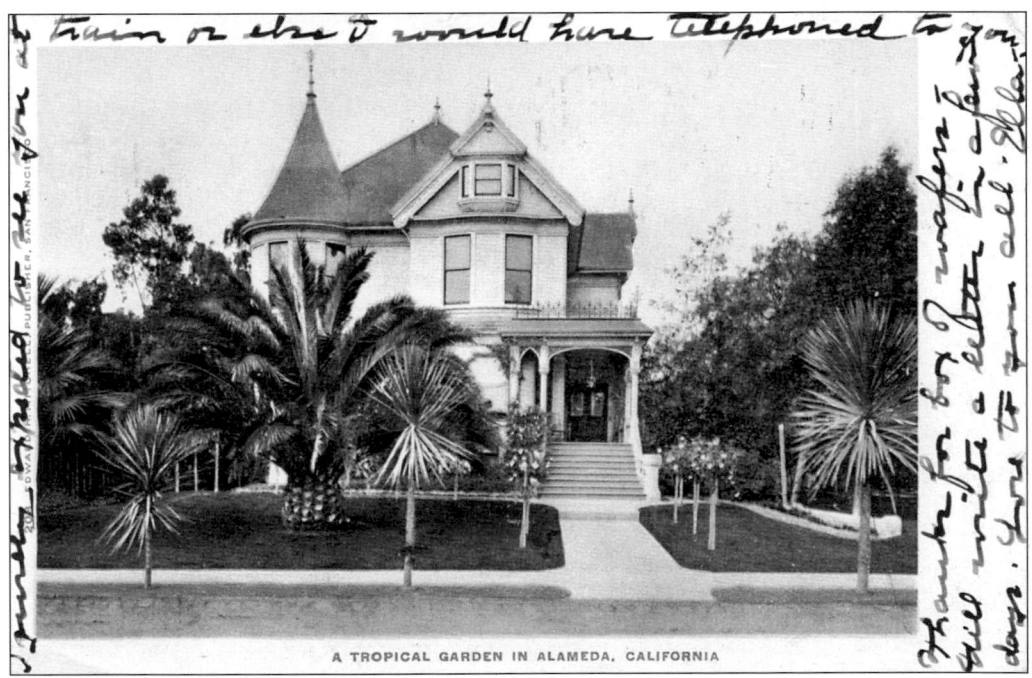

A TROPICAL GARDEN IN ALAMEDA, CALIFORNIA

The gorgeous Queen Anne home at 1021 Union Street was designed by Charles S. Shaner and was originally owned by Walter F. Haskell, who worked for Traveler's Insurance in San Francisco. Mailed in May 1905, this postcard illustrates the allure of Alameda's landscape and climate, as well as the exceptional architecture.

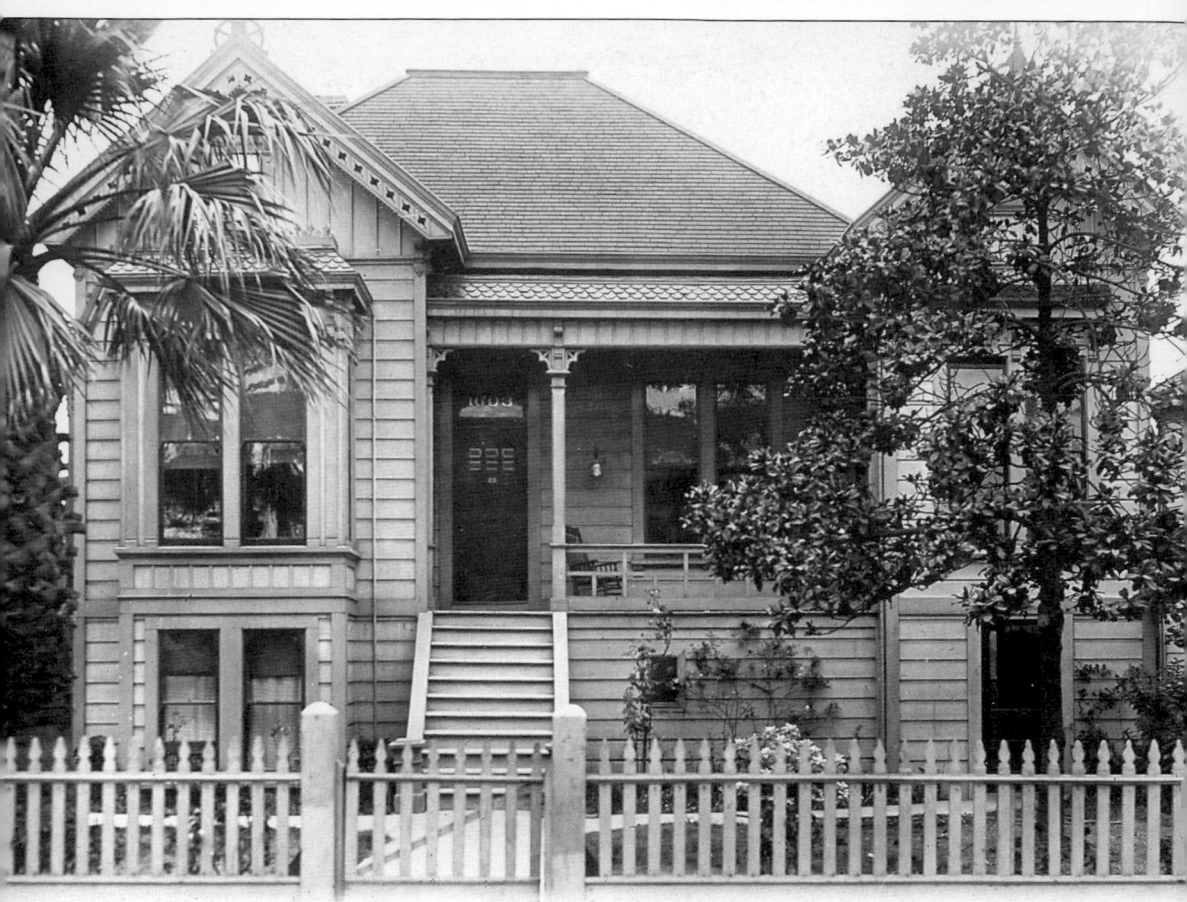

Sadly, this darling 1880s Victorian with the picket fence, the subject of this *c.* 1909 photographic postcard, no longer exists at 1603 Walnut Street.

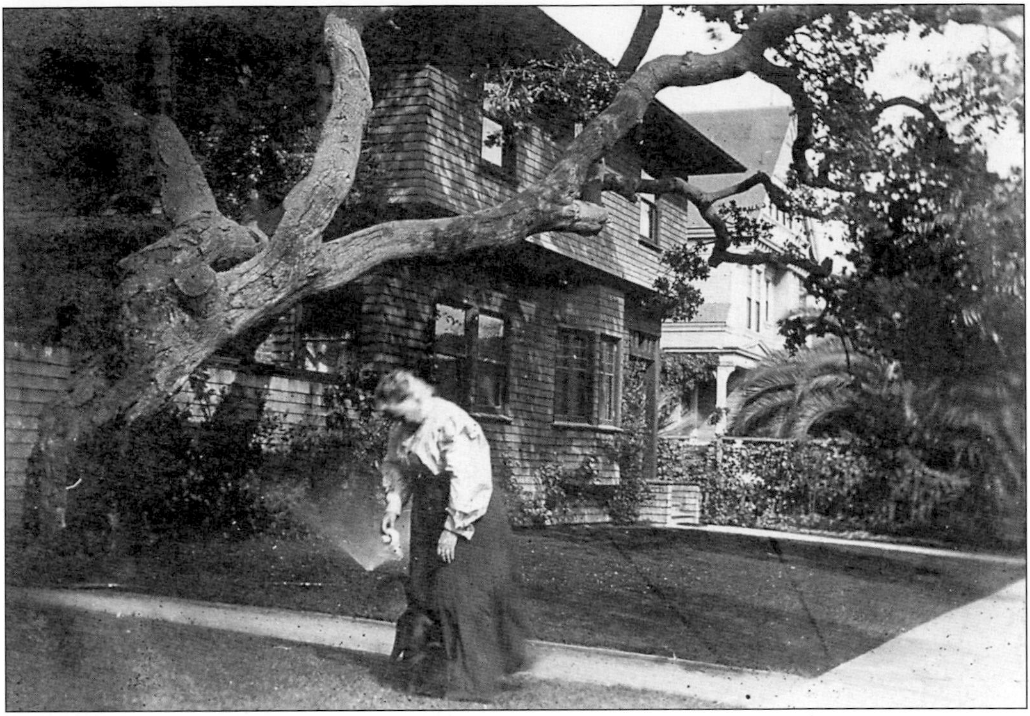

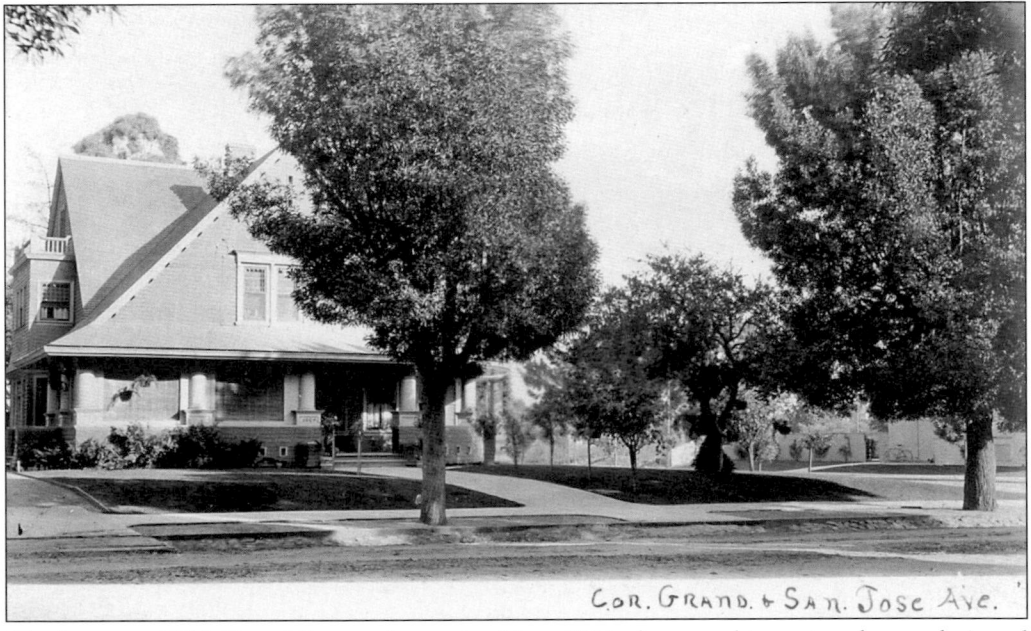

Alice Rix, owner of the Home of Truth, stands with her dog in front of her oak-shaded, brown-shingled home and parsonage at 1709 Alameda Avenue at the intersection of Grand Street in this *c.* 1906 photographic postcard. Designed by B. E. Remmel and built by Olaf Mageneson of Oakland in 1905, this house still stands.

The house at 1000 Grand Street, shown in this *c.* 1906 photographic postcard, was designed by architect C. H. Russell in 1900 and built at a cost of $8,000. It still decorates the corner of Grand Street and San Jose Avenue.

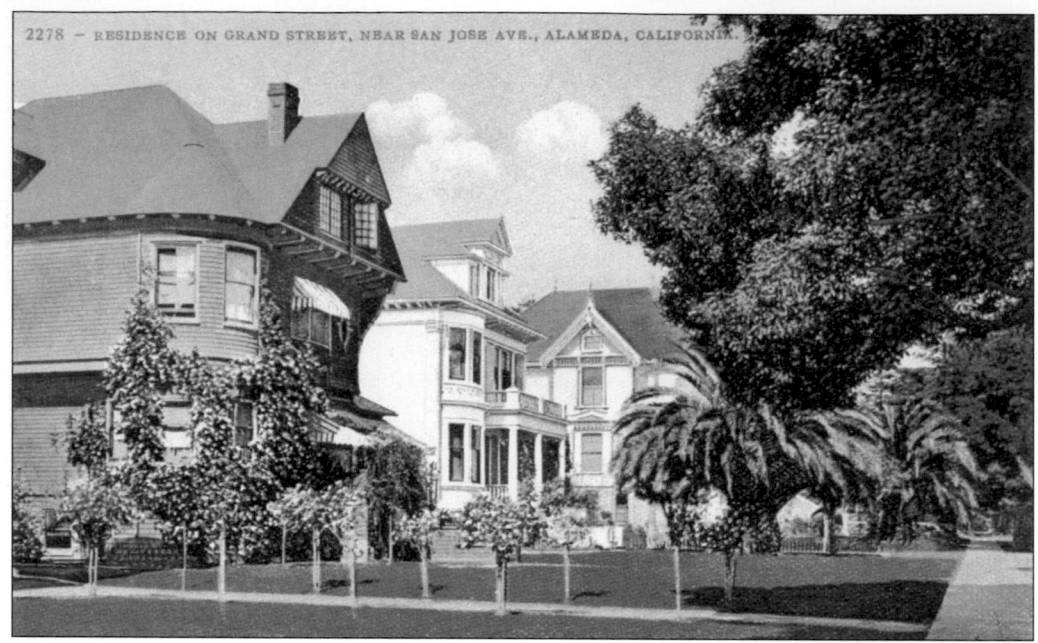

2278 - RESIDENCE ON GRAND STREET, NEAR SAN JOSE AVE., ALAMEDA, CALIFORNIA.

This *c.* 1912 view of the 900 block of Grand Street looks toward the intersection of San Jose Avenue. All three houses shown are still standing. The Queen Anne, brown-shingled house on the left was designed and built by A. W. Pattiani and Company in 1891. (Published by Edward H. Mitchell, San Francisco.)

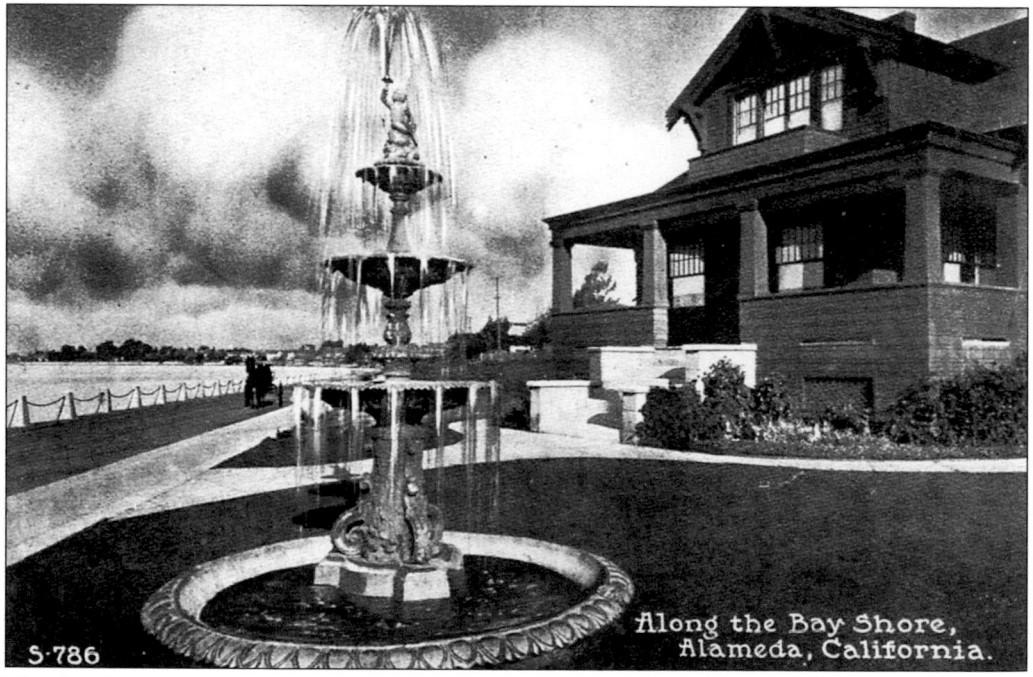

Along the Bay Shore, Alameda, California.

S-786

This lovely, brown-shingled house still stands at 821 Oak Street, where it once had a bay view and front yard fountain. It was built in 1909 by the Powell Brothers and was designed by the Duel and Wright firm. (Published by the Souvenir Publishing Company, San Francisco, *c.* 1912.)

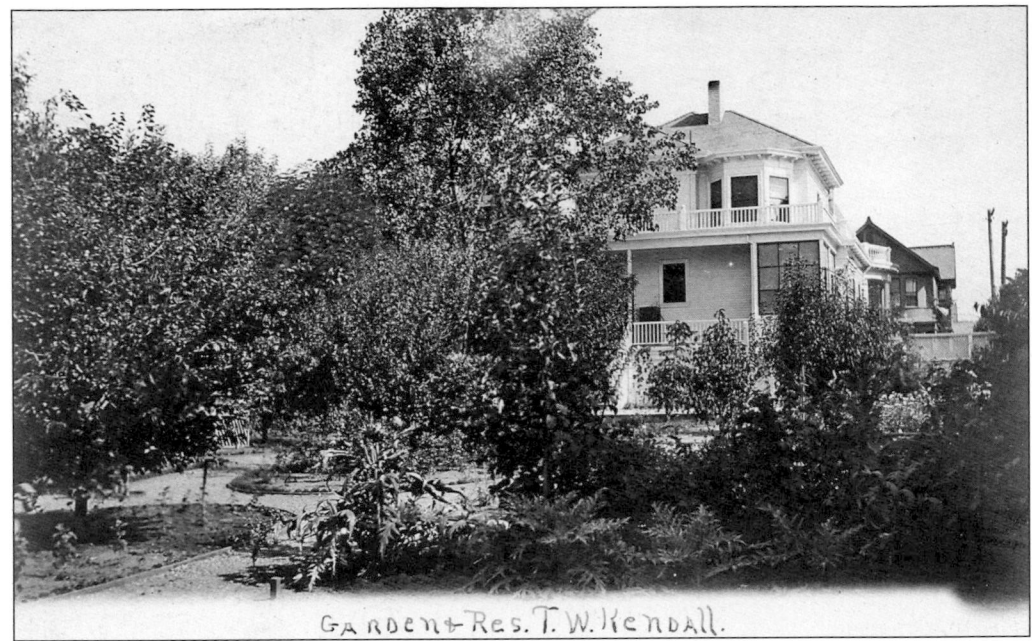

GARDEN & Res. T. W. Kendall.

This *c.* 1906 postcard shows the garden and home of T. W. Kendall, located on the bay shore at 1814 Clinton Avenue. According to telephone directories of the era, T. W. Kendall was in the mining business. This house, built in 1903, still stands, although the lot containing the side garden shown in the postcard was sold at some point, and a house was built there.

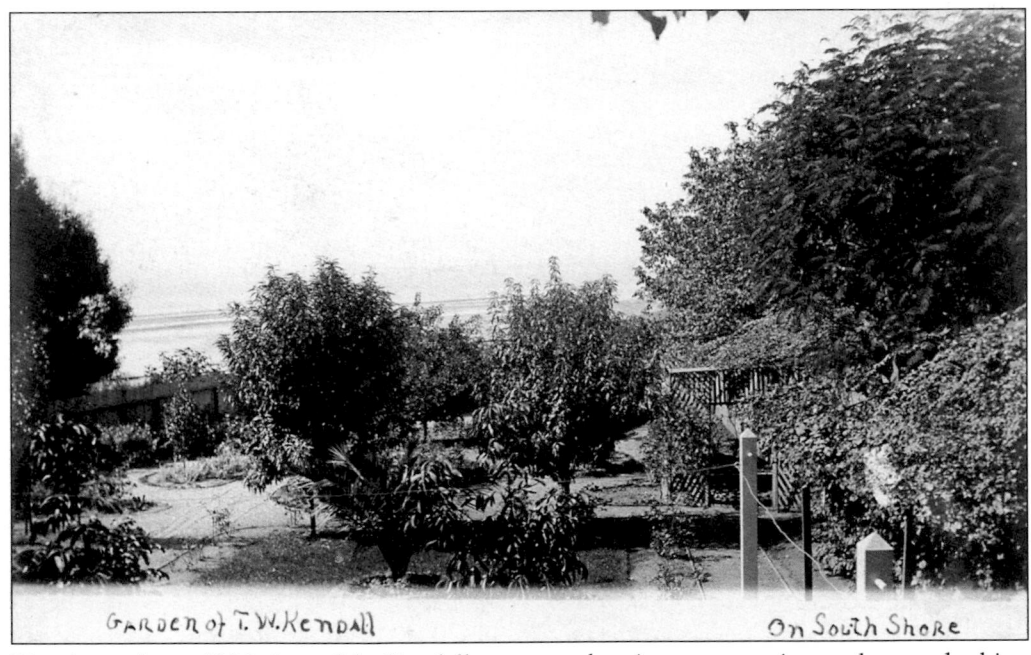

GARDEN of T. W. Kendall   On South Shore

Here is another *c.* 1906 view of the Kendall property, showing an expansive garden overlooking the bay.

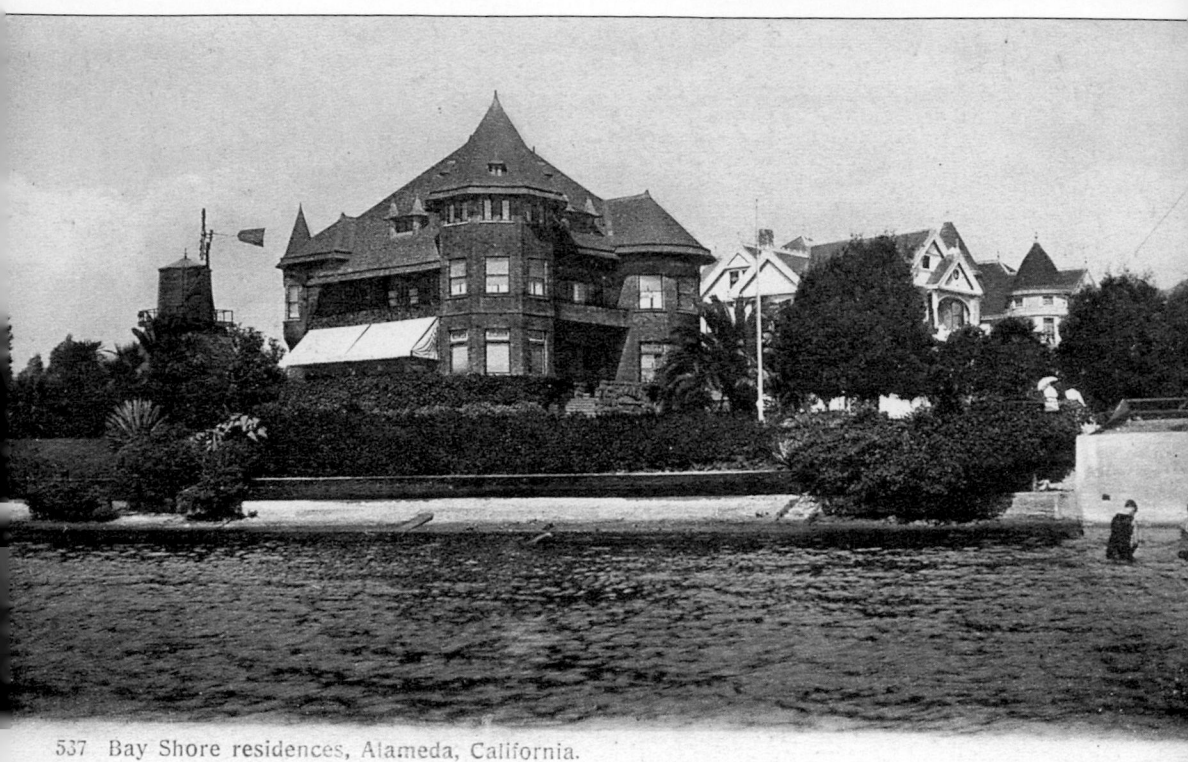

537 Bay Shore residences, Alameda, California.

Joseph A. Leonard's dramatic and unusual mansion can be seen here, where Union Street ended at the bay. Built in 1896 by Leonard, it was designed by architect and Leonard Company head draftsman C. H. Russell, for a cost of $20,000. Shortly after the home was completed, Leonard's prolific building phase came to an end. Economic troubles forced the closure of his business in 1898, and Leonard himself moved away from Alameda in 1900. By the time this *c.* 1907 postcard was published by the Cardinell-Vincent Company, the house had been sold to George W. Emmons. The house still stands at 891 Union, with minor external changes.

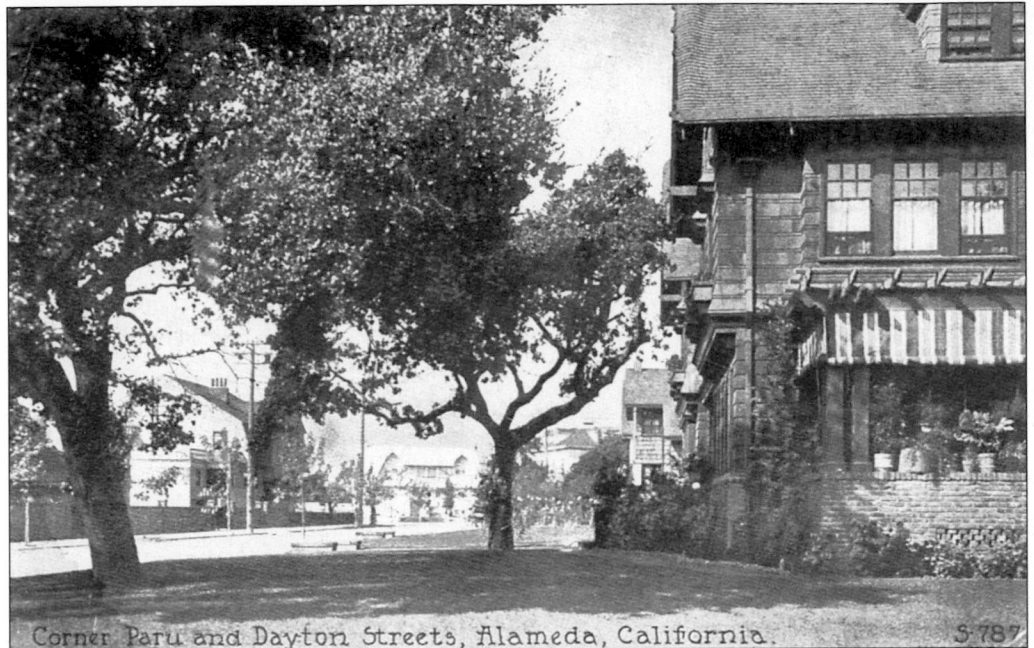

Corner Paru and Dayton Streets, Alameda, California.   S 787

This postcard, mailed in 1919, shows the spacious English Manor-style residence at the corner of Dayton Avenue and Paru Street. Completed in 1910, it was designed by the architectural firm of Murdock and Smith and built by Leard and Gates for the sum of $12,296. (Published by Souvenir Publishing Company, San Francisco.)

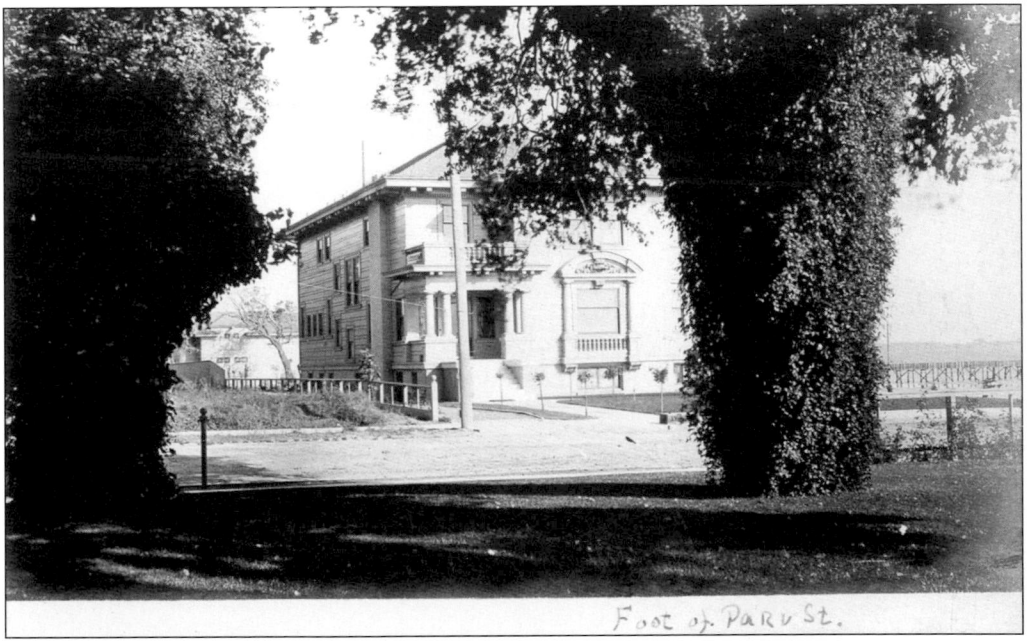

Foot of Paru St.

This *c.* 1906 photographic postcard of 700 Paru Street shows the Colonial Revival-style house at the foot of Paru, where it used to meet the bay. The home was built for Albert Clark of Clark and Sons Pottery Works, whose terra-cotta factory moved from Sacramento to Alameda in 1886. The plant operated until 1949.

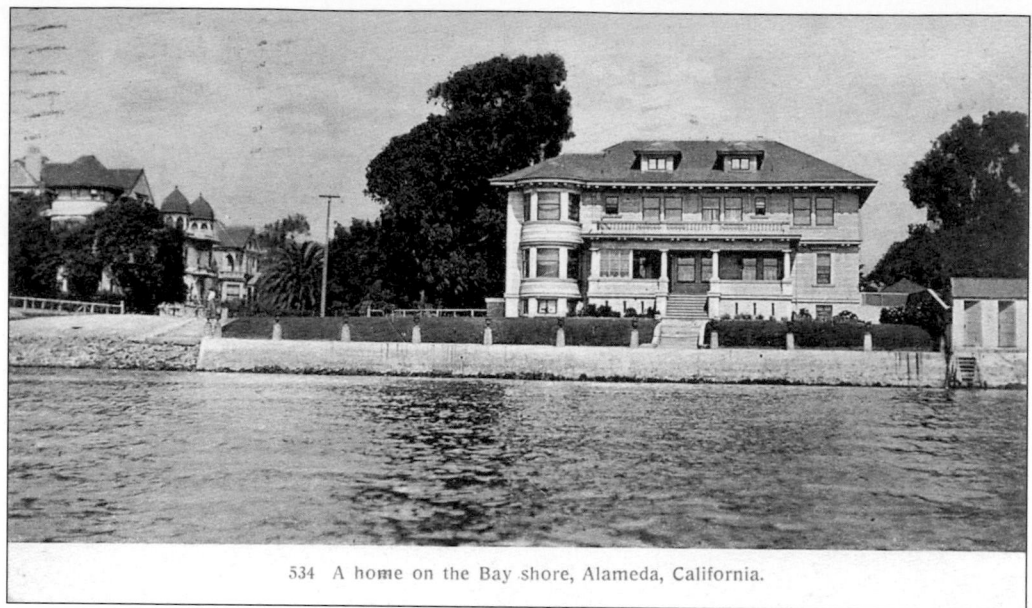

534 A home on the Bay shore, Alameda, California.

Built in 1904 for a cost of $11,518, this large residence at 700 Paru Street was designed by Cunningham and Politeo. The house still stands, with some external changes. (Published by the Cardinell-Vincent Company, Oakland, *c.* 1909.)

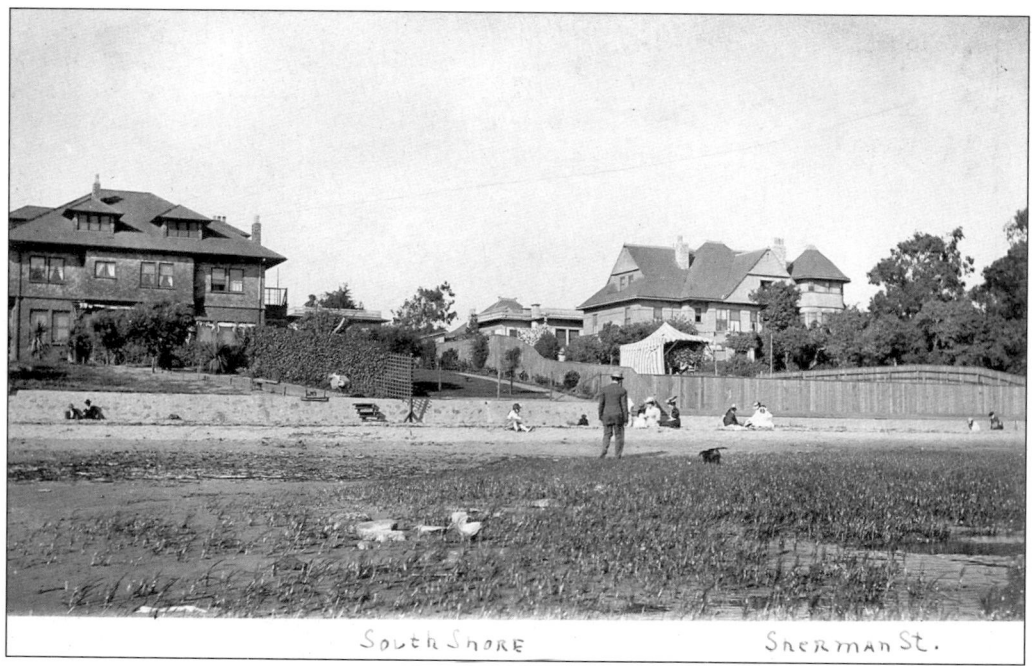

SOUTH SHORE   SHERMAN St.

In this *c.* 1906 postcard, a man walks his dog at low tide in the South Shore area between Sherman and Paru Streets, while small groups of people lounge on the beach below two enormous homes. The large, brown-shingled house on the left, which still stands at 1010 Sherman Street, was designed by B. E. Remmel and built by Cornelius and Brehaut in 1902.

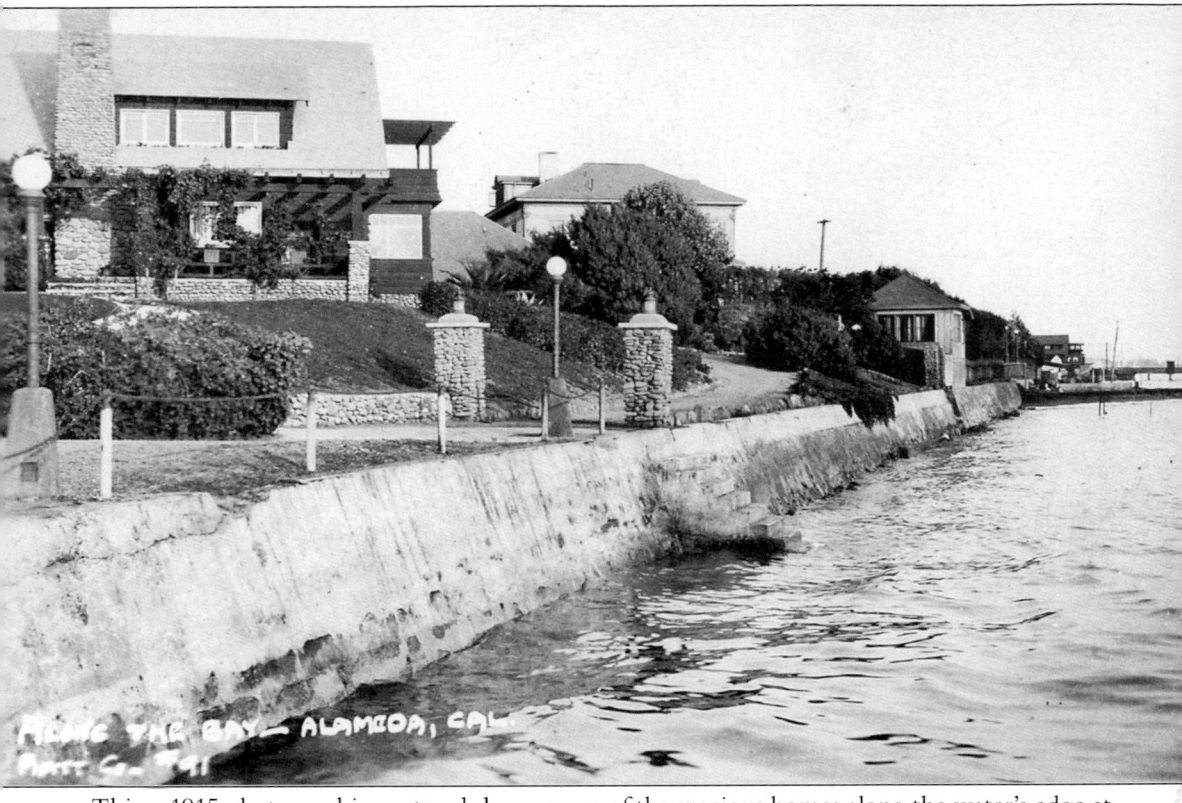

This *c.* 1915 photographic postcard shows some of the spacious homes along the water's edge at the end of Bay Street. On the left is 1100 Bay Street, a Craftsman-style house that was built in 1907. Because of the landfill and lagoon construction of the 1950s, the residents of these homes no longer enjoy the luxury of living on the bay shore.

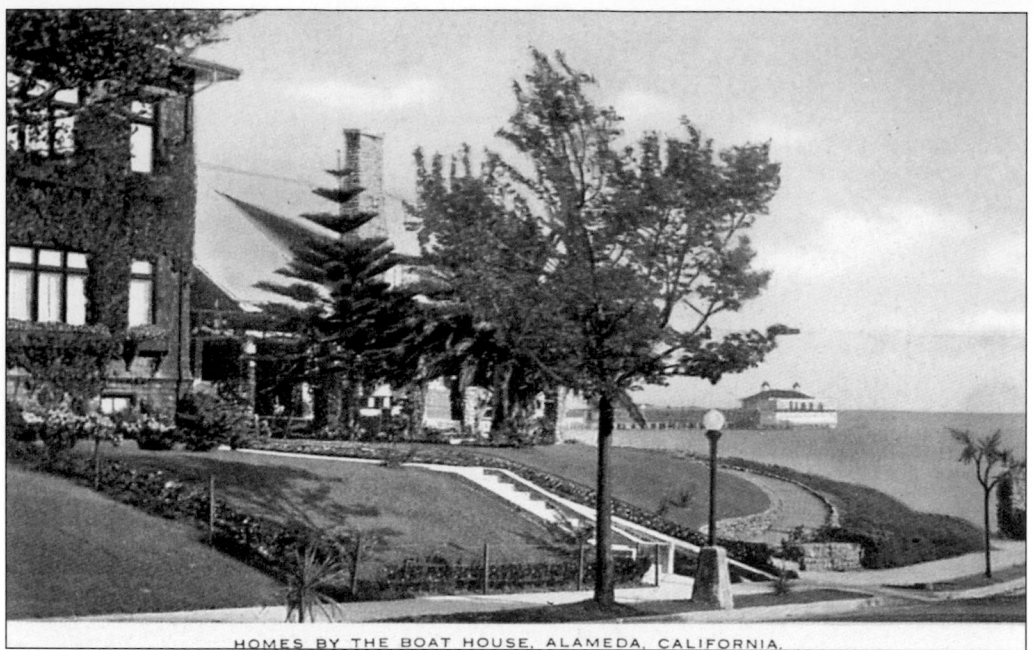

HOMES BY THE BOAT HOUSE, ALAMEDA, CALIFORNIA.

On the left is 1106 Bay Street, built in 1906 and originally owned by Frank V. Bordwell, a cashier at the Citizens Bank of Alameda on Park Street. On the right is 1100, built by Robert L. Holt in 1907. (Published by Pacific Novelty Company, San Francisco.)

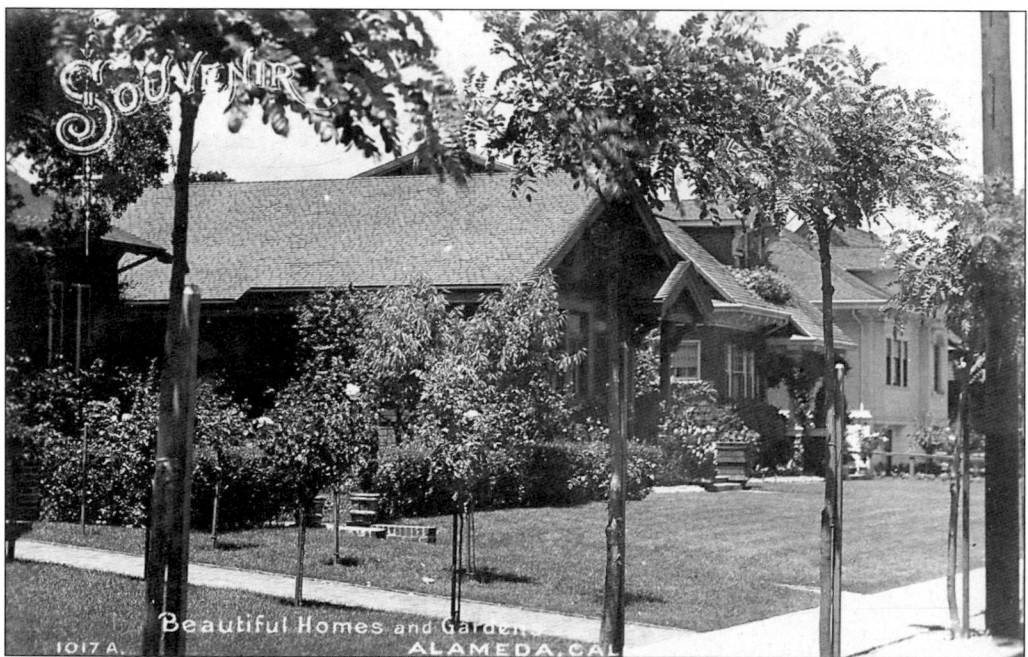

Souvenir

Beautiful Homes and Garden
1017 A.   ALAMEDA, CAL

This photographic souvenir postcard shows lovely cottages, lawns planted with roses, and young trees along the sidewalk. Although the image looks ideal, the writer complains that it is "too cold here for light clothes" when the postcard was mailed to Riverside in April 1913. (Published by American Industrial Photo Company, San Francisco.)

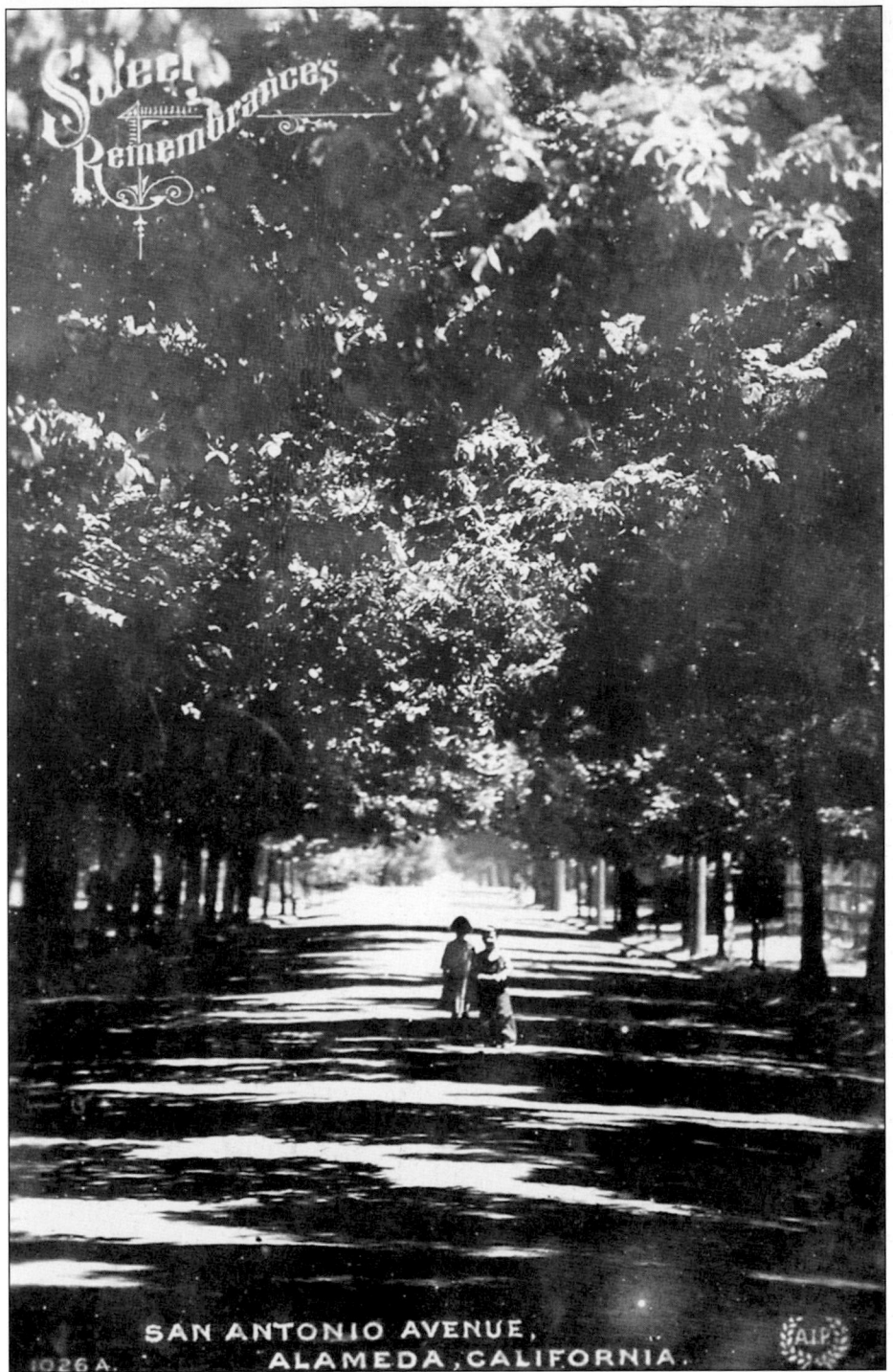

Mailed in October 1911, this photographic postcard shows the rural, small-town atmosphere of Alameda in the early 1900s. A small boy and girl stand in the middle of the dirt street in the shade of the large, leafy trees that lined San Antonio Avenue. (Published by American Industrial Photo Company, San Francisco.)

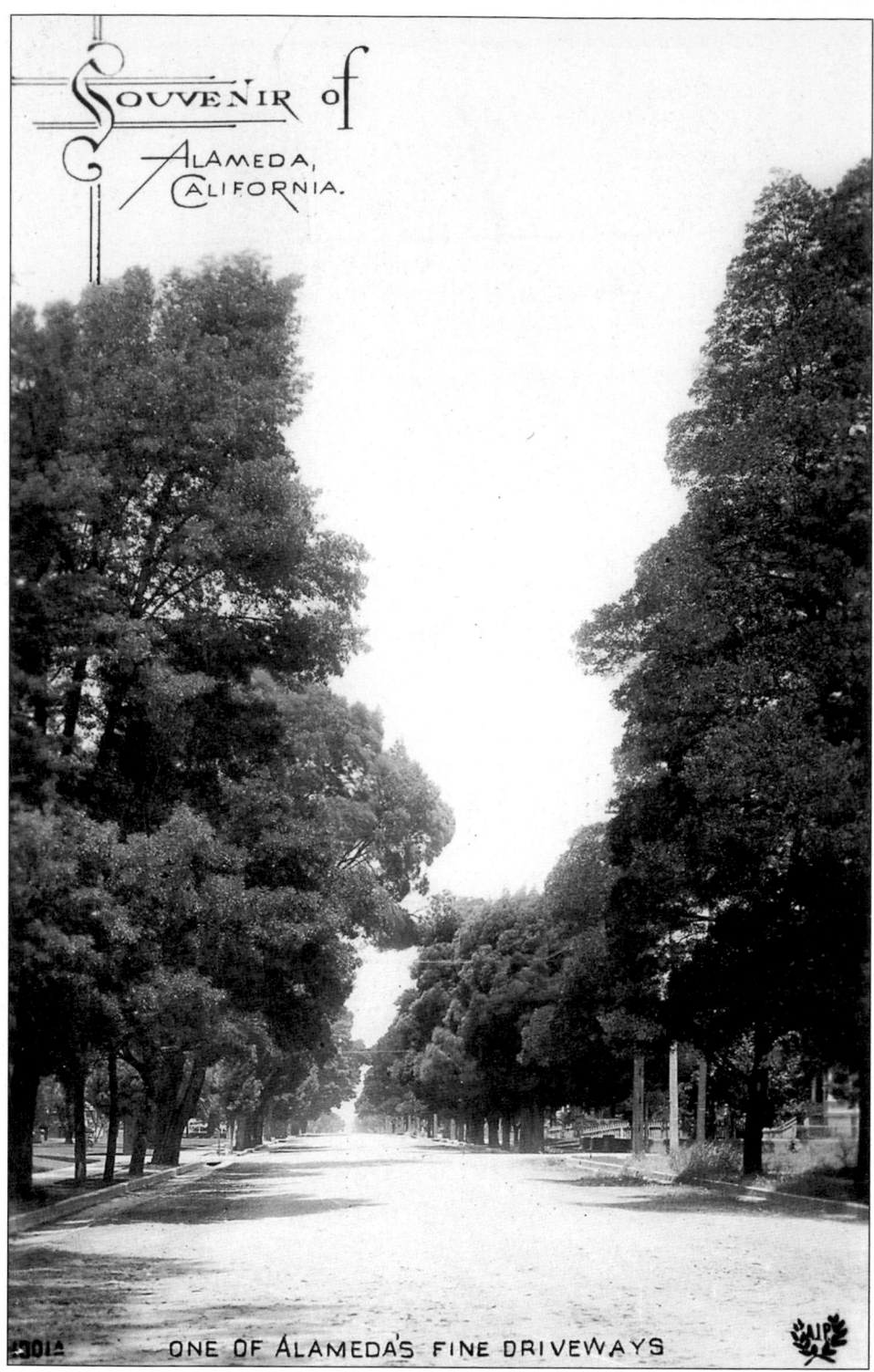

SOUVENIR of
ALAMEDA,
CALIFORNIA.

ONE OF ALAMEDA'S FINE DRIVEWAYS

The inviting tree-lined street pictured here probably leads to the bay shore. (Published by American Industrial Photo Company, San Francisco, *c.* 1912.)

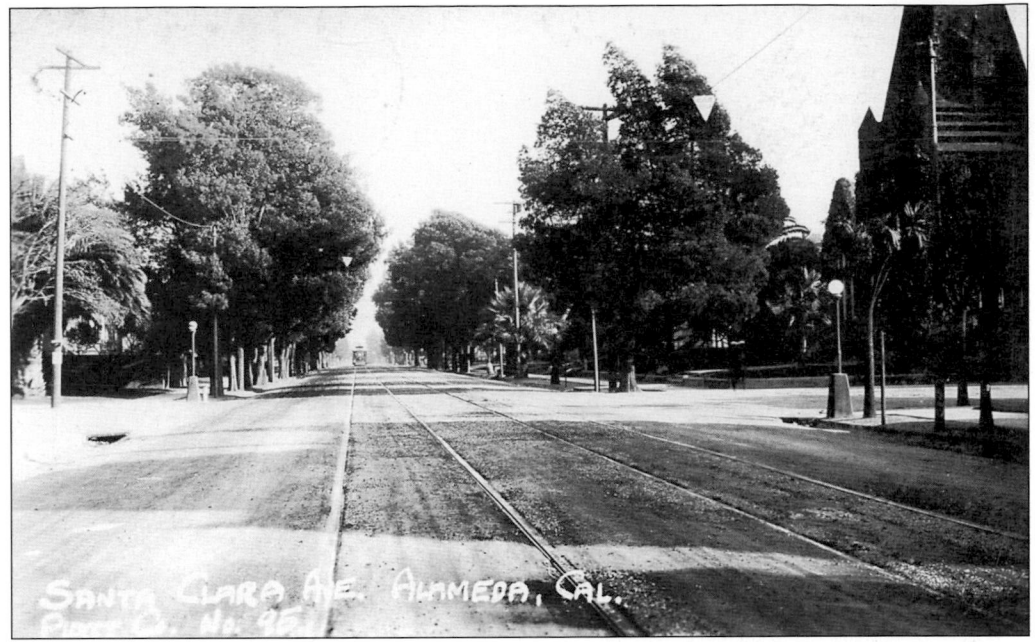

Looking southeast, this c. 1920 view shows the intersection of Santa Clara Avenue and Grand Street, complete with streetcar tracks. On the right is the Christ Episcopal Church.

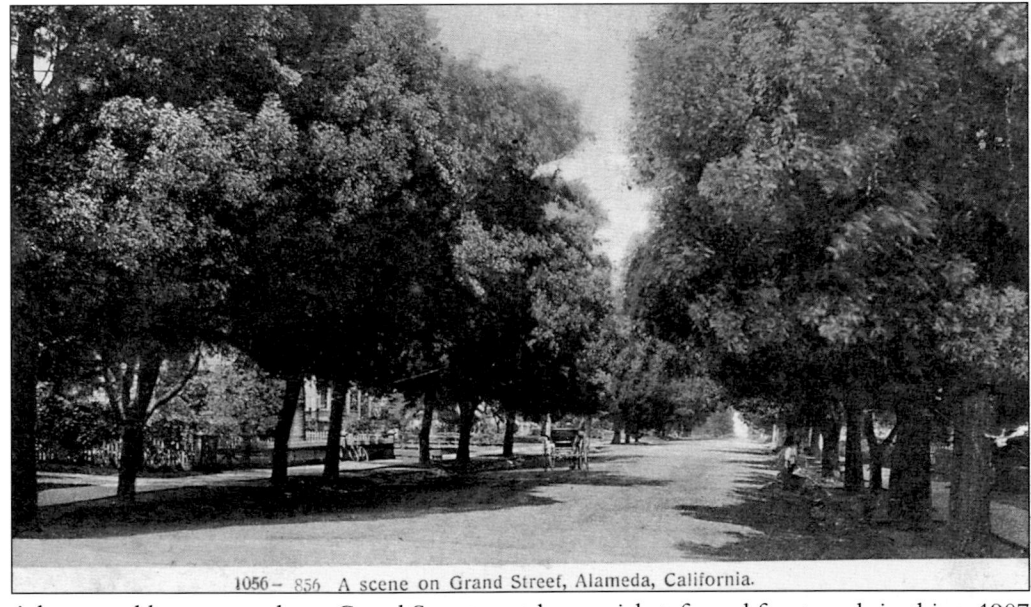

1056– 856 A scene on Grand Street, Alameda, California.

A horse and buggy travels on Grand Street, past large, picket-fenced front yards in this *c.* 1907 view. The wide, tree–lined street is still graced with stately houses. (Published by the Cardinell–Vincent Company, Oakland.)

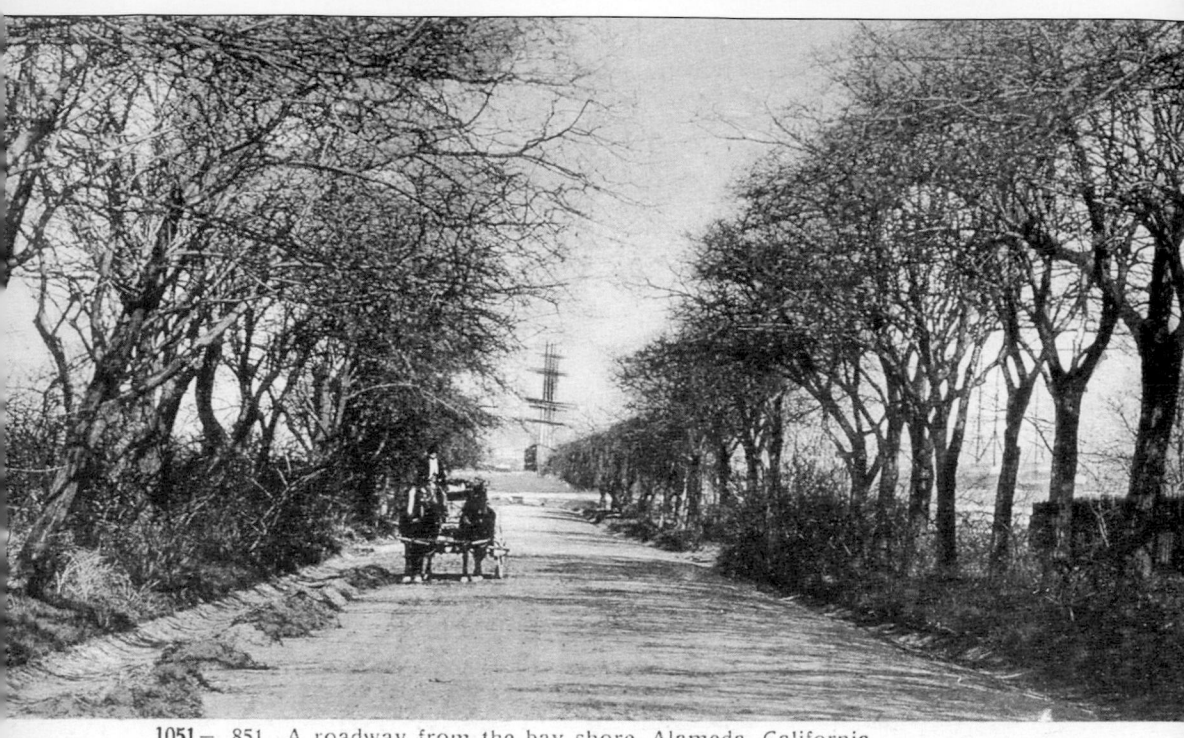

1051 – 851 A roadway from the bay shore, Alameda, California.

Two horses pull a wagon on this unidentified tree-lined roadway, most likely between Eighth Street and Grand. In the distance is a tall sailing ship on the estuary. Postmarked in February 1908, the author of the postcard gives her home address as 1421 High Street. (Published by Cardinell-Vincent Company, Oakland.)

Six

THE BAY SHORE

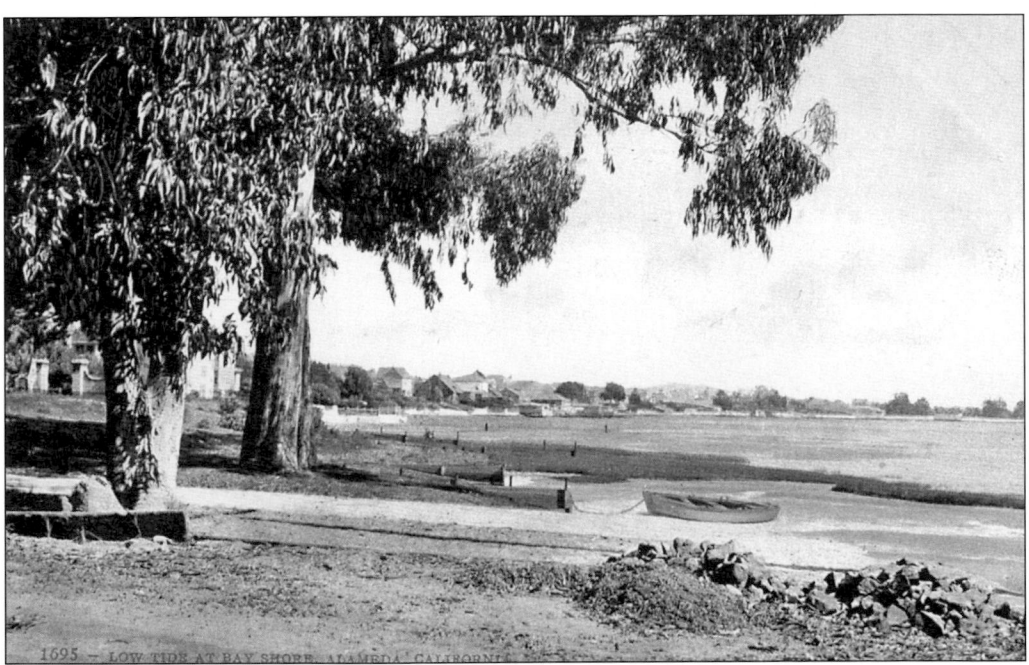

This *c.* 1909 postcard shows the foot of Grand Street, where it meets the bay, which became the site of the Oppenheimer home and Palmera Court after a 1910 landfill. (Published by Edward H. Mitchell, San Francisco.)

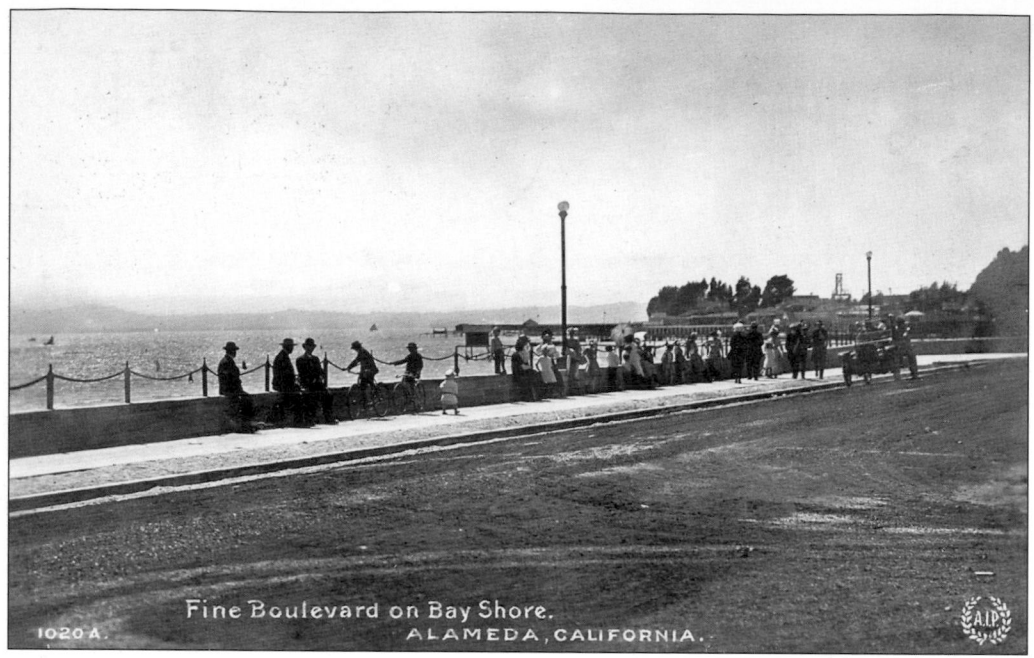

Fine Boulevard on Bay Shore.
1020 A.   ALAMEDA, CALIFORNIA.

Postmarked in October 1912, this view shows seawall at the end of Burbank Street at Portola Avenue. (Published by American Industrial Photo Company, San Francisco.)

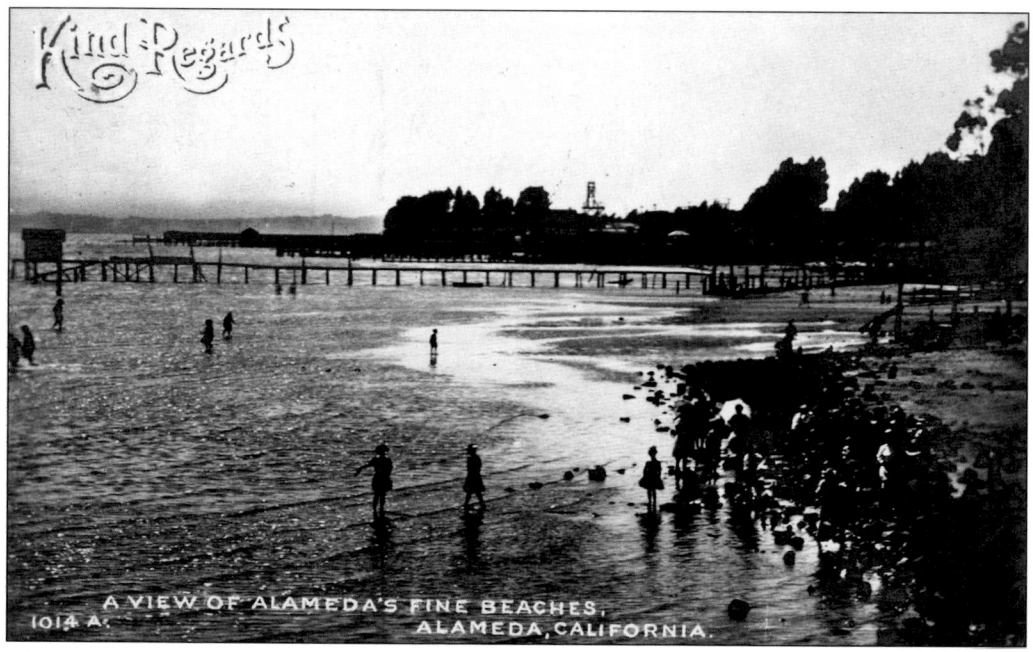

Kind Regards

A VIEW OF ALAMEDA'S FINE BEACHES,
1014 A.   ALAMEDA, CALIFORNIA.

This souvenir photographic postcard was mailed in April 1912, and the writer says, "I often go swimming at the beaches here." This refers to the beach next to Washington Park, which is now a baseball diamond. The distant high-diving platform at Surf Beach Park can be seen in the center of the image. (Published by American Industrial Photo Company, San Francisco.)

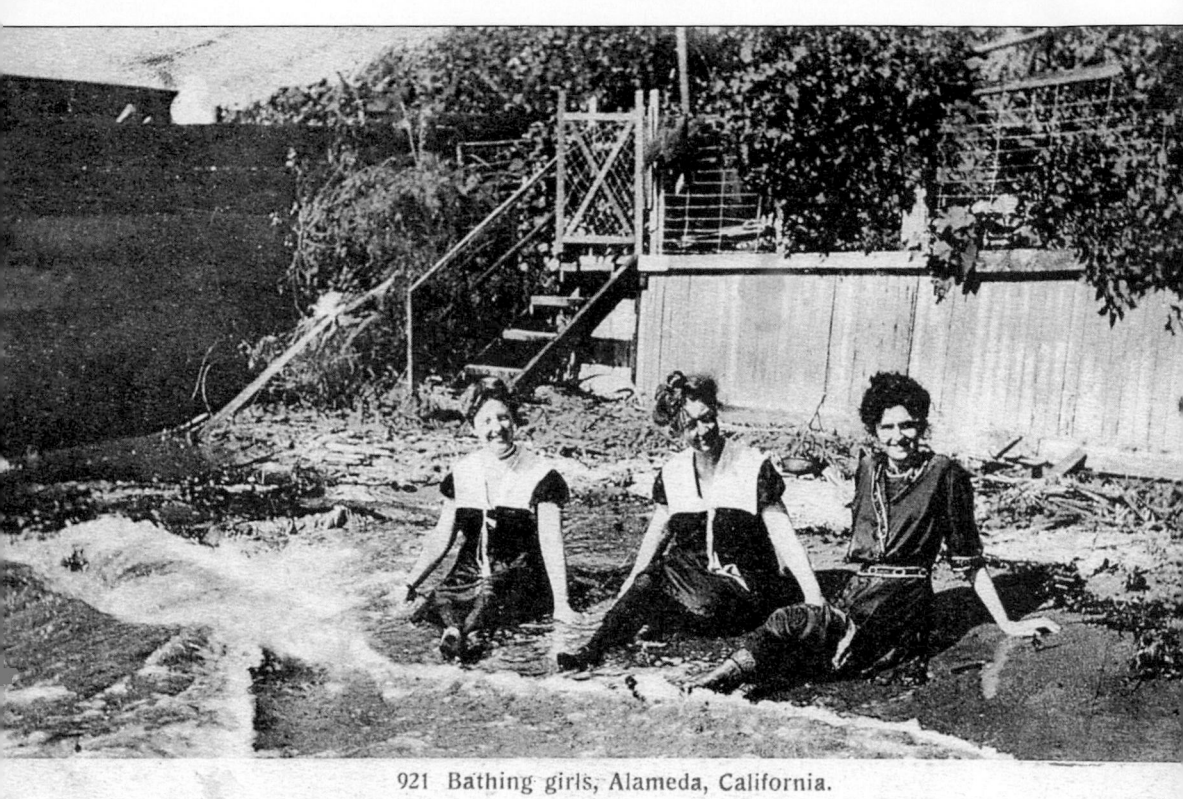

921 Bathing girls, Alameda, California.
1910

This *c.* 1910 postcard shows a well–covered, happy trio of bathing girls wearing the elaborate bathing costumes of of the day. The small beach on which they are sitting was located at the end of a residential street. These bathing areas no longer exist, due to the landfill projects of the 1950s. (Published by Cardinell-Vincent Company, Oakland.)

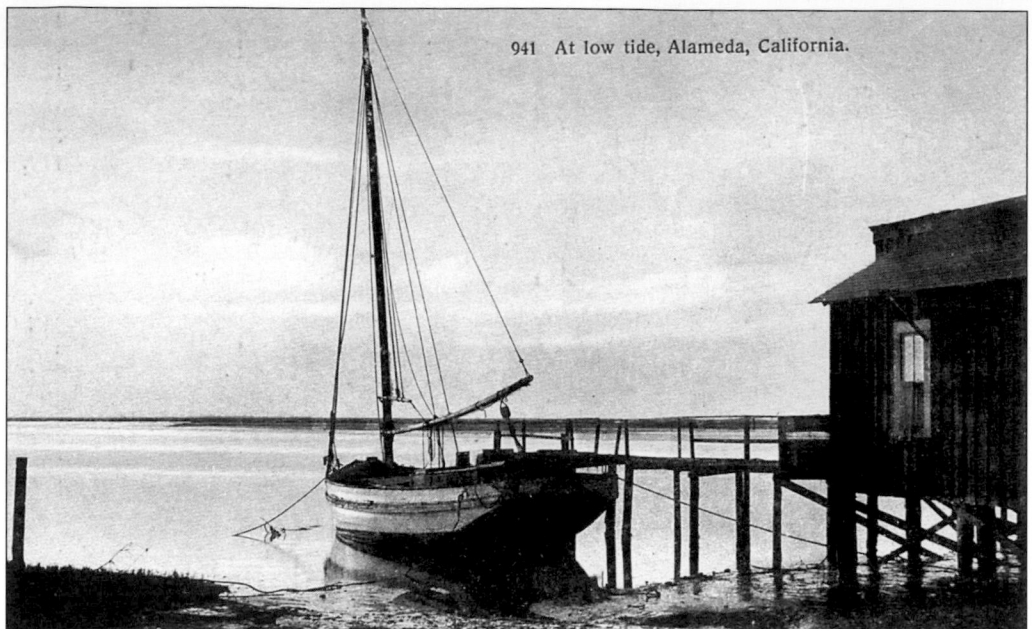

941 At low tide, Alameda, California.

This *c.* 1908 postcard shows a peaceful scene on the bay at low tide. (Published by Cardinell-Vincent Company, Oakland.)

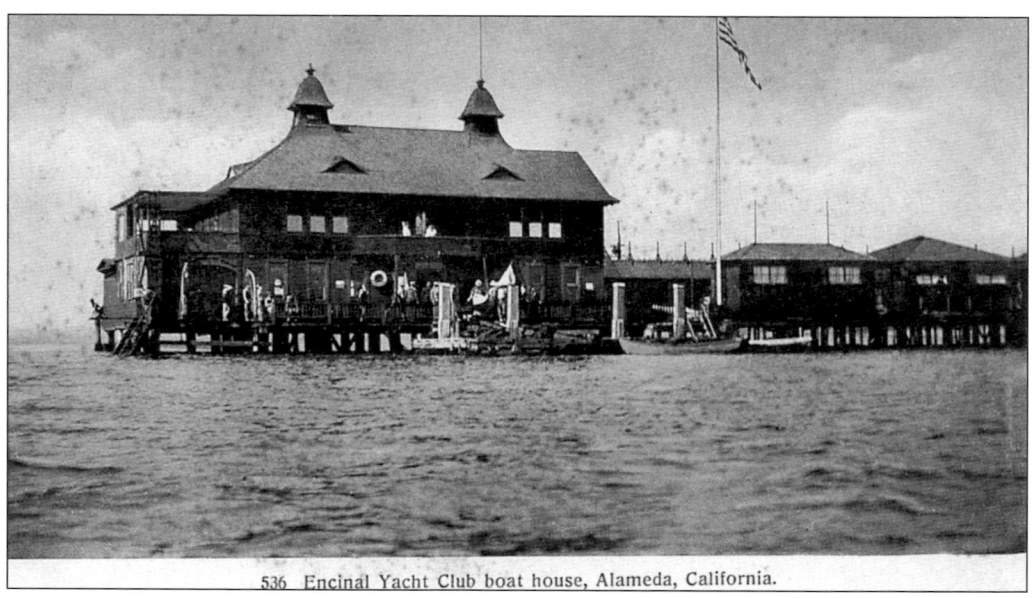

536 Encinal Yacht Club boat house, Alameda, California.

Established in 1891 by lawyer George T. Wright, the Alameda Boat Club headquarters was designed by noted local architect-builder Joseph A. Leonard. Its name was changed to the more prestigious-sounding Encinal Yacht Club in 1909. The building is long gone, but it used to be located at the end of a 1,000-foot pier near the termination of Grand Street at the beach. (Published by the Cardinell-Vincent Company, Oakland, *c.* 1910.)

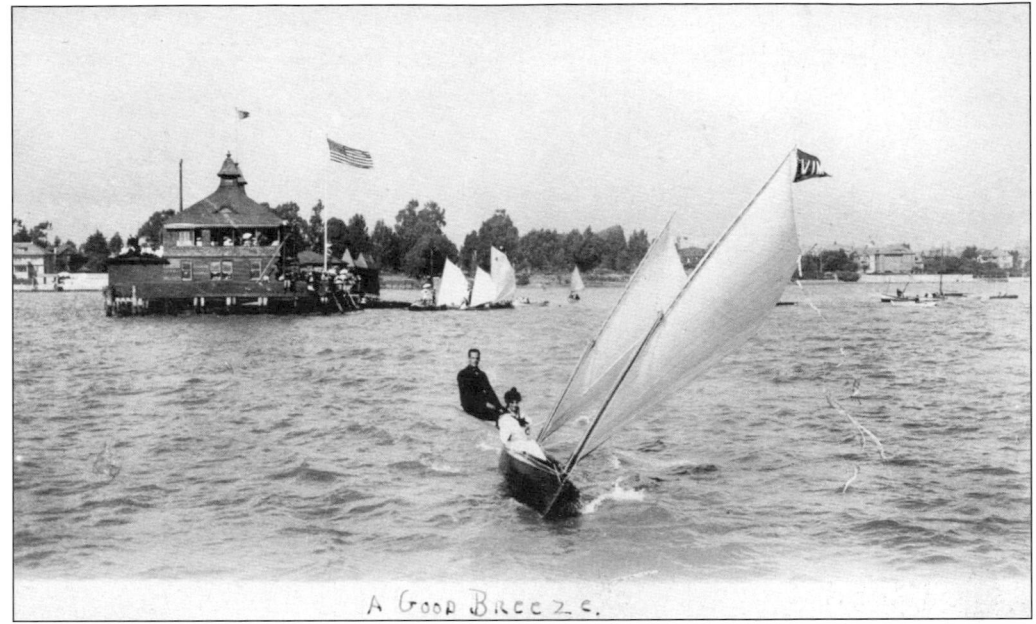

This c. 1906 photographic postcard shows a couple in a small sailboat enjoying the waves, views, and "a good breeze" on the bay. Behind them is the Encinal Yacht Club. On the shore at left is a large residence at the foot of Paru Street. On the right, between the boat's sails in the distance, is architect-builder Joseph A. Leonard's residence on Union Street.

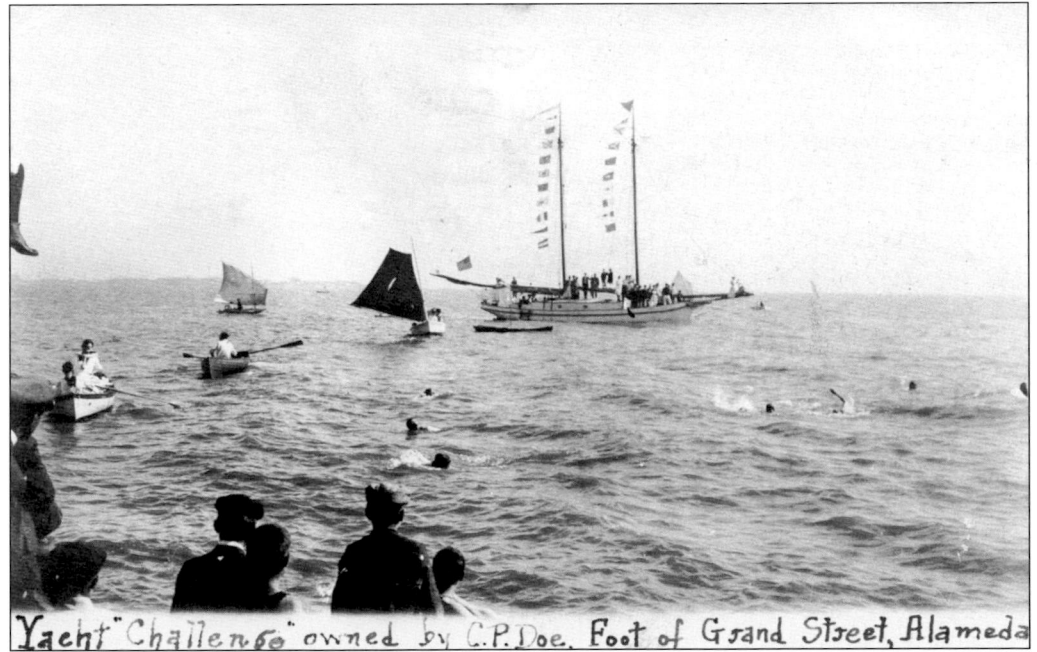

This c. 1906 photographic postcard shows the yacht *Challenge*, owned by C. P. Doe, sailing on the waters off the foot of Grand Street. Swimmers and small boats surround the craft. The postcard writer mentions going to hear a lecture by photojournalist and author Jacob Riis the night before.

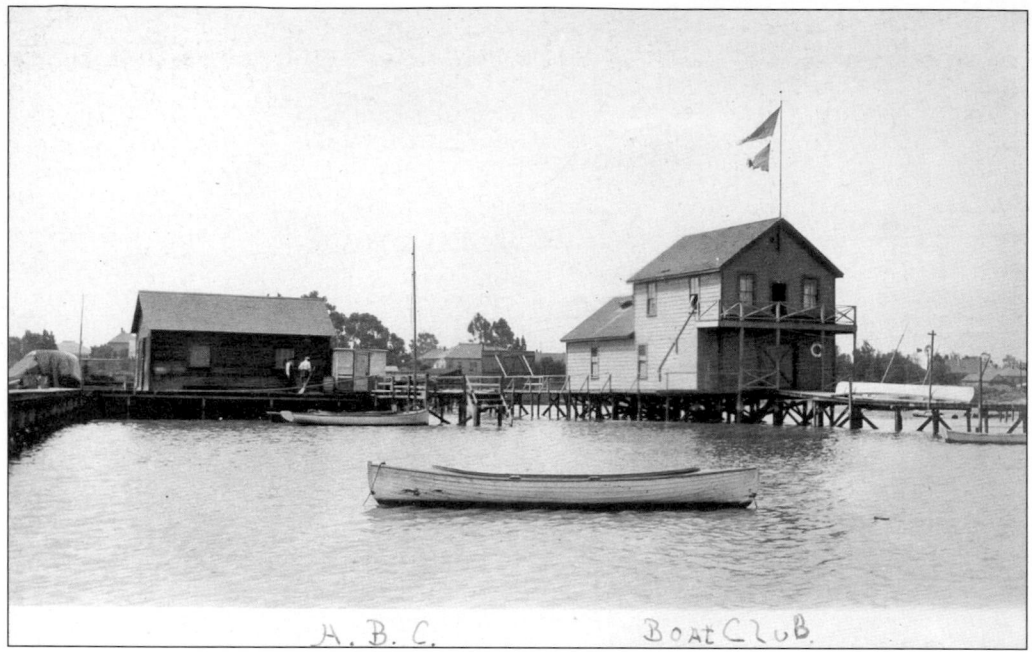

A. B. C.   Boat Club.

Originally nothing more than a houseboat and a small collection of rowboats and sailboats belonging to boat builder Jules Hartman, the Alameda boating club was located at the end of Chestnut Street and was officially completed and opened on May 30, 1890, after much expansion. A very popular rowing club in its formative years, the Alameda Boat Club lasted until 1942, when it lost its site and never reopened. This photographic postcard dates from *c.* 1906.

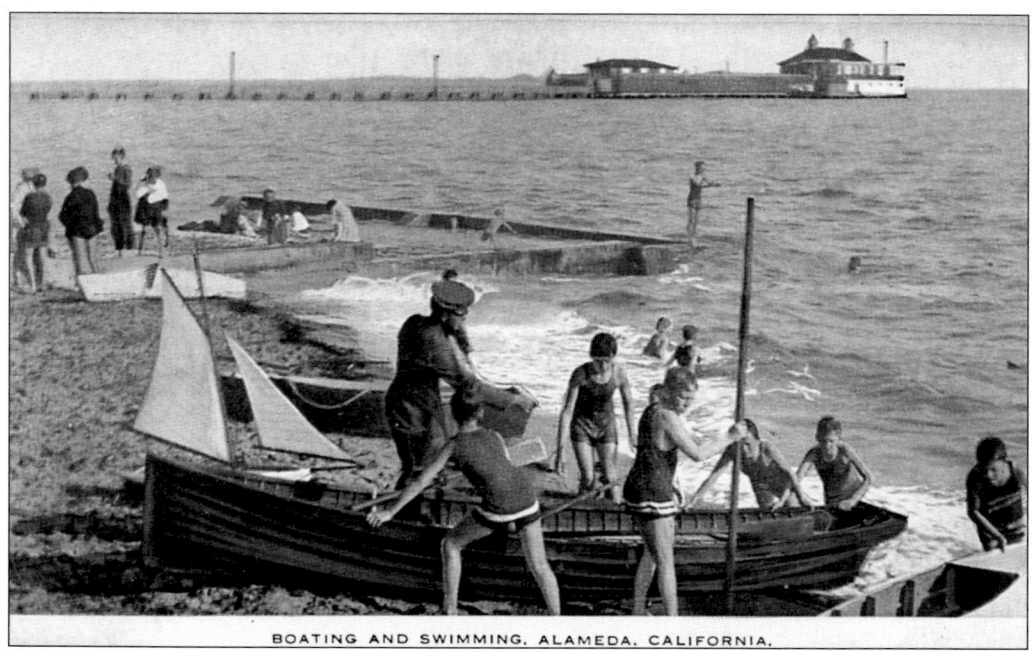

BOATING AND SWIMMING, ALAMEDA, CALIFORNIA.

Children frolic in the bay near where Sherman and Paru Streets ended at the beach in this 1920s-era postcard. The Encinal Yacht Club can be seen in the distance. (Published by Pacific Novelty Company, San Francisco.)

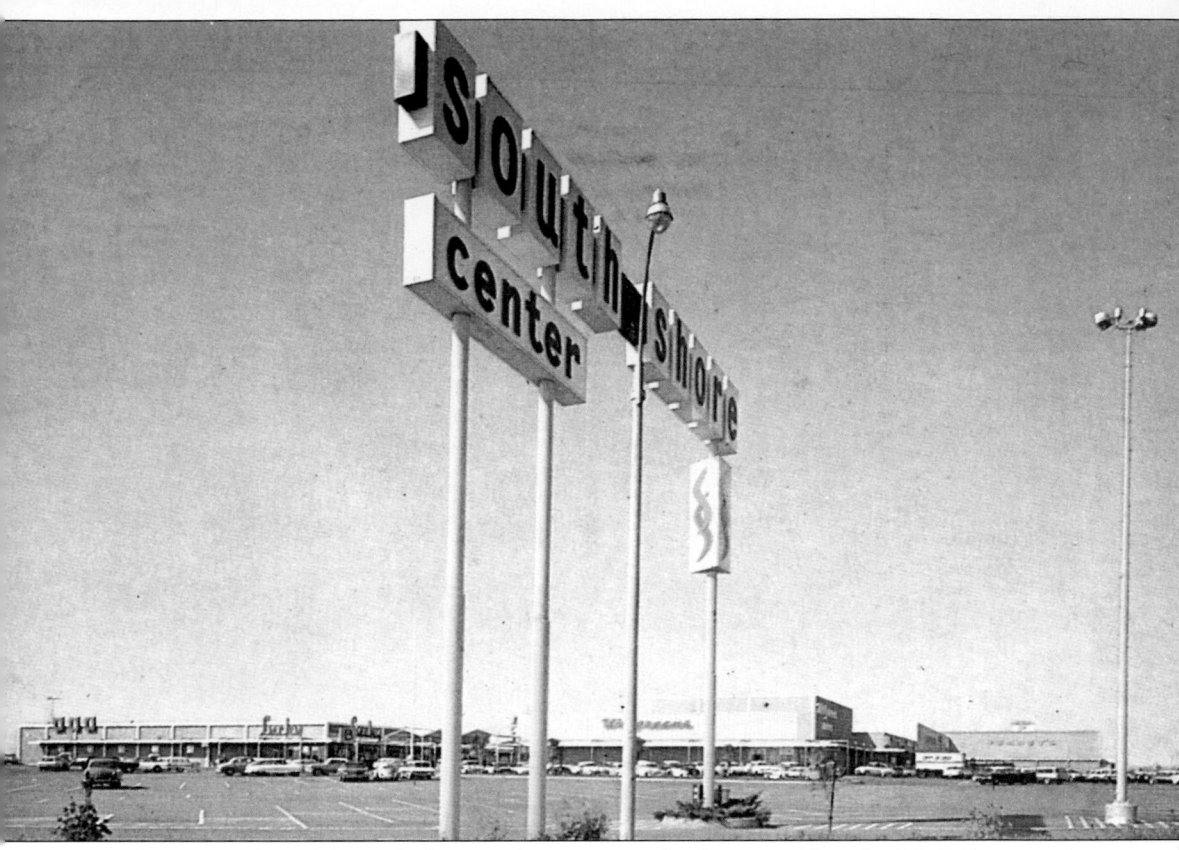

Tidelands on Alameda's south shore and Bay Farm Island were sold to the Utah Construction company on January 4, 1955. An ordinance to fill in about 1,200 acres for new developments was created and subsequently put to a vote on May 24, 1955, after much controversy. The final count in the vote was tallied—7,002 "yes" votes to 5,385 "no" votes. To the chagrin of many waterfront property owners, Alameda would be extended. The massive dredging operation for the South Shore Project commenced on November 7, 1955, and was completed a little over a year later on November 16, 1956. This *c.* 1963 postcard shows an early view of the much-heralded (at the time) South Shore Center, which opened on August 21, 1958, amidst Hawaiian music, prize giveaways, carnival rides, and a celebratory atmosphere. (Published by Smith News Company, San Francisco.)

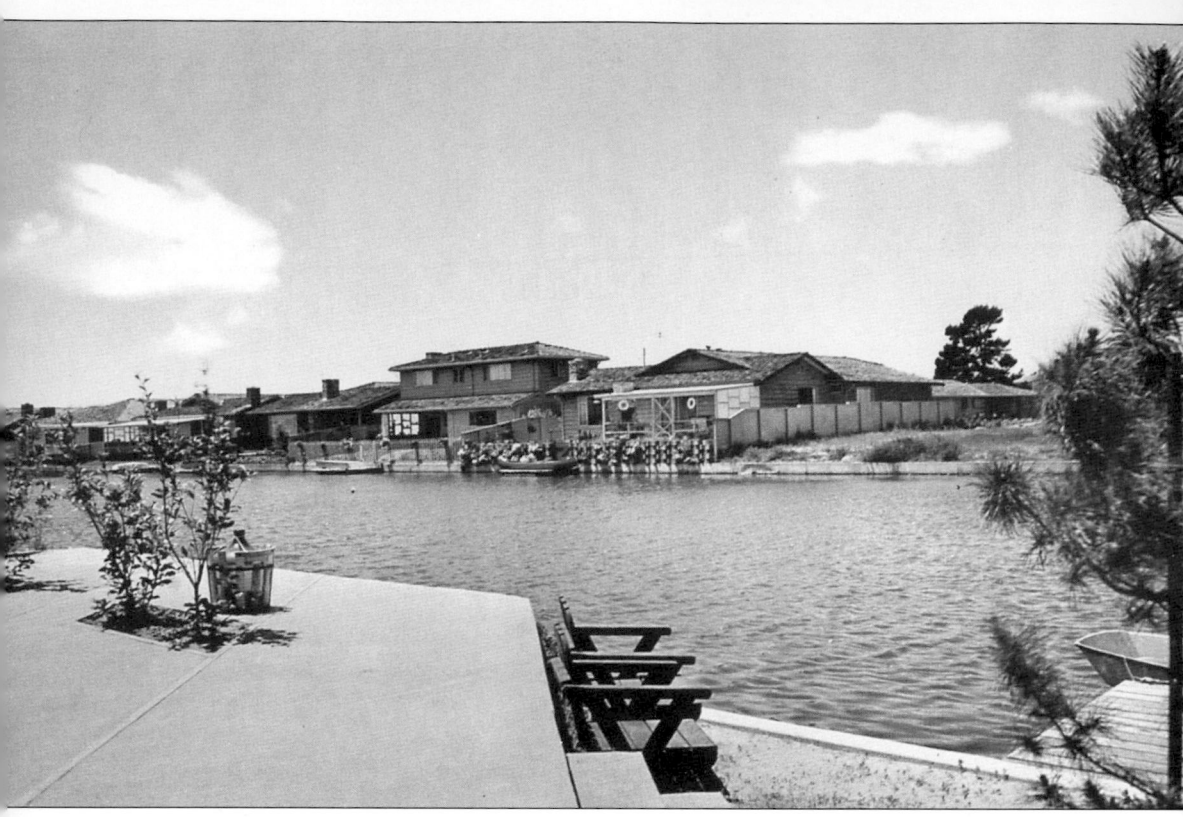

One of the plans developed during the large South Shore Project of the mid–1950s was to add several land-locked lagoons in residential areas. Although the addition had some practical effects, such as aiding drainage, the main reason for the lagoons was probably to create and sell new waterfront real estate. The idea was considered as early as November 1954, and the official plan was approved on September 26, 1956, after delays caused by negotiations between the Utah Construction Company and the Alameda Planning Board regarding the size of the lagoons. (Published by the Alameda Chamber of Commerce.)

Seven

AMUSEMENTS AND CELEBRITIES

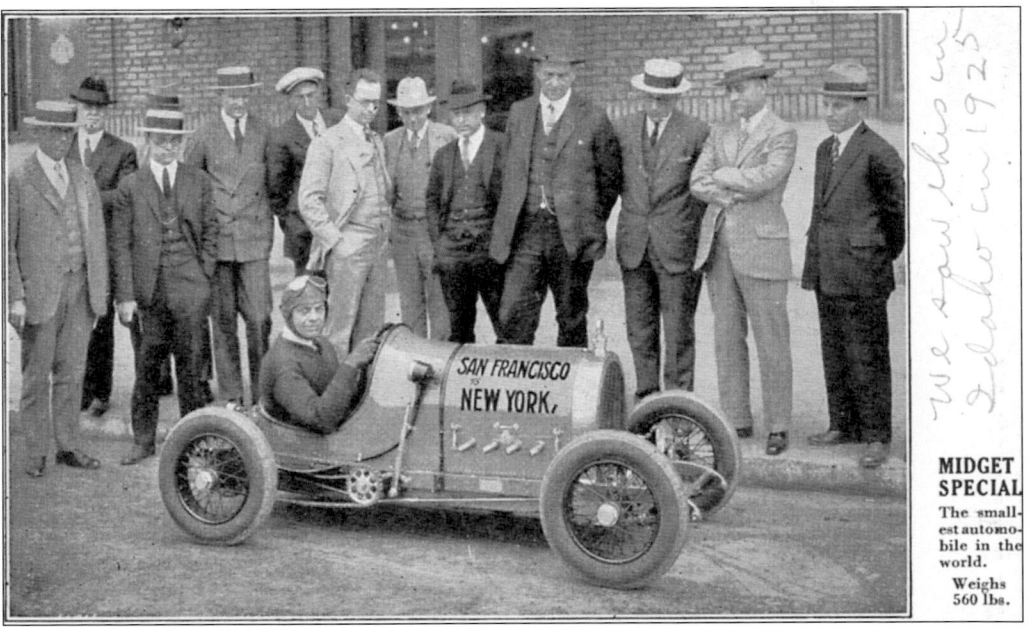

This *c.* 1924 printed photographic postcard shows Gus Petzel and his Midget Special car, hailed here as "the Smallest Automobile in the World." Petzel designed and built the Midget Special at his home at 1207 Grand Street (now replaced by a church) and attempted to drive this diminutive and uncomfortable-looking vehicle from San Francisco to New York on the Lincoln Highway. No word yet if he made it or not.

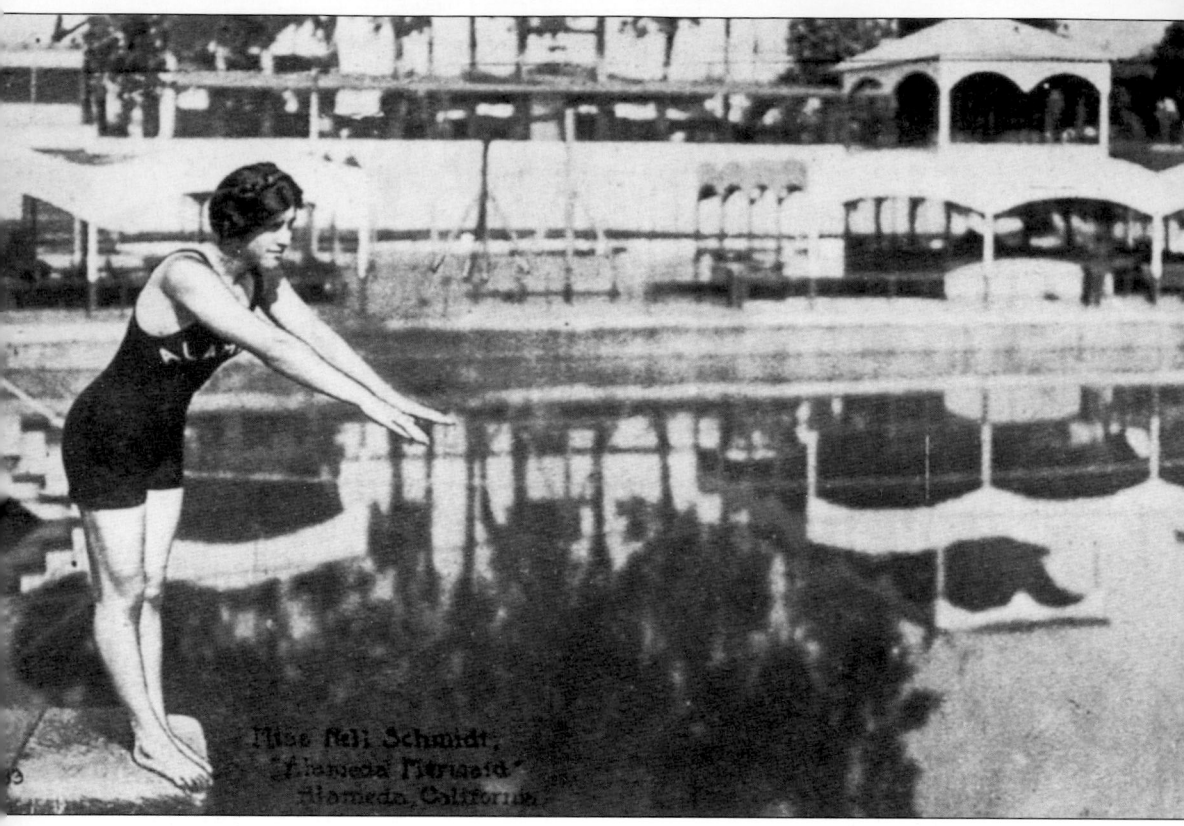

A *c. 1915* postcard shows Miss Nell (or Nellie) Schmidt, the "Alameda Mermaid" who, at age 20, was the first woman and the third person to swim across the San Francisco Bay. On August 12, 1912, she crossed from the Vallejo Street wharf in San Francisco to Oakland. During her eight-mile journey, which lasted three hours and six minutes, Schmidt was fed milk and coached by F. M. Riehl, who in 1872, was the first man to swim across the bay. After setting a record for being the first person to circle San Francisco's Seal Rocks near the Cliff House one month later in September 1912, Schmidt took the Pantages Theatre Company up on its offer of fame and fortune. Billed as the Alameda Mermaid, she dazzled audiences with her diving and swimming act on a six-week United States tour. She then brought her show back to Oakland before the slow slide into obscurity. Her mother, "Ma" Schmidt, ran the Cottage Saloon, which she eventually closed in favor of the more family-oriented Cottage Baths, opened in 1893. The baths' clientele included such famous names as Ethel Barrymore, Al Jolson, and Jack London.

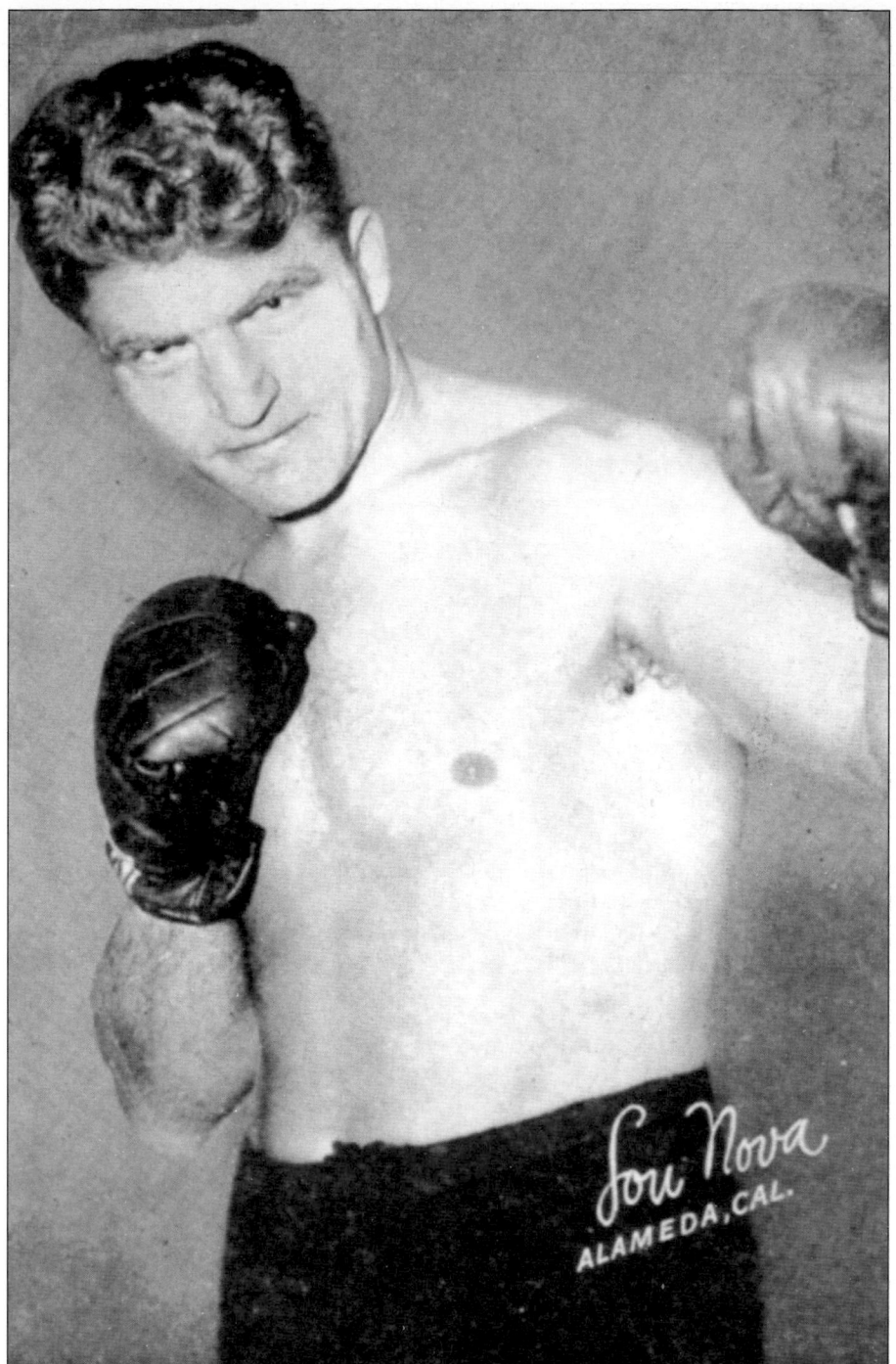

A *c.* 1935 arcade card shows the U.S. and world amateur heavyweight boxing champion of 1935, Alameda resident Lou Nova. Known for his "Cosmic Punch," he knocked out Max Baer twice and fought him in the first televised heavyweight boxing match in 1939. He was, however, unable to take the heavyweight title from Joe Louis in 1941. Nova also practiced yoga before it was popular, and had a B-movie acting career in the 1940s and 1950s.

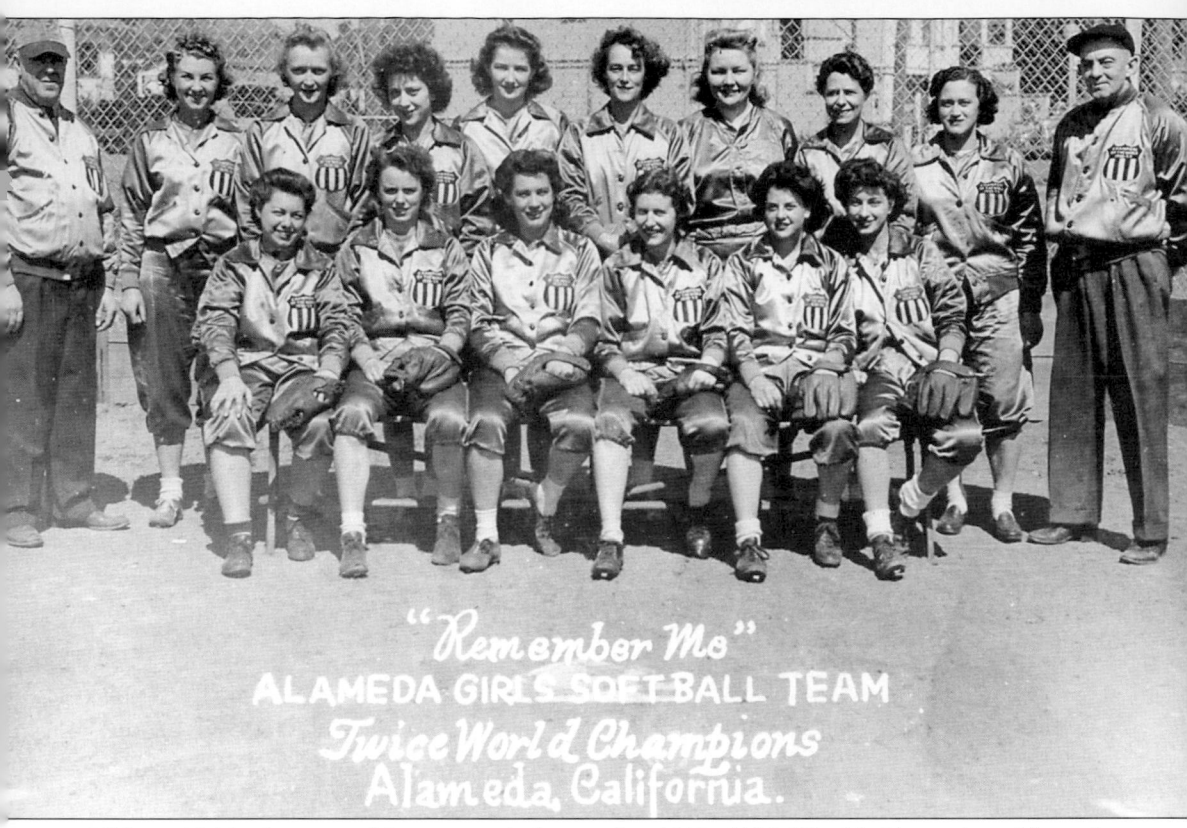

"*Remember Me*"
ALAMEDA GIRLS SOFTBALL TEAM
Twice World Champions
Alameda, California.

This *c.* 1940 photographic postcard shows the 1938–1939 World Champion Alameda Girls Softball Team, which was the first team of either gender west of the Mississippi to win the World Championship. In existence for 12 years, the team once won 103 straight games (some against men's teams) and never lost a league or tournament title. Team members included 1932 Olympic javelin thrower Gloria Russell Hillenbrand and top California bowler Claire Knabenshus.

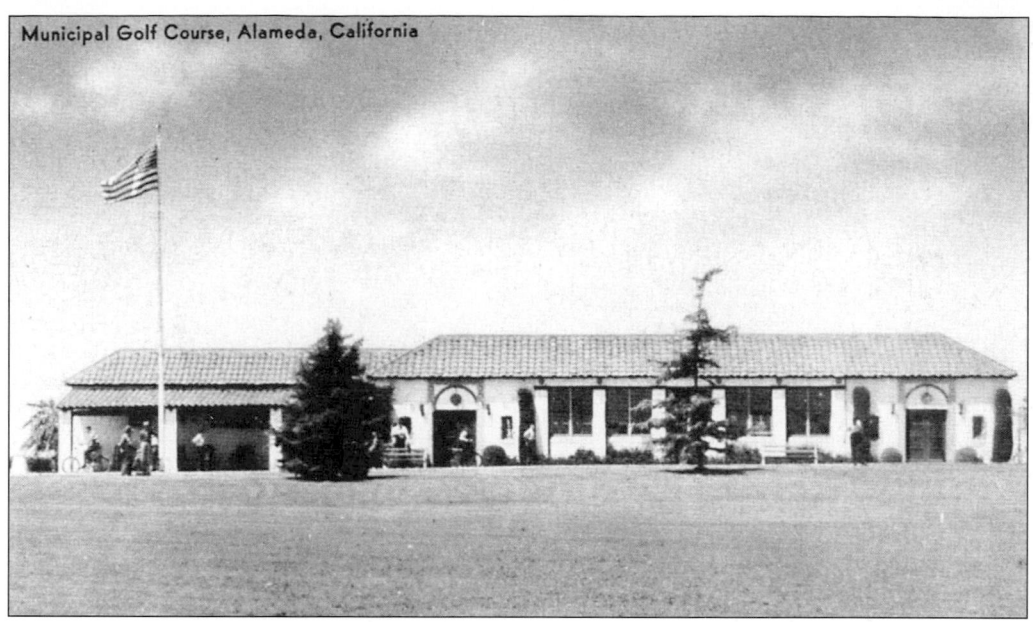

Municipal Golf Course, Alameda, California

Construction began on the municipal golf course in November 1925, and it opened on May 27, 1927. This building was designed by Carl Werner, the architect who was also responsible for Alameda High School. By 1952, it was lauded as the most popular course in Northern California. Operated by the city, the course has been home to large tournaments. (Published by Greenwood Printers Limited, Oakland.)

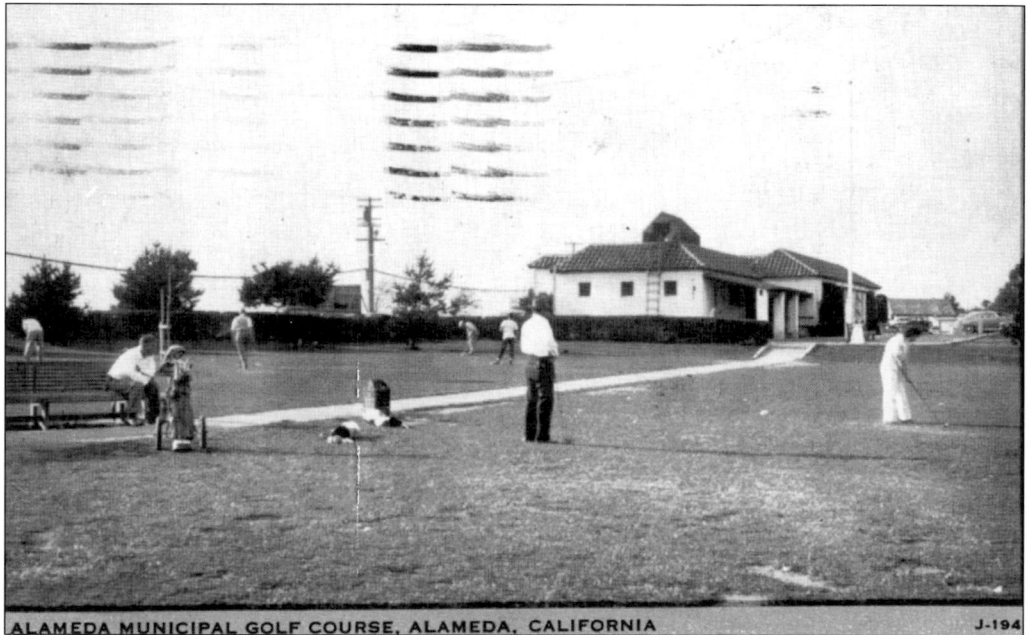

ALAMEDA MUNICIPAL GOLF COURSE, ALAMEDA, CALIFORNIA   J-194

Postmarked in July 1946, this postcard to friends back in Wichita, Kansas, tells of the writer's intentions to go "out to this golf course today." It is now called the Chuck Corica Golf Course in honor of the former Alameda mayor who helped to prevent the sale of the course for residential development. (Published by Wayne Paper Box and Printing Corporation, Fort Wayne, Indiana.)

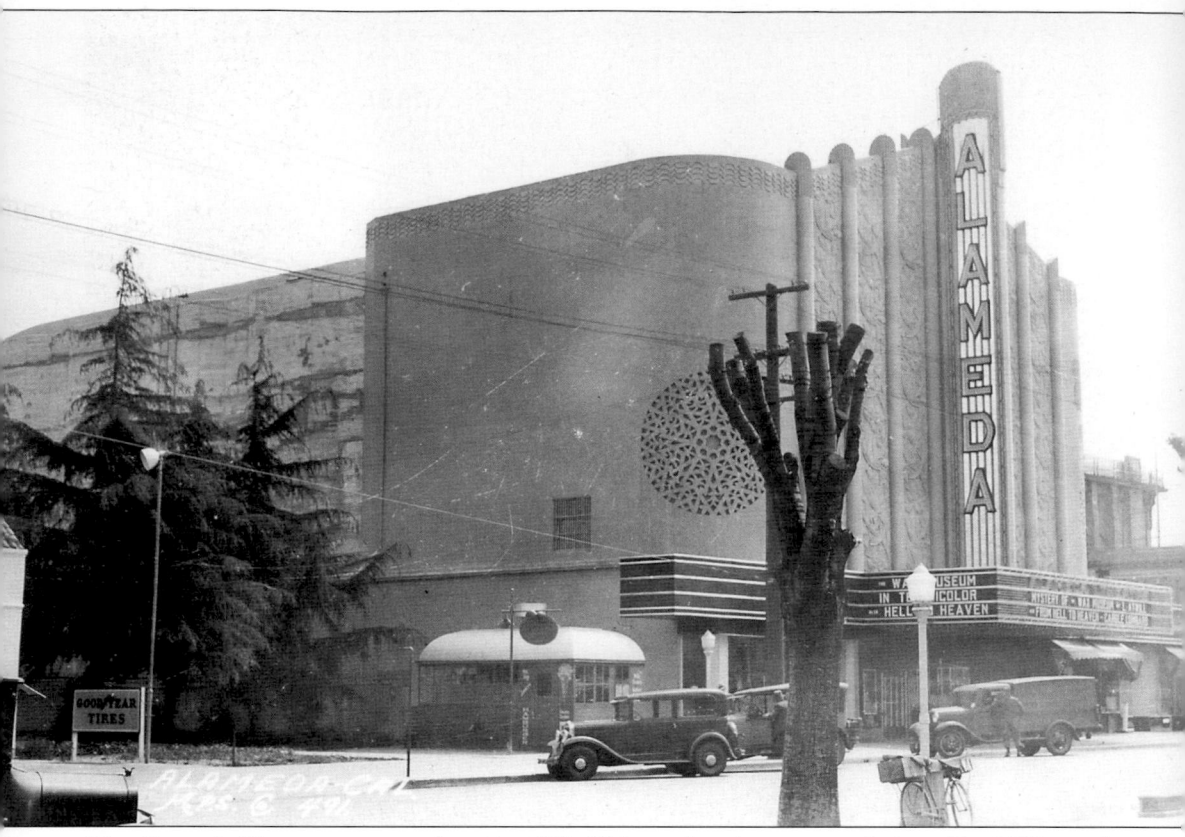

The Alameda Theatre was completed in 1932. This art deco beauty was designed by Miller and Pfleuger of San Francisco; Pflueger also designed the Paramount Theatre in Oakland. The blade sign above the marquee is the oldest neon sign in Alameda. The grand opening of the theatre on August 16, 1932, was attended by California governor James Rolph Jr., and the movie shown that night was *Rebecca of Sunnybrook Farm.* In this 1933 postcard image, *The Mystery of the Wax Museum* with Lionel Atwill, and *From Hell to Heaven,* starring Carole Lombard, are showing at the theatre. The building still stands, but movies ceased being shown in 1979. After serving as a venue for live music, gymnastics, and other uses, many hope that it will be restored to its original movie-house grandeur.

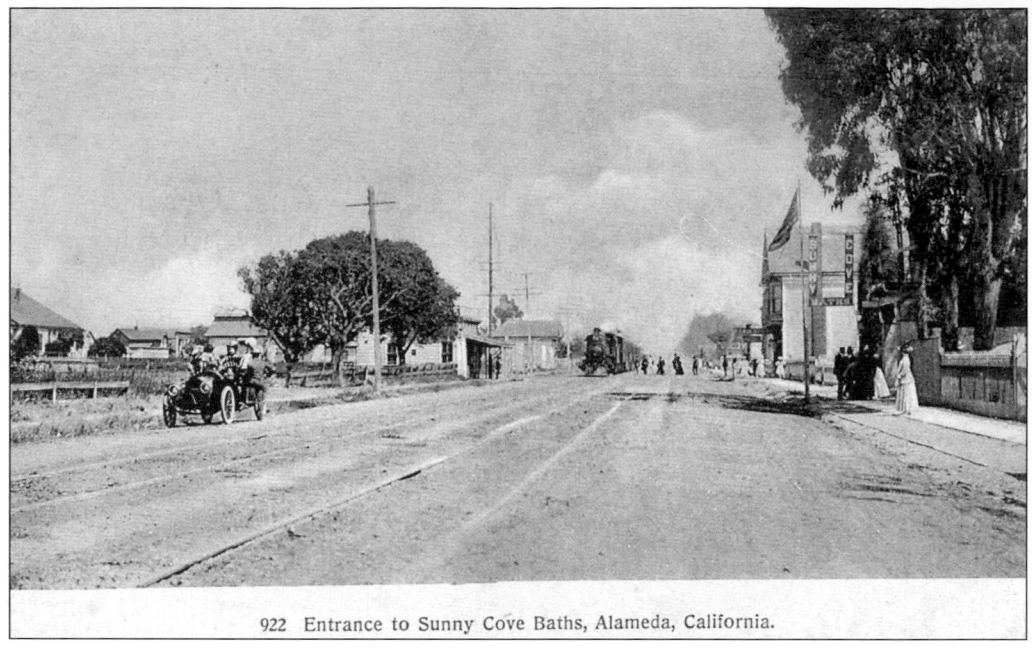

922 Entrance to Sunny Cove Baths, Alameda, California.

This *c.* 1908 postcard shows Central Avenue looking east, with the entrance to Sunny Cove Baths on the right. Farther up on the left is Fifth Street. Established in 1878, Sunny Cove stayed in business until 1947. (Published by Cardinell-Vincent Company, Oakland.)

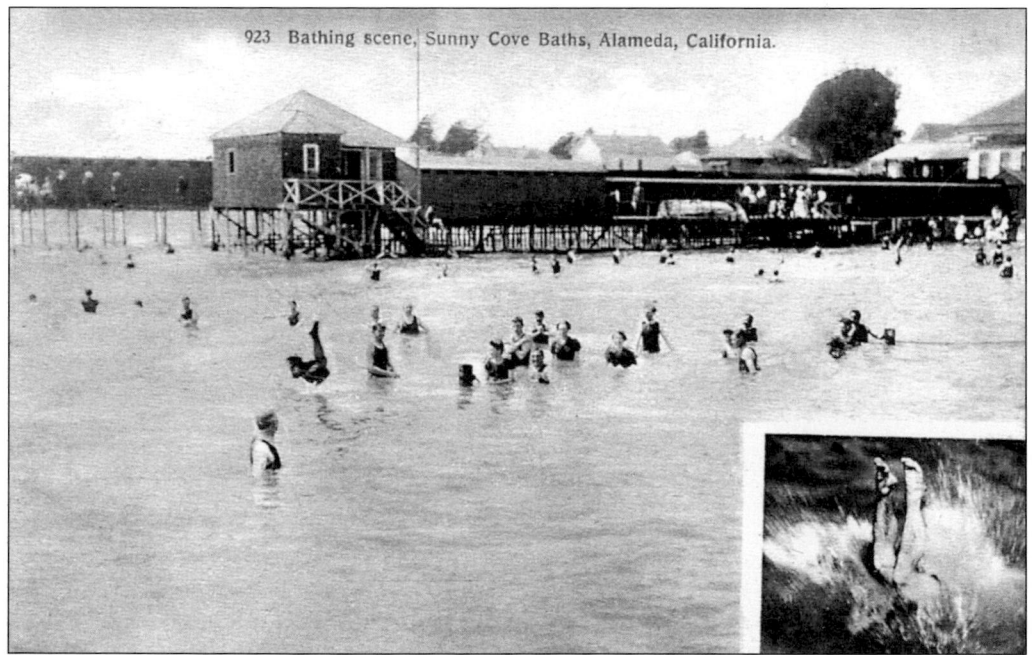

923 Bathing scene, Sunny Cove Baths, Alameda, California.

An 1878 entry in the Alameda Encinal refers to the Sunny Cove Baths as having "the most commodious grounds and finest sand beach." Easy access to this swimming area was provided by the close proximity of the Fifth Street streetcar station. (Published by Cardinell-Vincent Company, Oakland.)

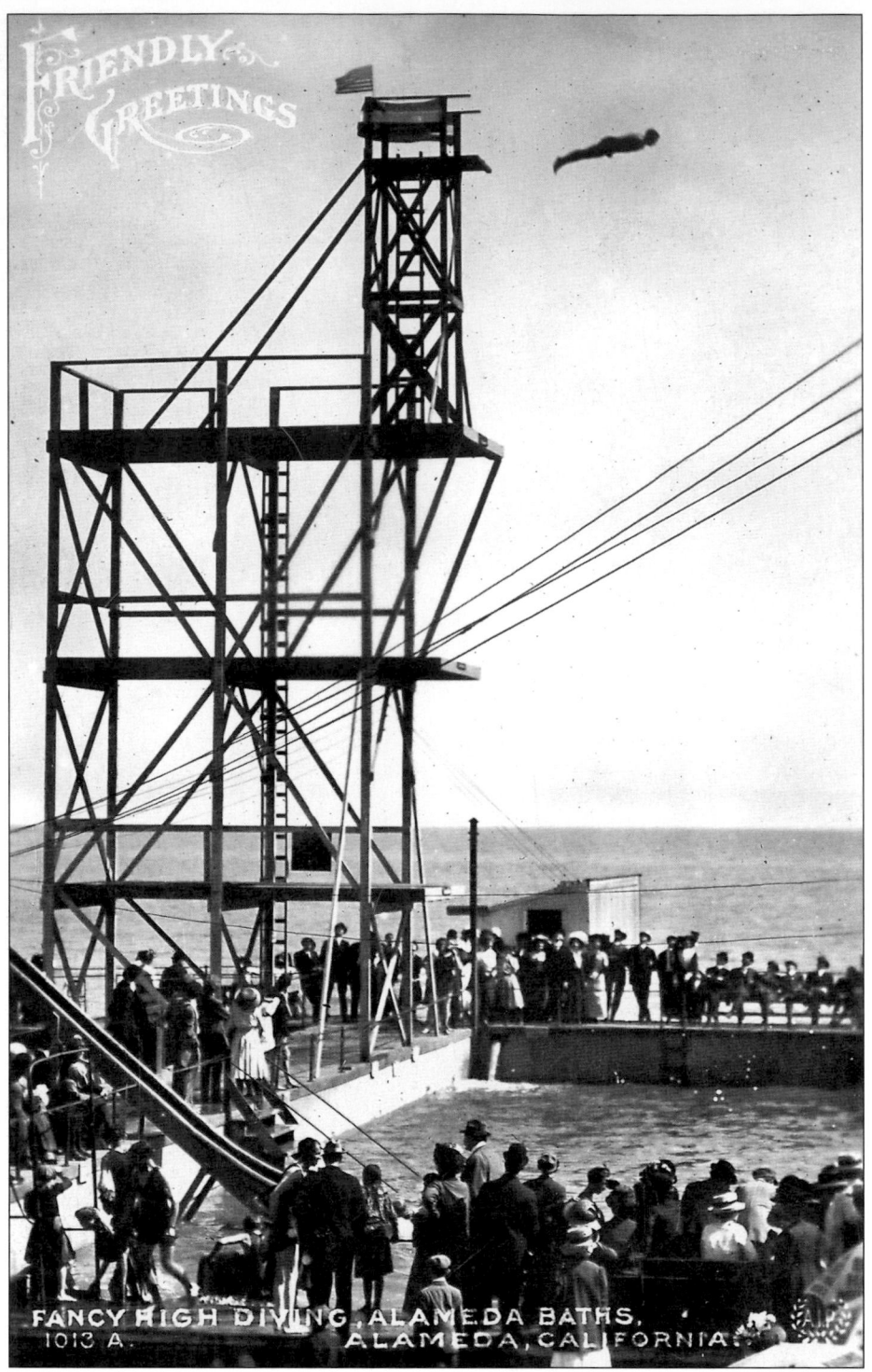

FANCY HIGH DIVING, ALAMEDA BATHS,
1013 A. ALAMEDA, CALIFORNIA.

A diver is caught midair in this *c.* 1912 photographic souvenir postcard of the high-diving platform at Surf Beach Park. It was located on Central Avenue between Sixth Street and Webster. (Published by American Industrial Photo Company, San Francisco.)

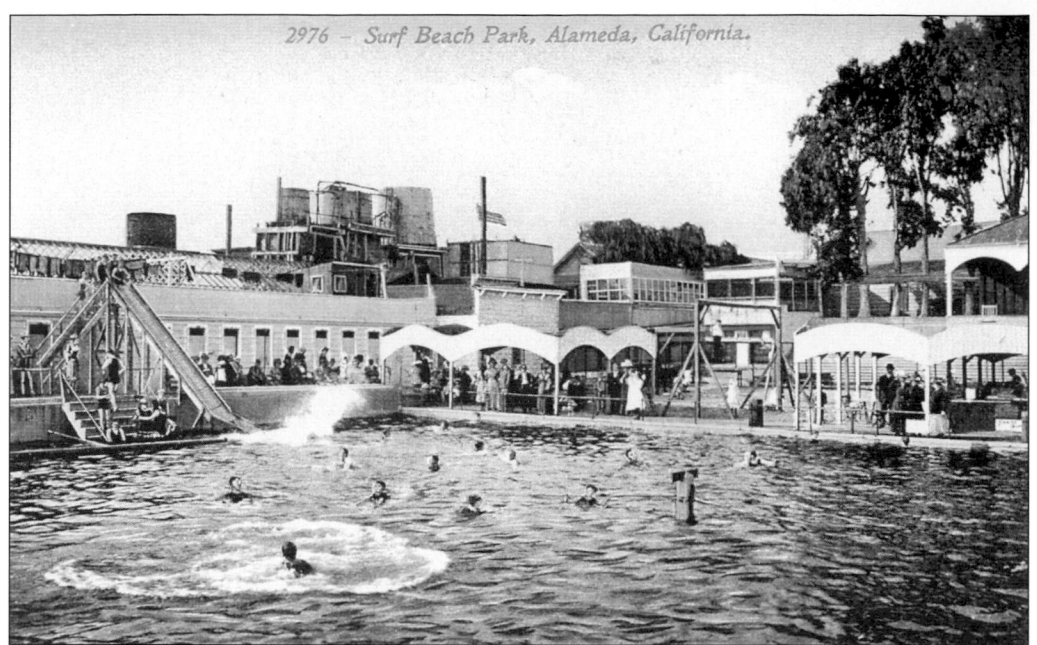

Swimmers enjoy the slides and pool at Surf Beach Park, c. 1915. On top of the building at left, bathing suits dry in the sun on a clothesline. Opened in 1908, the park was absorbed into Neptune Beach around 1920. (Published by Edward H. Mitchell, San Francisco.)

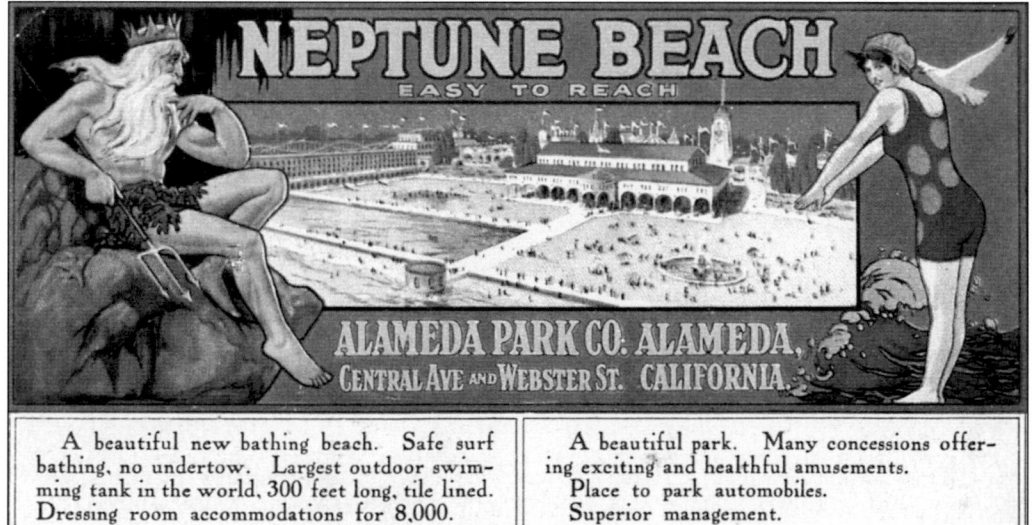

The fanciful imagery of this delightful c. 1917 oversized advertising postcard must have brought many revelers to "easy to reach" Neptune Beach.

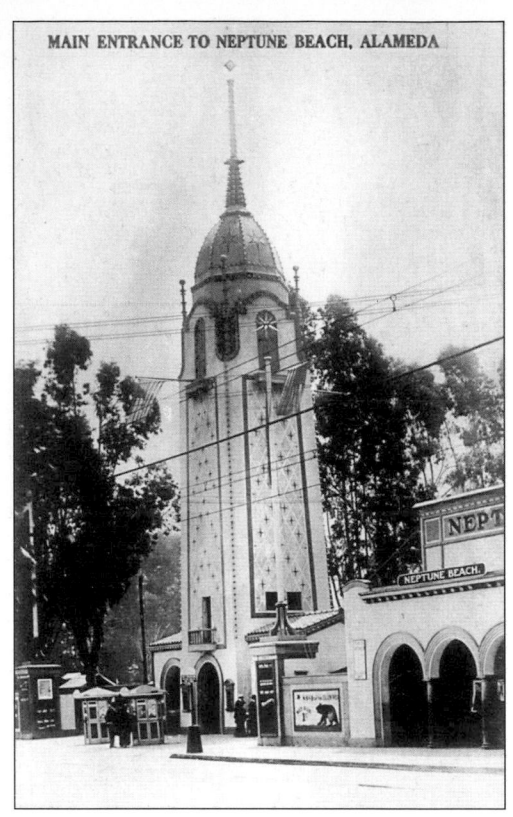

MAIN ENTRANCE TO NEPTUNE BEACH, ALAMEDA

Neptune Beach opened on March 31, 1917. Exposition contractor Robert C. Strehlow developed it in partnership with the Alameda Park Company and later took over complete ownership of Neptune Beach with his family. This c. 1915 photographic postcard shows the entrance to Neptune Beach at the south end of Webster Street at Central Avenue. The Moorish-style tower with a star motif was decorated with inlaid tile and an octagonal, domed roof with spires. The Southern Pacific Red Train station next door to the entrance made it a convenient destination for fun and frolic. (Published by Pacific Photo Company, San Francisco.)

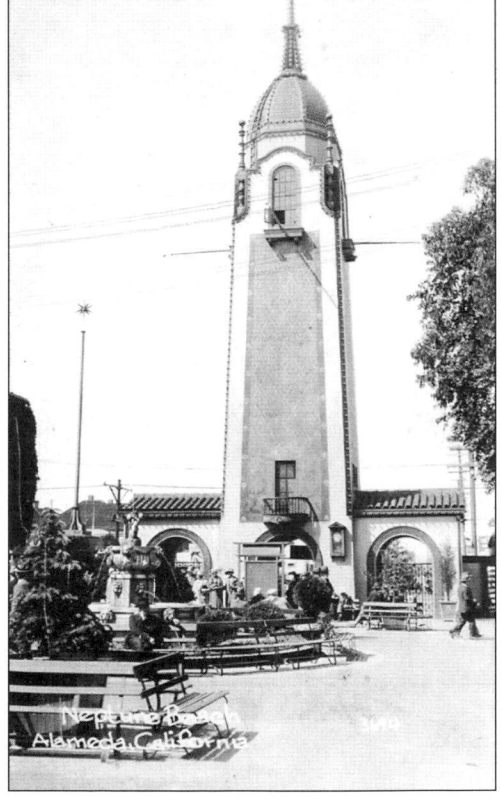

The Neptune Beach entrance tower is seen c. 1925 from inside the park. The postcard writer says, "This is a picture of the entrance for Neptune Beach, where Doris and I go every Sunday." She later writes, "I rode on the Speedway, ha, it sure was fun. Doris rode too, of course, but for an old woman like me, well it was lots of fun anyway."

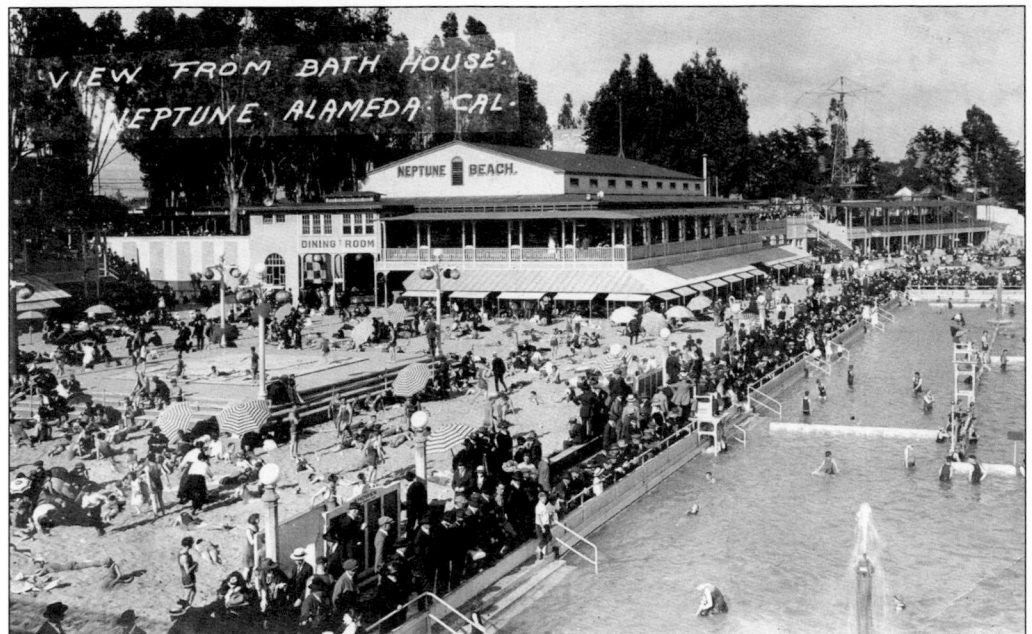

Neptune Beach gave Alameda the nickname "the Coney Island of the West." In the center of this *c.* 1921 photographic postcard is the dance hall and adjoining dining room. The small pool is on the right, and the fairway can be seen in the background.

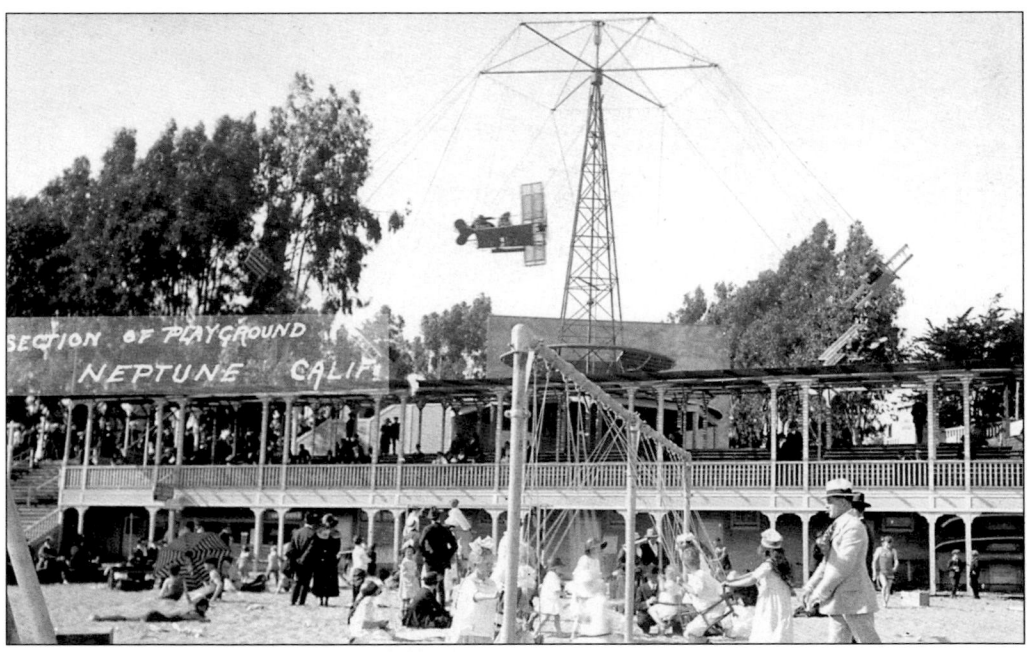

The action and excitement of the Neptune Beach fairway can be seen in this early 1920s postcard. A flying biplane ride towers above. Neptune-brand candy was sold in a red wrapper, and the most popular snow cone flavor was "bluebird." Along with the regular attractions, special events drew crowds, such as appearances by King Neptune and his entourage on Easter Sunday.

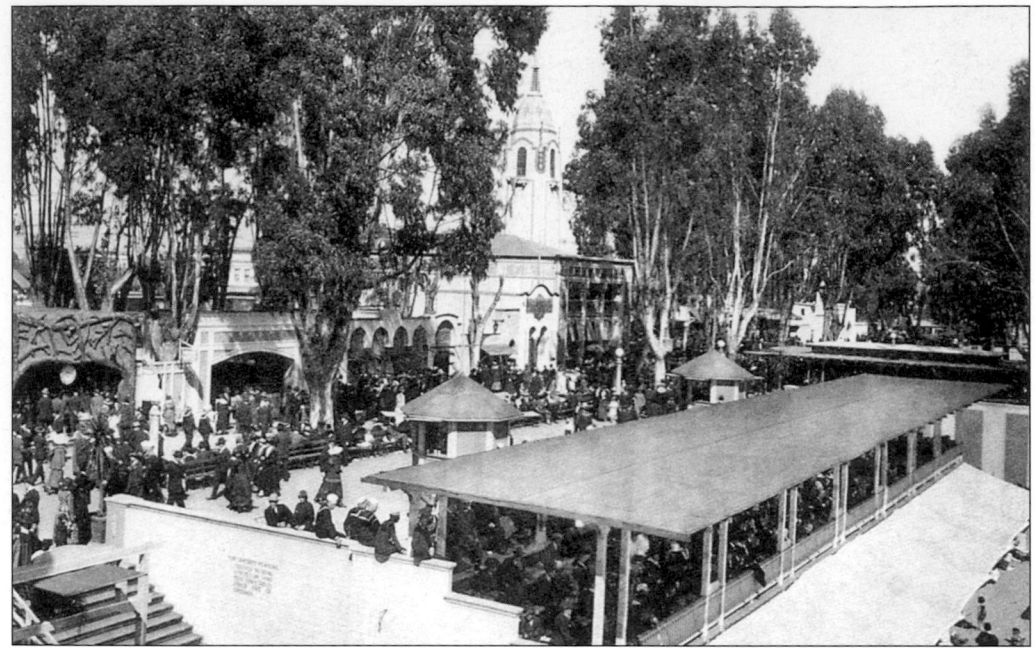

Sailors watch the crowds pass by the concession stands on the Neptune Beach midway in this *c.* 1918 postcard. Live goldfish and canaries were given away as prizes at the game booths, and bathing girl revues were a crowd-pleaser. (Published by Post Cards of Quality, New York.)

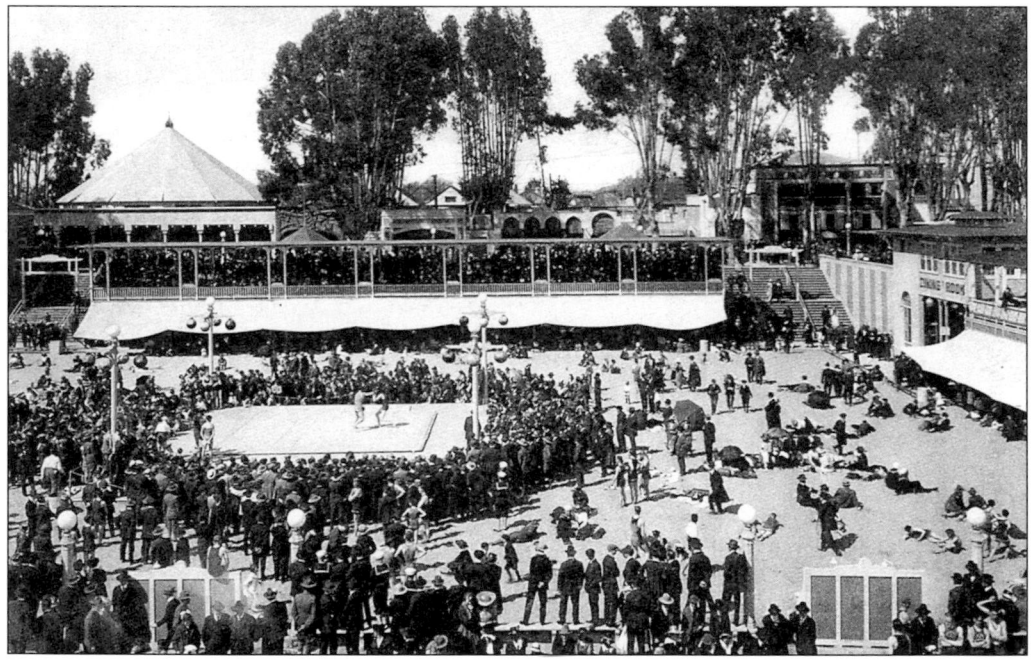

A boxing match draws a large, predominantly male crowd in this *c.* 1918 postcard of the midway, also known as the "Street of Damascus." Neptune Beach was the scene of many boxing and wrestling matches, as well as other sporting events. Note the merry-go-round in the background on the left. (Published by Post Cards of Quality, New York.)

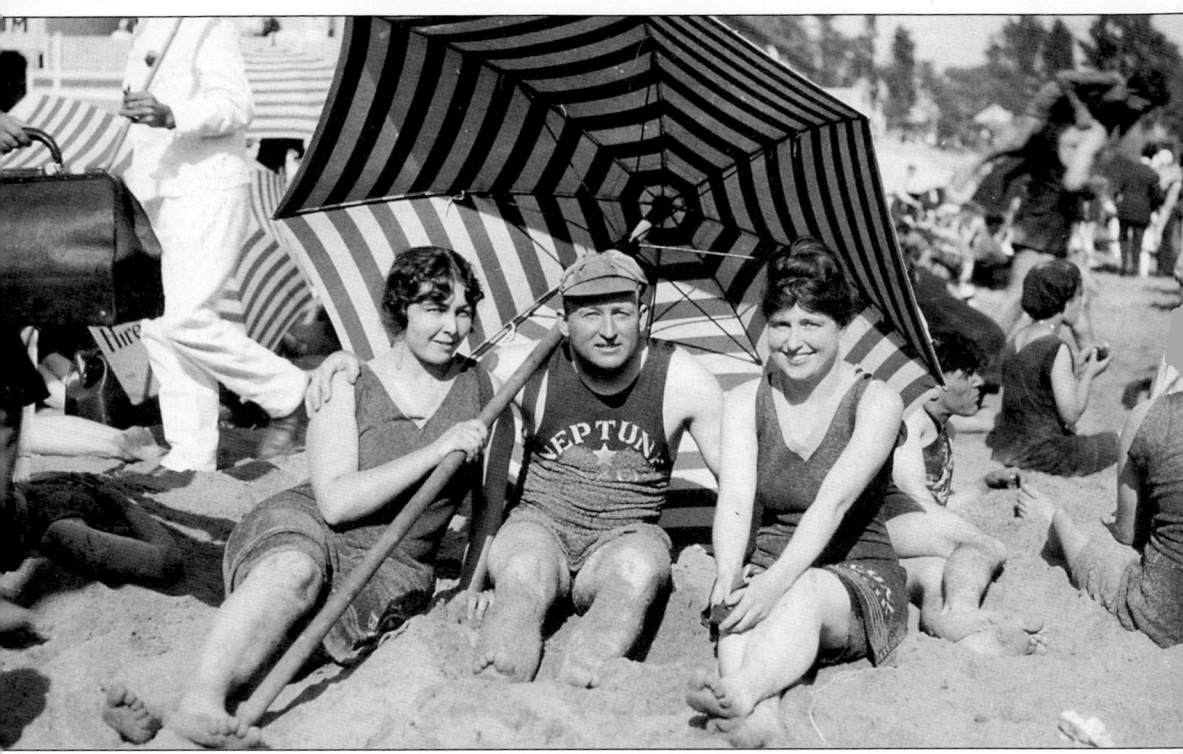

A happy trio enjoys the sun and sand of Neptune Beach *c.* 1919, wearing rented bathing suits while sitting under a striped beach umbrella. In 1917, bathing suits were required to have at least a nine-inch inseam. In 1924, local clubwomen complained that the beach was rife with "immoral" bathing attire, which they considered "scant, immodest, and transparent." They called for a standard in coverage, which was never adopted. Unfortunately, bathing suit controversies and wonderful scenes like this came to an end as the Depression sent the park into bankruptcy. After its closure in 1940, the equipment was sold, with the Ferris wheel traveling to Los Angeles, and the merry-go-round to Playland at the Beach in San Francisco. The buildings were demolished, the pools buried, and the property later used as a U.S. Maritime Service Officers' Training School during World War II.

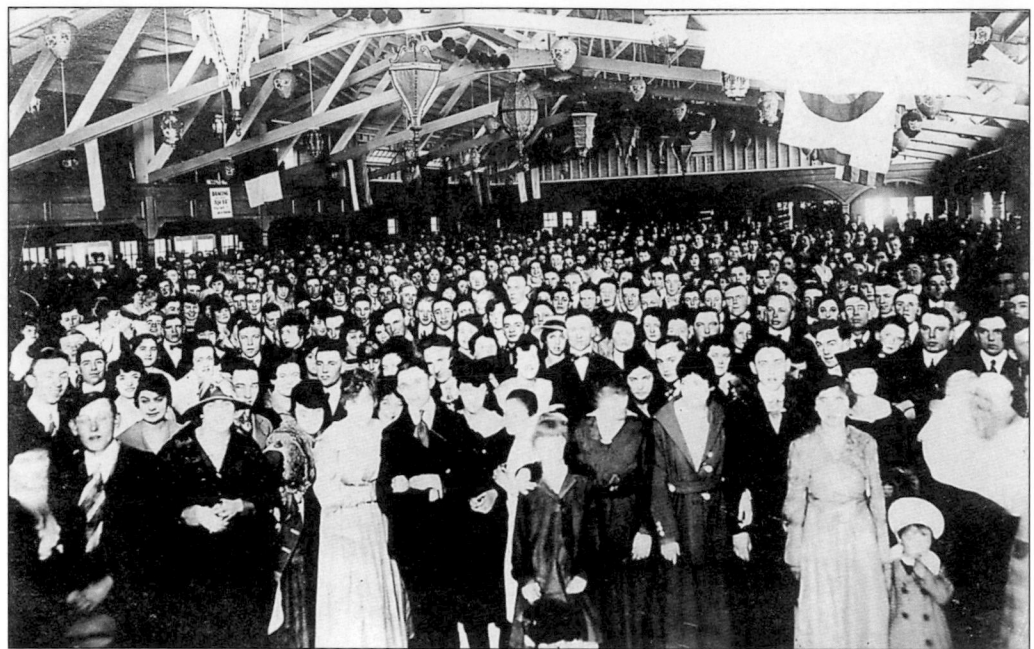

A happy crowd of dancers stops for a moment to face the camera under decorative flags and paper lanterns in the Neptune Beach dance pavilion, *c.* 1920. A restaurant also shared space in this large central building. (Published by Pacific Photo Company, San Francisco.)

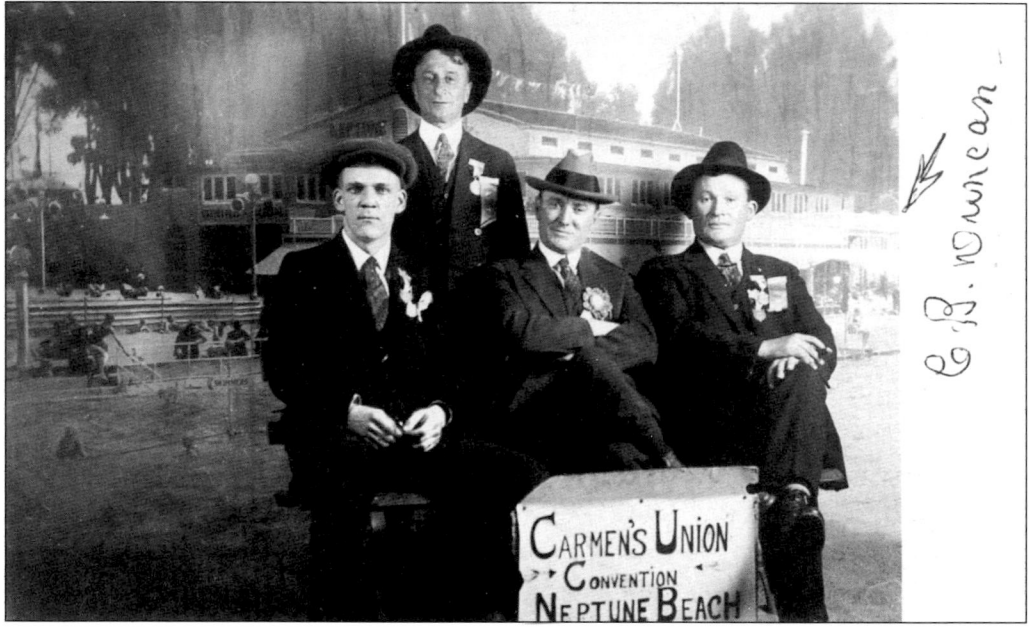

Four members of the Carmen's Union (for railroad car men) take time out from their railroad convention activities to pose in the Neptune Beach photographer's studio, *c.* 1925. Photographic images like these, taken in front of a painted backdrop, were common souvenirs from the early 1900s through the 1940s.

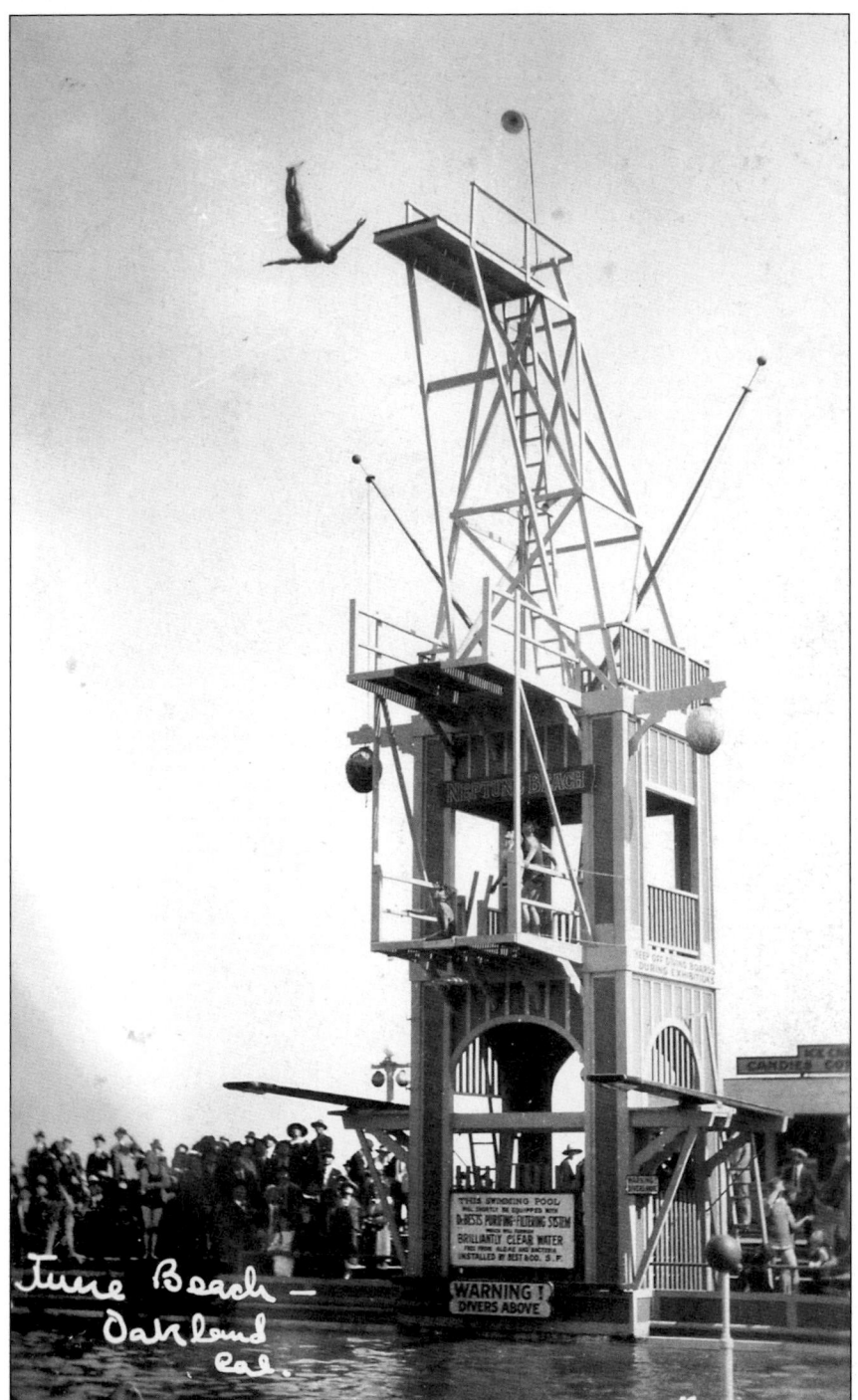

A diver is caught midair in this *c.* 1919 photographic postcard of the diving platform. Several legendary 1920s swimming races took place at Neptune Beach, including Olympic gold medalists Duke Kahanamoku and Johnny Weissmuller (of *Tarzan* movie fame), who had a record-breaking season in 1926. The Neptune Club held numerous swim meets, and in 1927 and 1928, a 14-mile race around the island brought competitors from around the world.

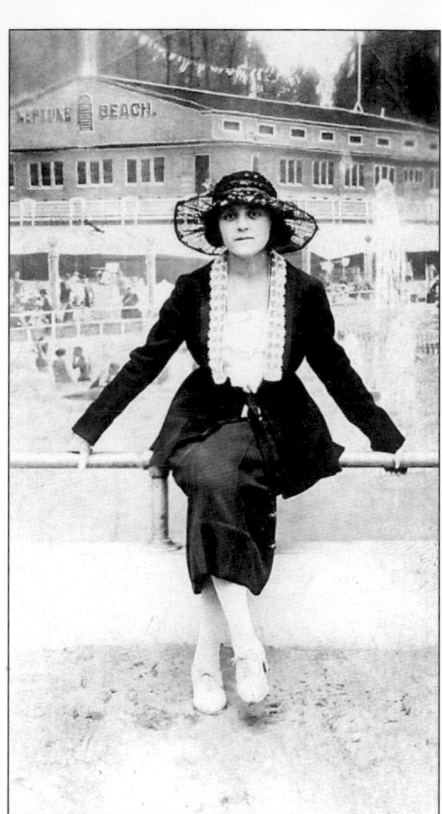

A stylish beauty with a fancy hat poses in the Neptune Beach studio, *c.* 1919.

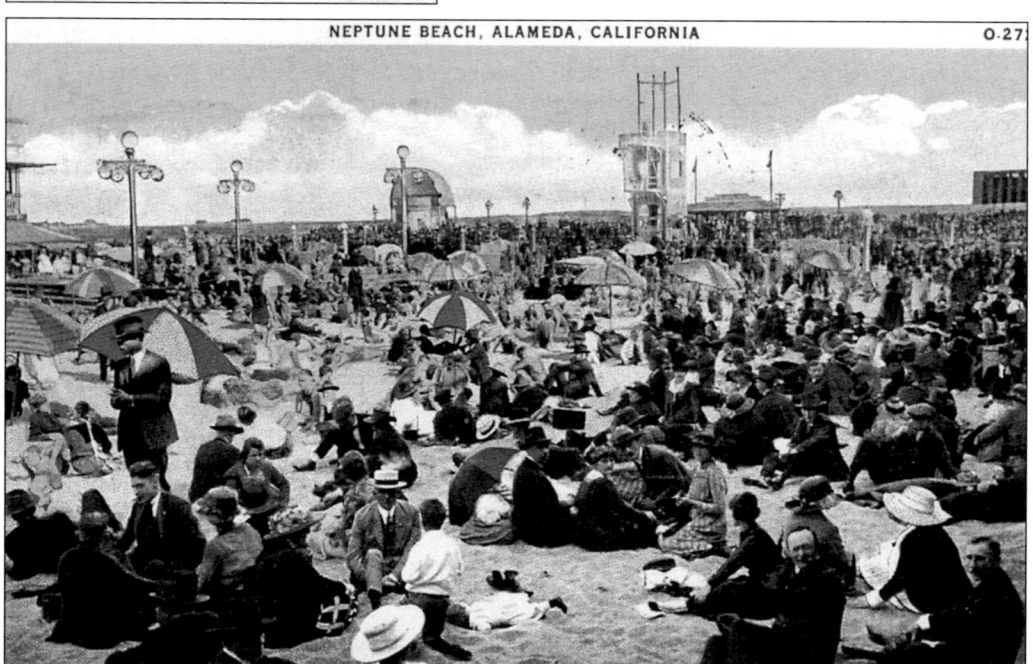

An overdressed crowd, most likely sweltering in the heat, nevertheless enjoys the sights and sounds of Neptune Beach. The high-diving platform looms in the background. Mailed in 1929, this postcard was published by the Pacific Novelty Company, San Francisco.

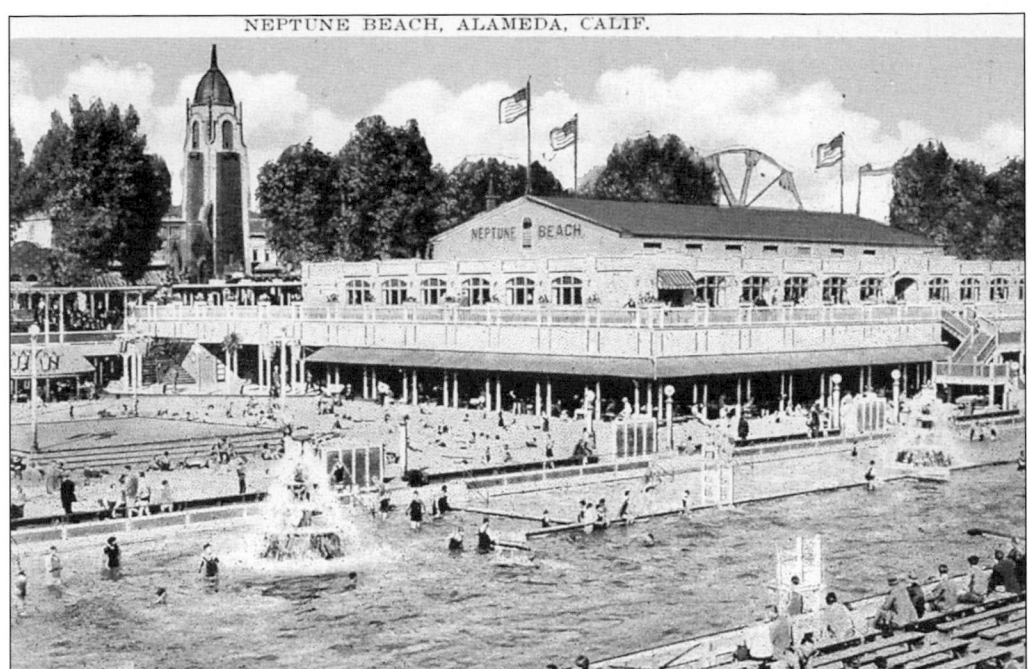

NEPTUNE BEACH, ALAMEDA, CALIF.

Swimmers enjoy the water and fountains in the small pool, seen in this early 1920s postcard of Neptune Beach. On the left is the dance pavilion and the entrance tower in the background. (Published by the Western Notion and Novelty Company, Oakland.)

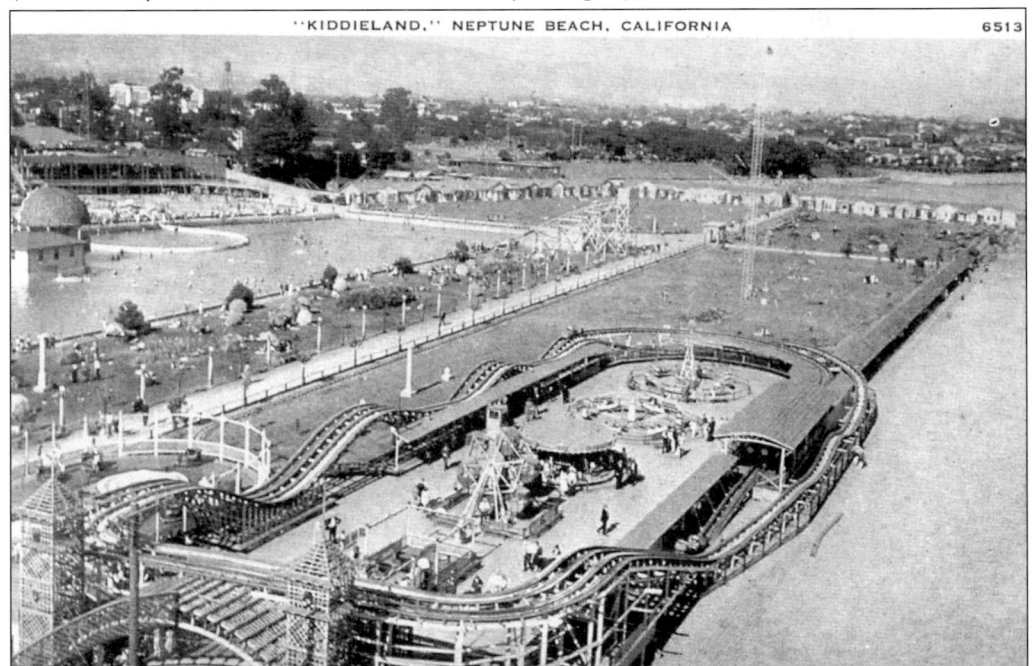

"KIDDIELAND," NEPTUNE BEACH, CALIFORNIA   6513

A c. 1930s view of Kiddieland's children's rides at Neptune Beach, which included a miniature Ferris wheel, a merry-go-round, a small roller coaster, a train, and swan boats. By this time, Strehlow owned the park with his family, having bought out his original partners in 1923. (Published by the Pacific Novelty Company.)

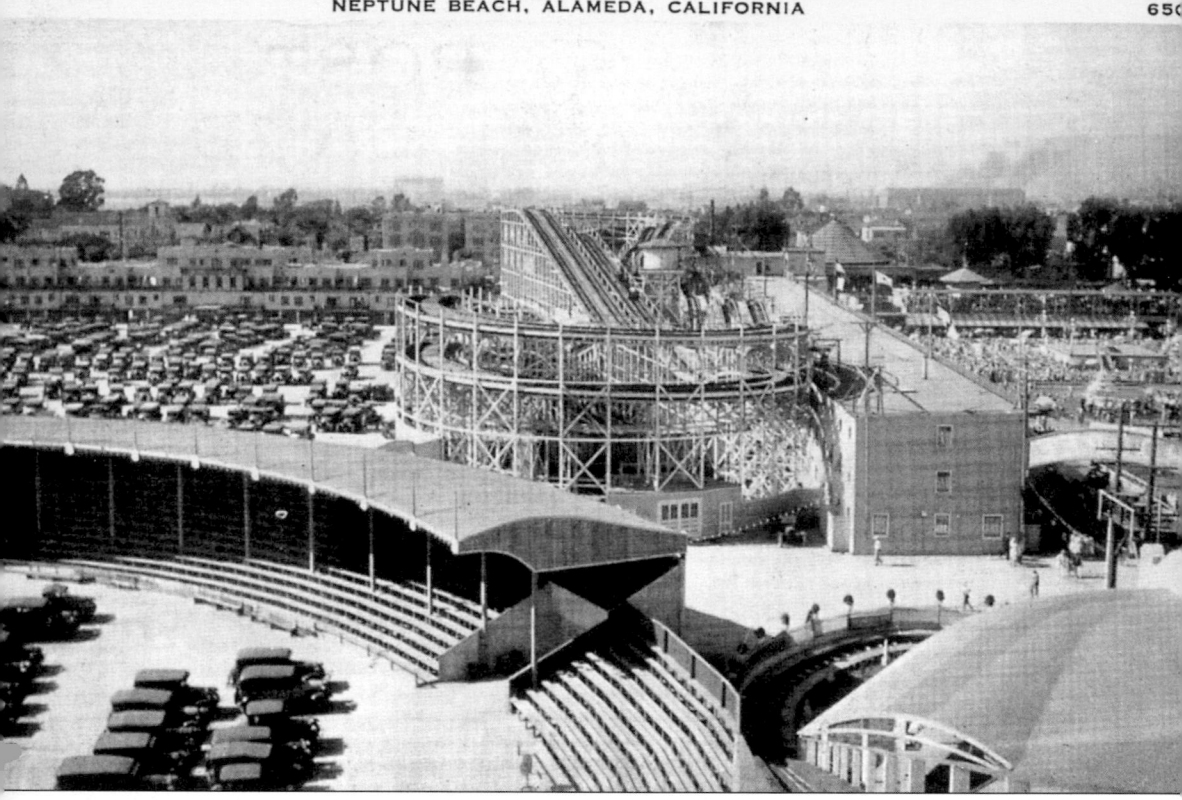

The roller coaster known as The Whoopie can be seen in this *c.* 1932 view of Neptune Beach. In the background on the left is the Neptune Court apartment building that Robert Strehlow built during the mid-1920s expansion. The 39-unit building housed summer tourists and long-term residents, including Strehlow himself. The 1925 structure is the only remaining relic of Neptune Beach. (Published by the Pacific Novelty Company.)

Eight

HOTELS AND MOTELS

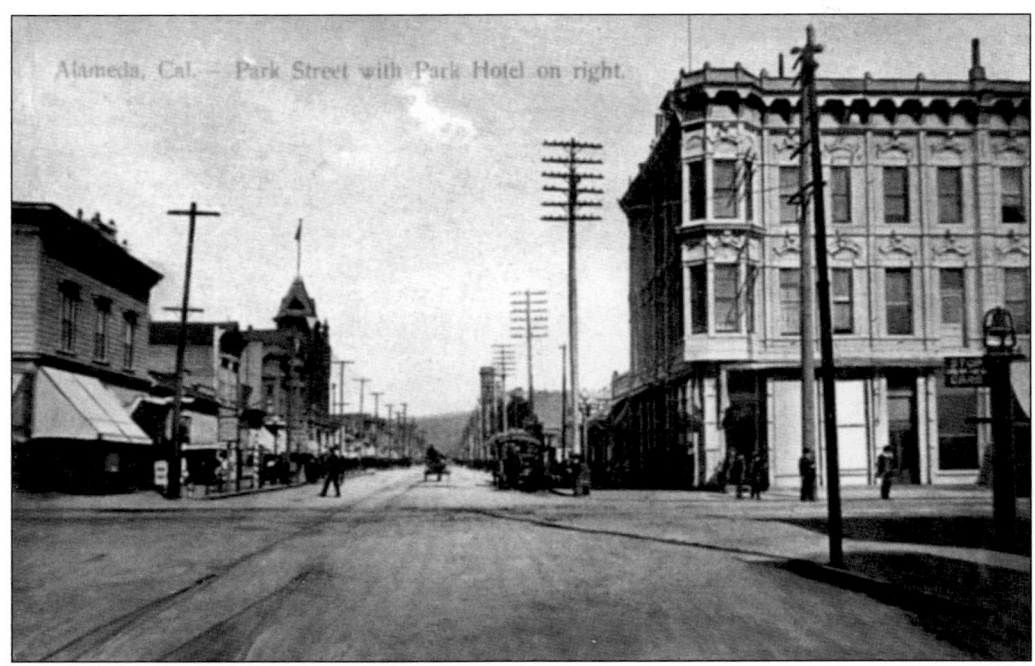

This *c.* 1910 view is of Park Street at the intersection of Encinal Avenue. On the right is the Park Hotel, which was built in 1878–1879 by A. A. Fair to accommodate passengers of his narrow-gauge railroad. In its prime, the hotel's first floor served as a waiting area for the trains and as a Western Union office. Later renamed the El Centro Hotel, it was demolished in 1965 after fire damage and structural decline. (Published by the Pacific Novelty Company, San Francisco.)

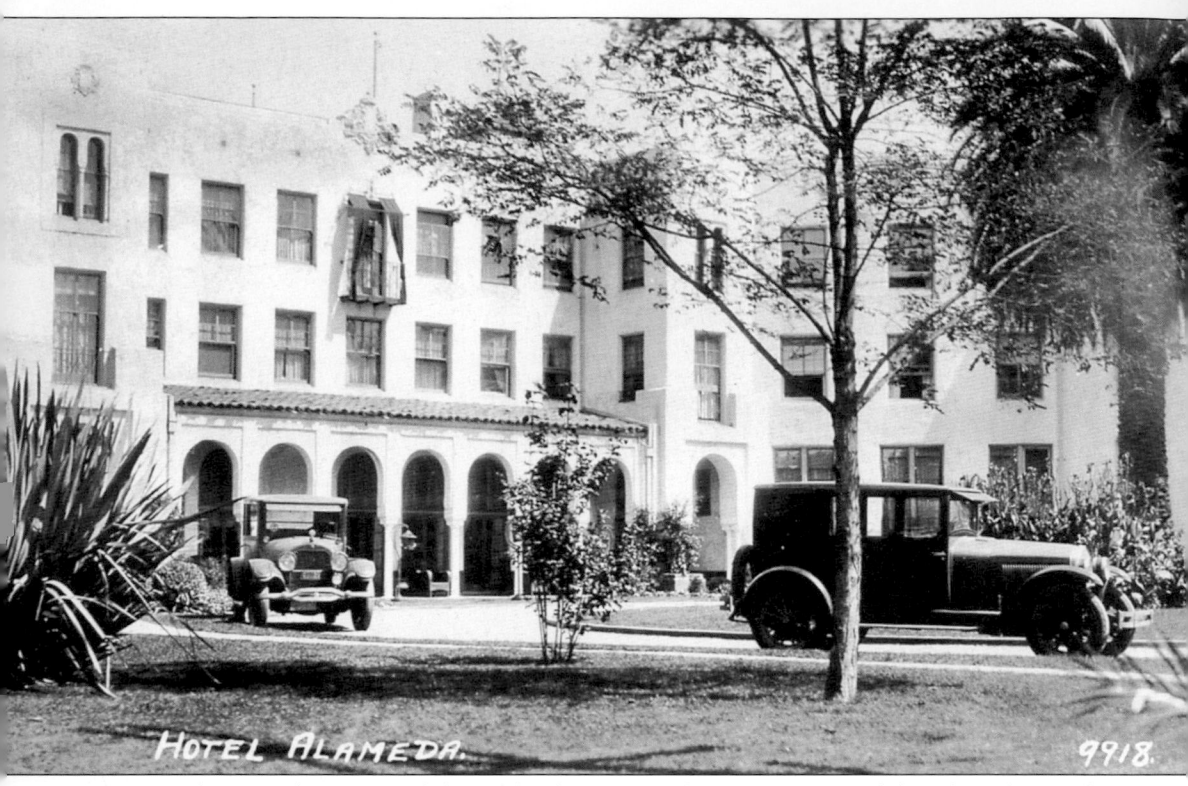

HOTEL ALAMEDA.   9918.

A *c.* 1930 photographic postcard shows the driveway and main entrance of the Alameda Hotel. Designed by the architectural firm of Slocum and Tuttle and built in 1927–1928, the hotel still graces a large corner lot at Broadway and Central Avenue. Financed by stock shares sold to local residents, the hotel held dinner dances in the ballroom, with music provided by popular orchestras, from the opening in the late 1920s until the Depression. Famous visitors included Errol Flynn, who was in town supervising work on his yacht, as well as Jackie Cooper and Wallace Beery during the filming of *Treasure Island* in 1934.

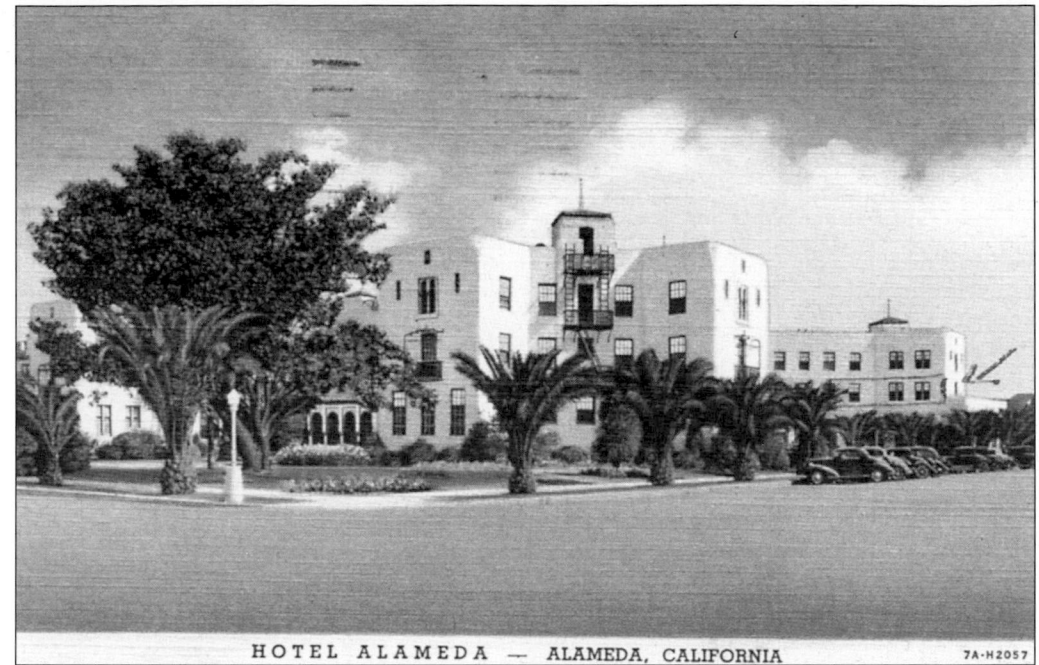

HOTEL ALAMEDA — ALAMEDA, CALIFORNIA   7A-H2057

This 1937 postcard shows the Alameda Hotel at the intersection of Central Avenue and Broadway. The hotel's amenities included furnished rooms and apartments, a coffee shop, cafe, cocktail lounge (the popular La Taverna bar, which opened after the end of Prohibition), and a ballroom. During World War II, the main lobby was transformed into the Allied Officers Club, which was a center for visiting officers of all nations. (Published by Curt Teich and Company, Chicago.)

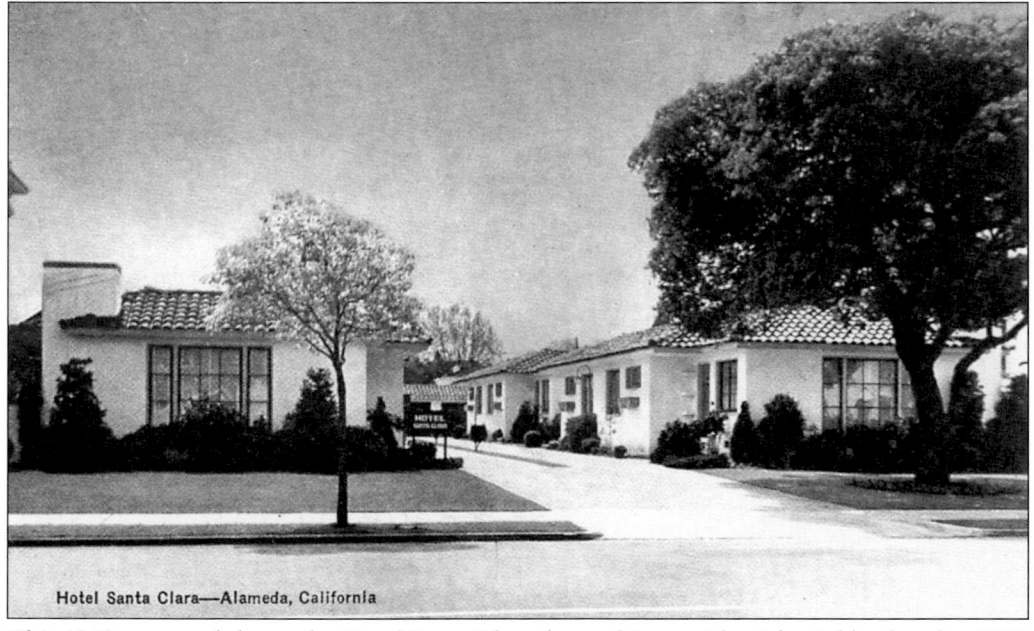

Hotel Santa Clara—Alameda, California

This 1940s postcard shows the Hotel Santa Clara, located in a residential neighborhood at 1830 Santa Clara Avenue. Built in July 1938 by P. Spaulding, this hotel now serves as apartments. (Published by John MacIver.)

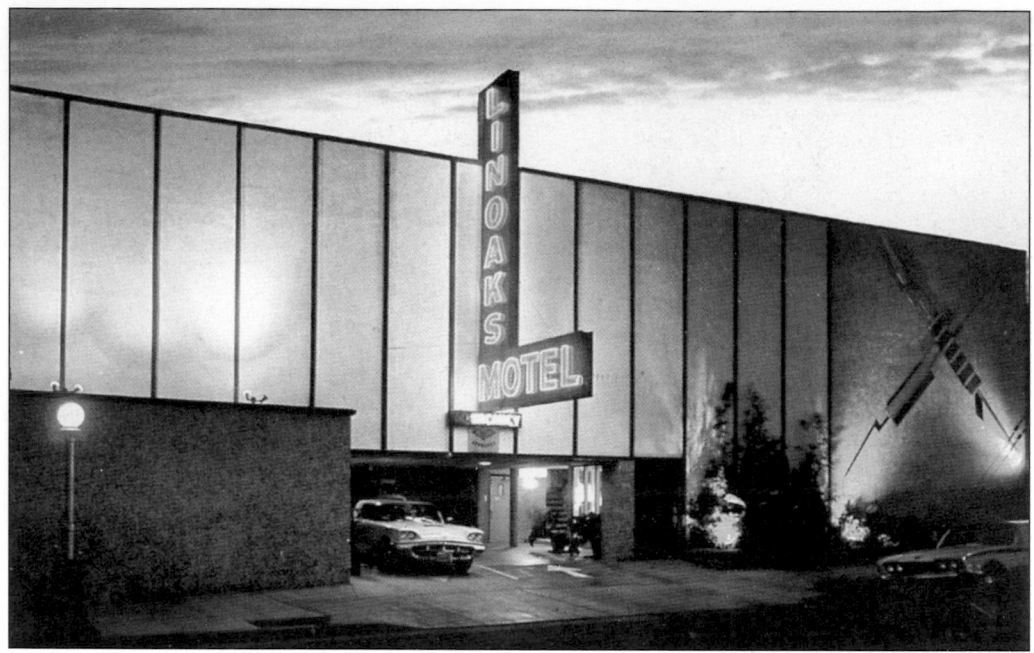

This early 1960s chrome postcard captures the Linoaks Motel entrance and neon sign. Opened on October 9, 1959, the motel was located at the corner of Lincoln Avenue and Oak Street, hence the name. (Color by Mike Roberts, Berkeley.)

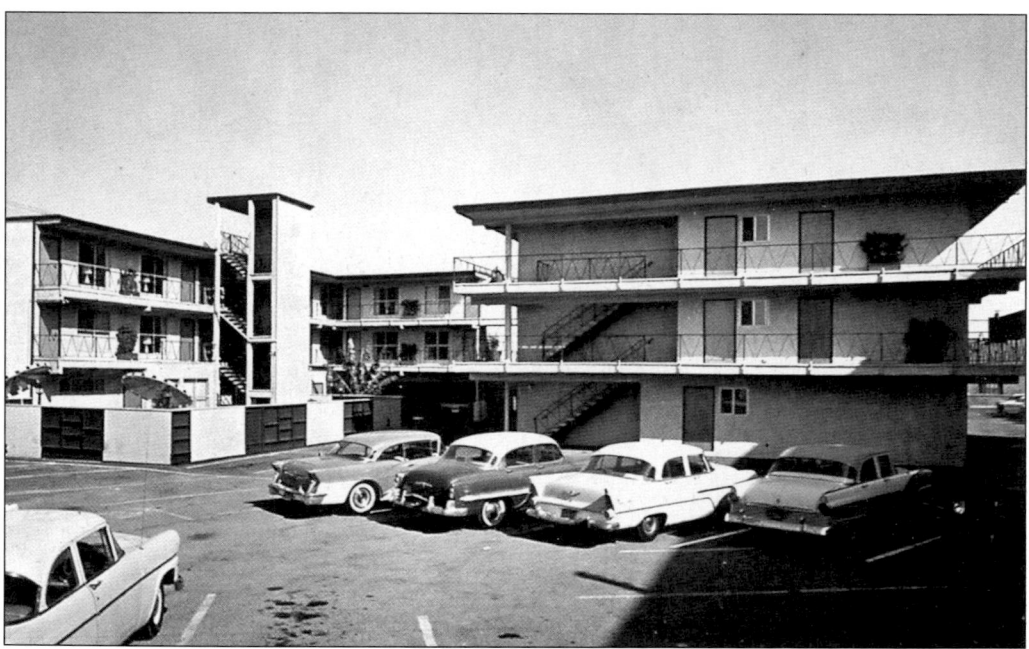

Taken in the side parking lot of the Linoaks Motel, this *c.* 1959 view shows a "modern" three-story structure "located in the heart of beautiful Alameda." The motel was demolished in 2004. (Color by Mike Roberts, Berkeley.)

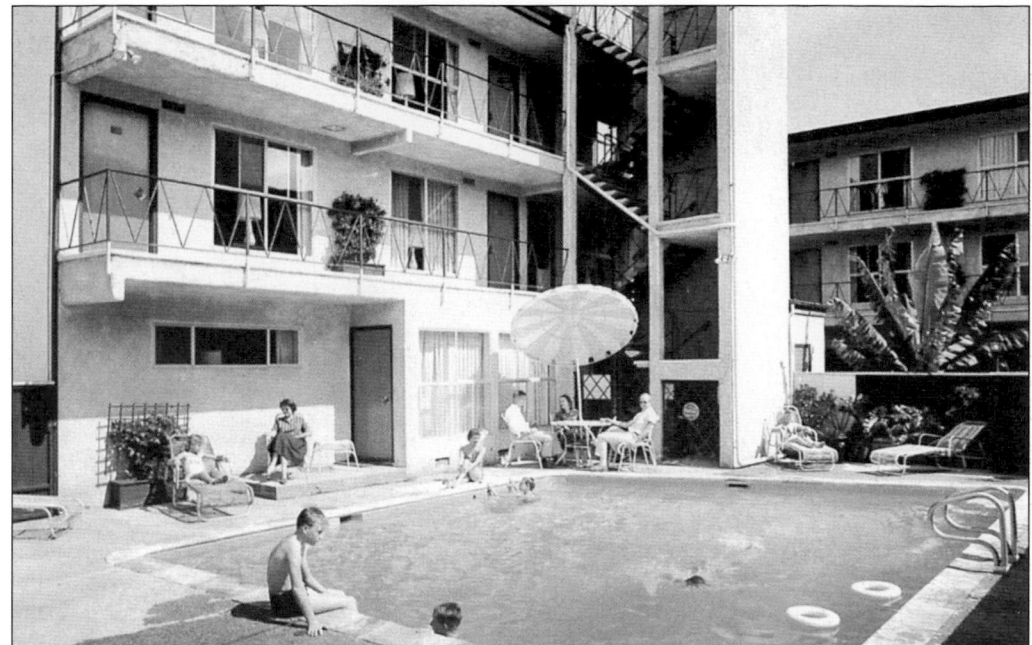

This *c.* 1959 poolside scene was taken long before the Linoaks Motel's sad decline. This picture is described on the back of the postcard as "a beautiful heated pool surrounded by lounging furniture." At the time it opened, a local newspaper described the room decor as "Swedish modern." (Color by Mike Roberts, Berkeley.)

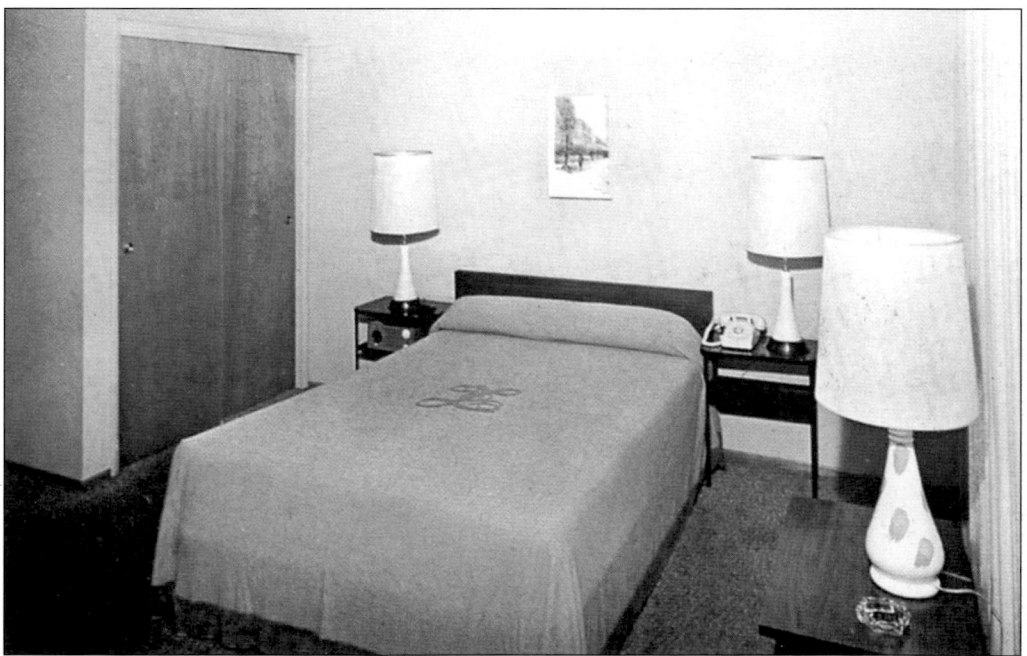

According to the information on the back of this chrome postcard, the Linoaks Motel offered "smartly appointed rooms together with kitchenette units, room phones, complimentary TV, radio, newspaper, coffee"—not to mention the overabundance of lamps that illuminated this particular room. (Color by Mike Roberts, Berkeley.)

Royal Inn of Alameda

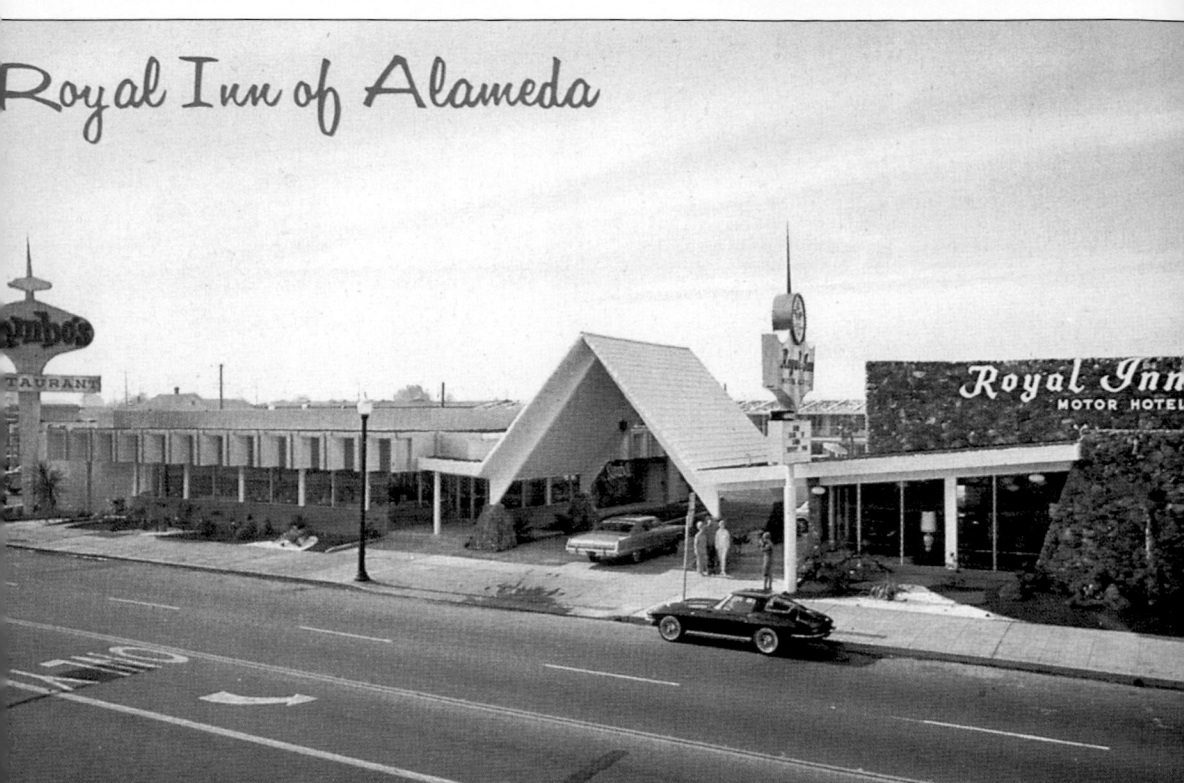

This *c.* 1973 chrome postcard is of the Royal Inn, "Alameda's newest luxury motor hotel," which provided such exotic comforts as suites with bars, sauna baths, and color televisions. A Sambo's restaurant and Lost Knight Cocktail Lounge on the premises added to the excitement. Originally built in 1945, this motel underwent a drastic remodeling, probably around 1967. Both the restaurant and motel are now under different ownership. (Color by Mike Roberts, Berkeley.)

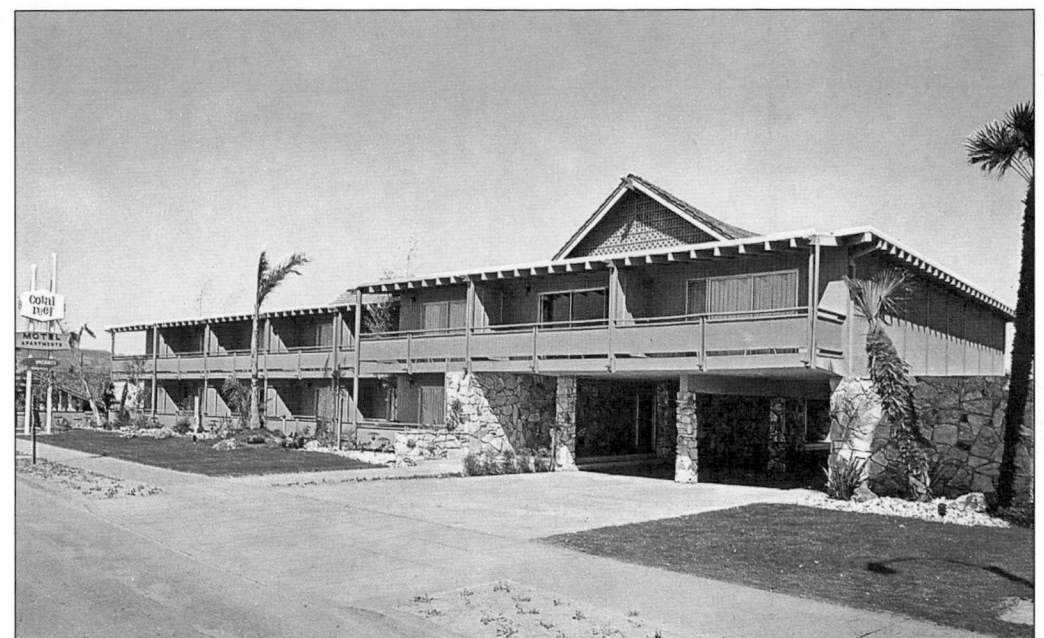

This is an outside view of the Coral Reef Motel at 400 Park Street, one block from the beach, *c.* 1970. The motel's amenities included family units, televisions, phones in all rooms, and teletype reservations. (Color by Mike Roberts, Berkeley.)

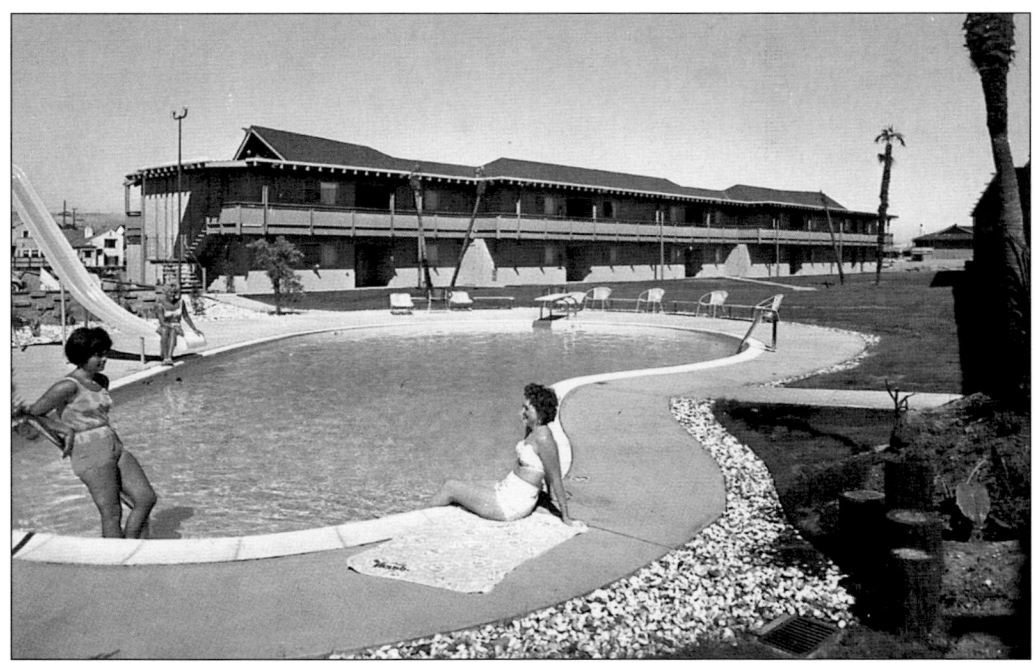

Bathing beauties lounge by the Coral Reef Motel kidney-shaped pool some time in the 1960s. Located in the South Shore area, the motel was built in 1963 by George Samson and still stands today, with slight cosmetic changes. (Color by Mike Roberts, Berkeley.)

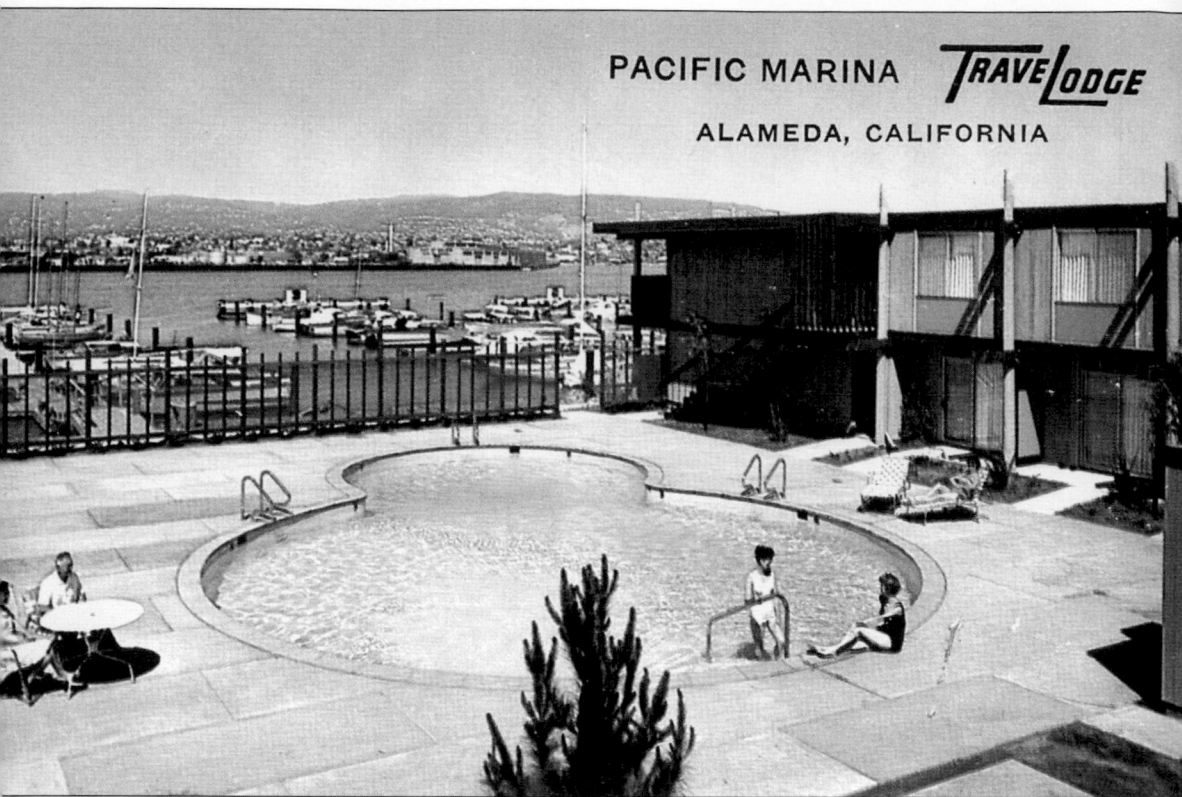

PACIFIC MARINA *Trave*Lodge

ALAMEDA, CALIFORNIA

A 1960s chrome postcard shows the pool, patio, and harbor beyond, at the Pacific Marina TraveLodge. Designed by the nationally-known architectural firm of Campbell and Wong, the motel opened in 1961.

Nine

TRANSPORTATION

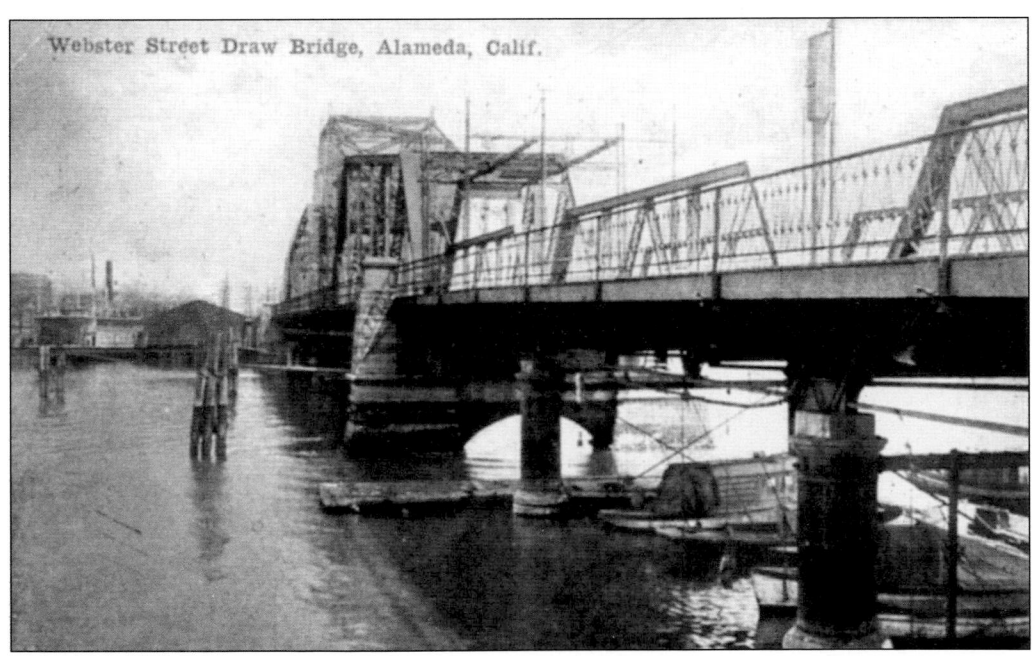

The 1881 Webster Street Bridge was replaced with this iron-truss swing bridge that opened to traffic on February 1, 1900. Streetcars going to and from Oakland used this span, shown here in a *c.* 1907 postcard.

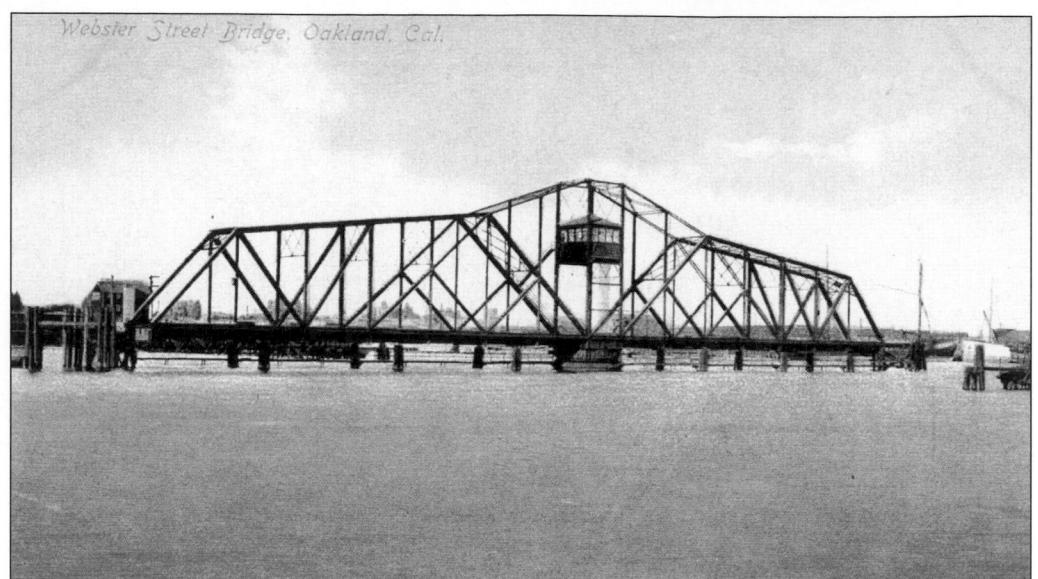

On January 7, 1926, the steamer *Lancaster* destroyed the Webster Street Bridge, only three years before the Posey Tube was to render it obsolete. Since the tunnel was still under construction, the bridge was rebuilt at a cost of $134,000, used for a short time, and then dismantled in October 1928. The bridge was later auctioned off to Sacramento County for only $3,100, where it began anew as a span across the American River. (Published by the Newman Postcard Company, Los Angeles, *c.* 1909.)

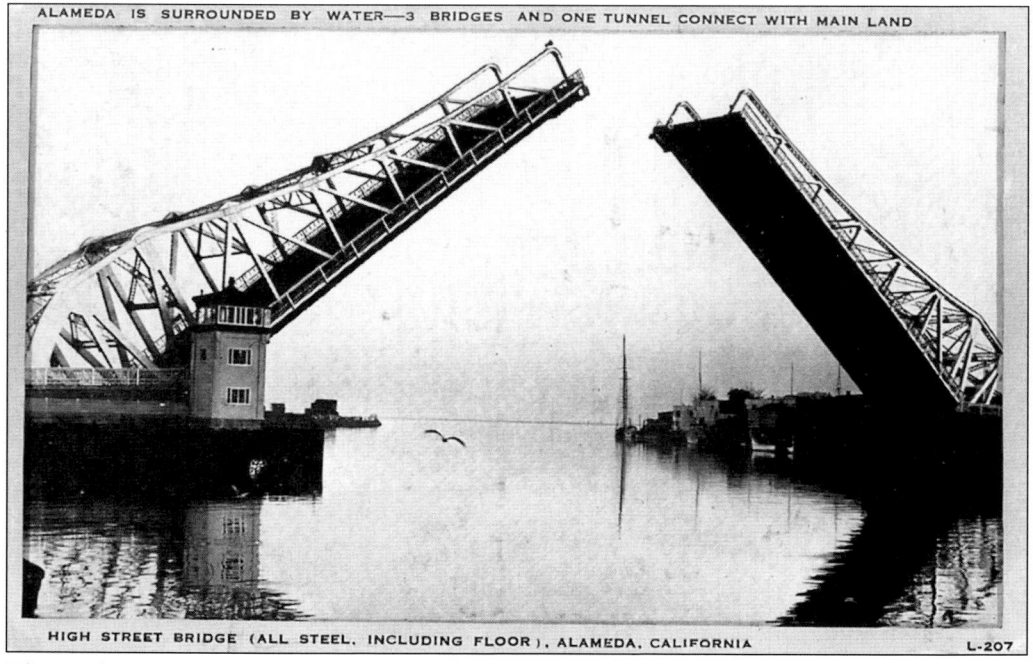

The High Street Bridge was built in 1901 by the Army Corps of Engineers over the canal, which had not yet been completed. (Postcard manufactured by the Wayne Paper and Box Printing Corporation, Fort Wayne, Indiana, *c.* 1942.)

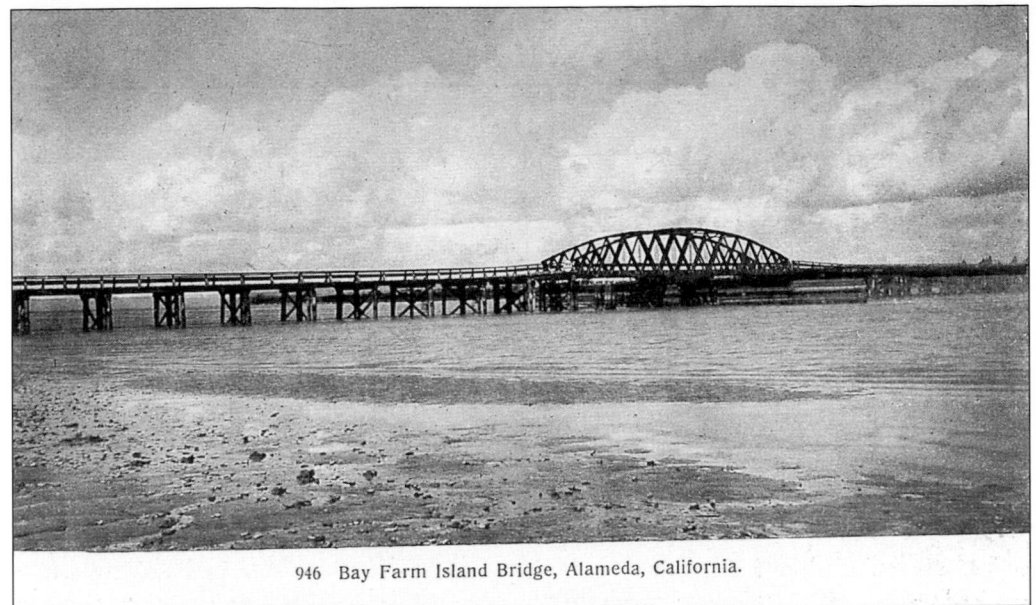

946 Bay Farm Island Bridge, Alameda, California.

The first crossing to Bay Farm Island was constructed in 1854. Upkeep on the wooden structure proved to be too costly, and it was taken down in 1860. The next Bay Farm Island Bridge was completed in January 1875, and built by the Pacific Bridge Company. This *c.* 1907 postcard shows the third bridge, built in 1902, which included a portion of the 1881 Webster Street Bridge. (Published by the Cardinell-Vincent Company, Oakland.)

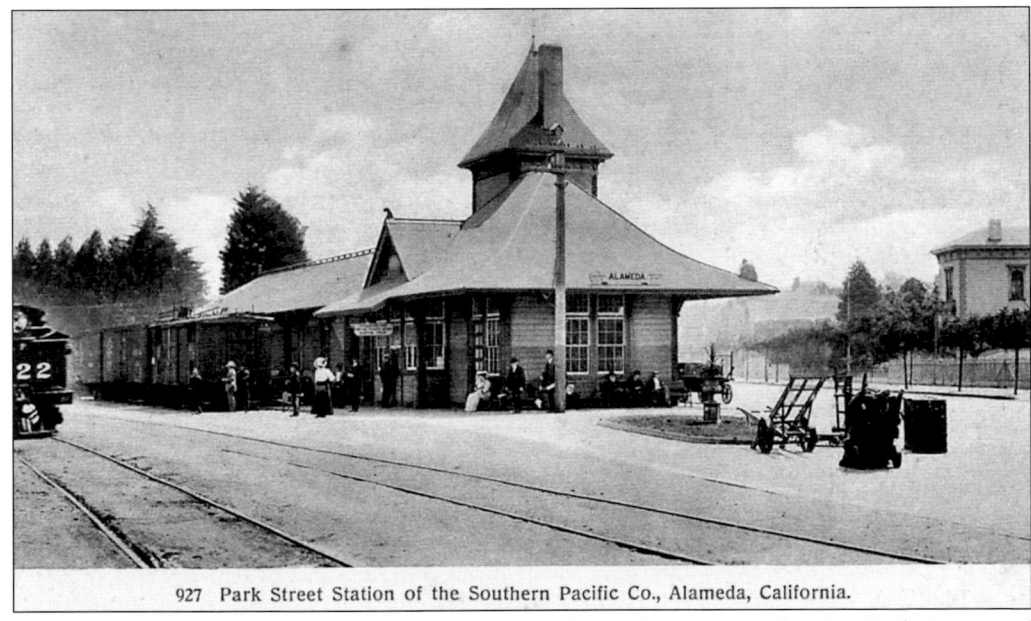

927 Park Street Station of the Southern Pacific Co., Alameda, California.

The Park Street Station was established by the South Pacific Coast Railroad at Park Street and Encinal Avenue in 1878. It was renamed South Park Street Station in 1911. (Published by the Cardinell-Vincent Company, Oakland, *c.* 1908.)

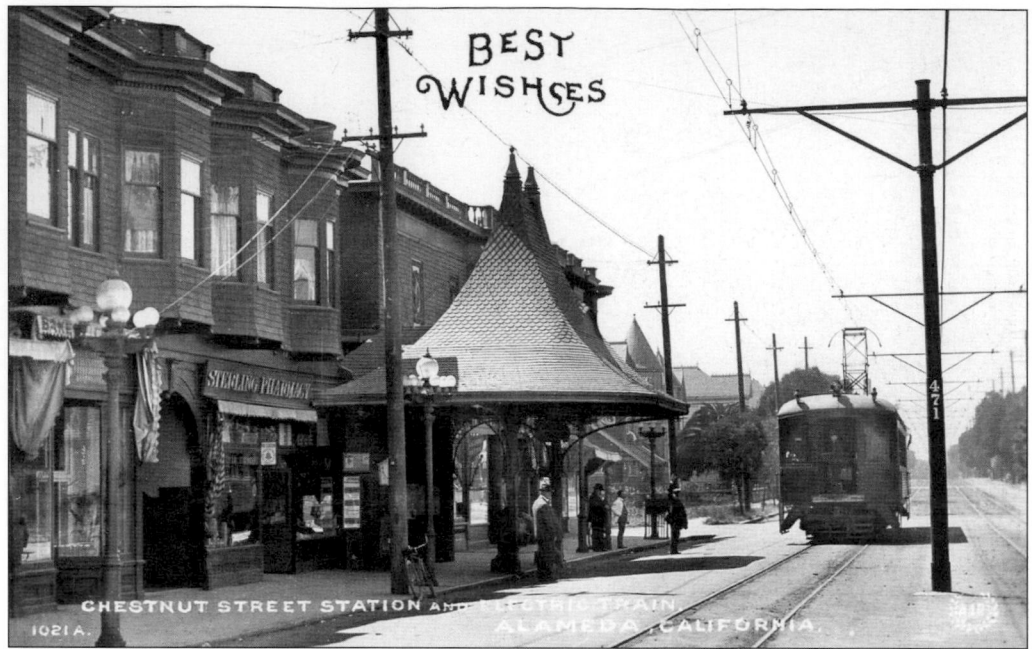

This *c.* 1910 photographic postcard shows the Chestnut Street Station and electric train, which was located between Chestnut and Lafayette Streets on the south side of Encinal Avenue. Designed by Joseph A. Leonard, who also donated land for the site, it was built in 1890 and was demolished in the early 1940s. (Published by American Industrial Photo Company, San Francisco.)

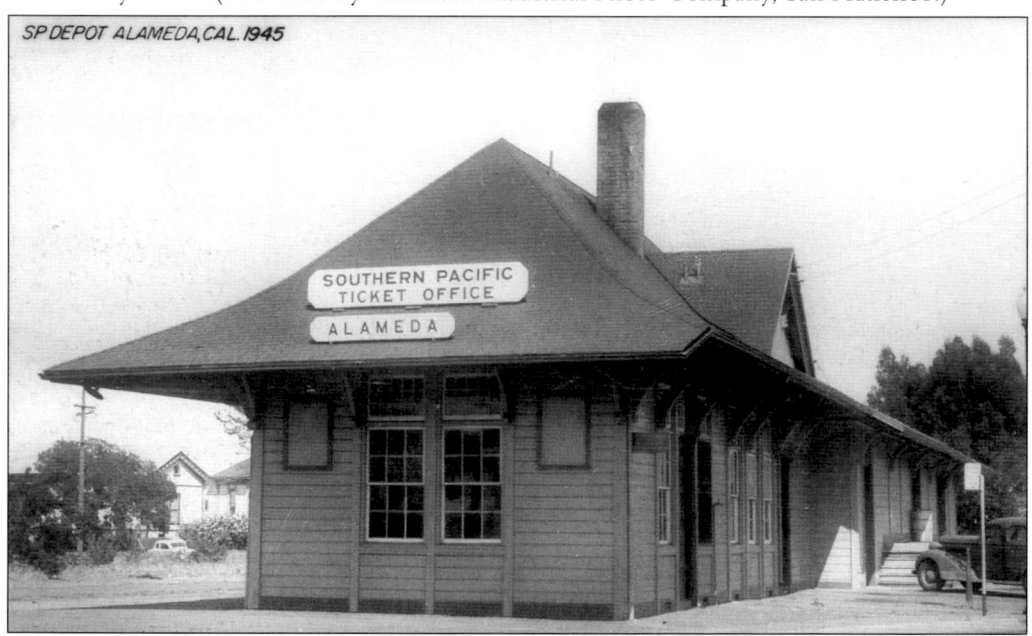

This postcard shows a 1945 photographic image of the Southern Pacific Railroad depot. Built in 1901 at Park Street and Lincoln Avenue, this line was last used on May 1, 1954, much to the relief of the residents on Lincoln Avenue, who had complained about the noise for years. The depot was shuttered in 1957 and demolished in 1961. The tracks on Lincoln, between Park and Webster, were eventually paved over to create a four-lane avenue.

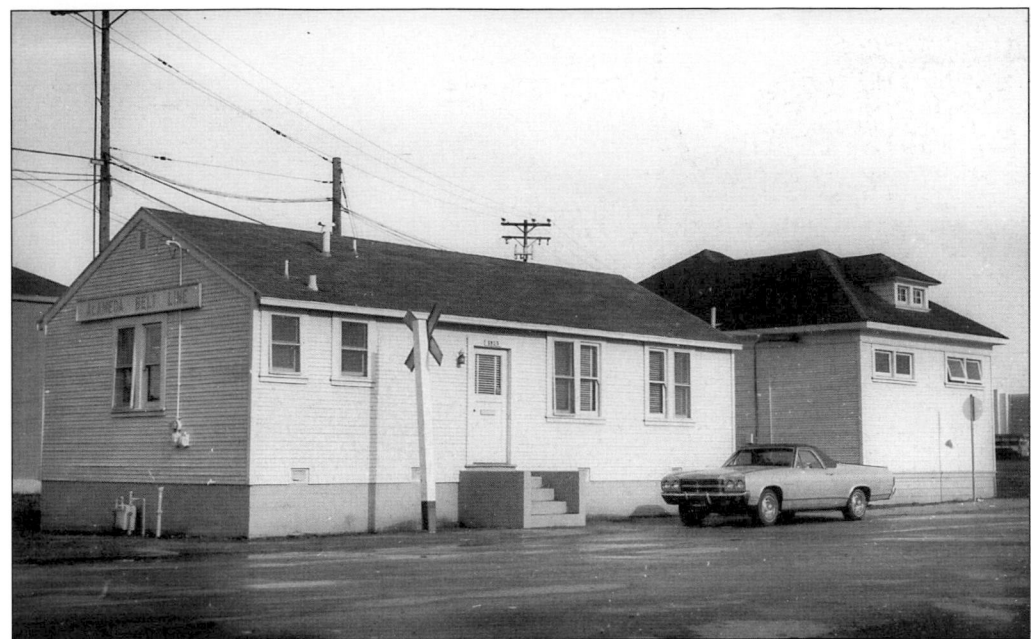

This is a 1971 view of the Alameda Belt Line depot, which was originally created in 1918 as a one-mile line for industrial use, freight, and switching cars. In the mid-1920s it was acquired by Western Pacific-Santa Fe and expanded along the city's northern end. Operations dwindled during the 1970s and by 1989, it had been reduced to only a switching area on Sherman Street.

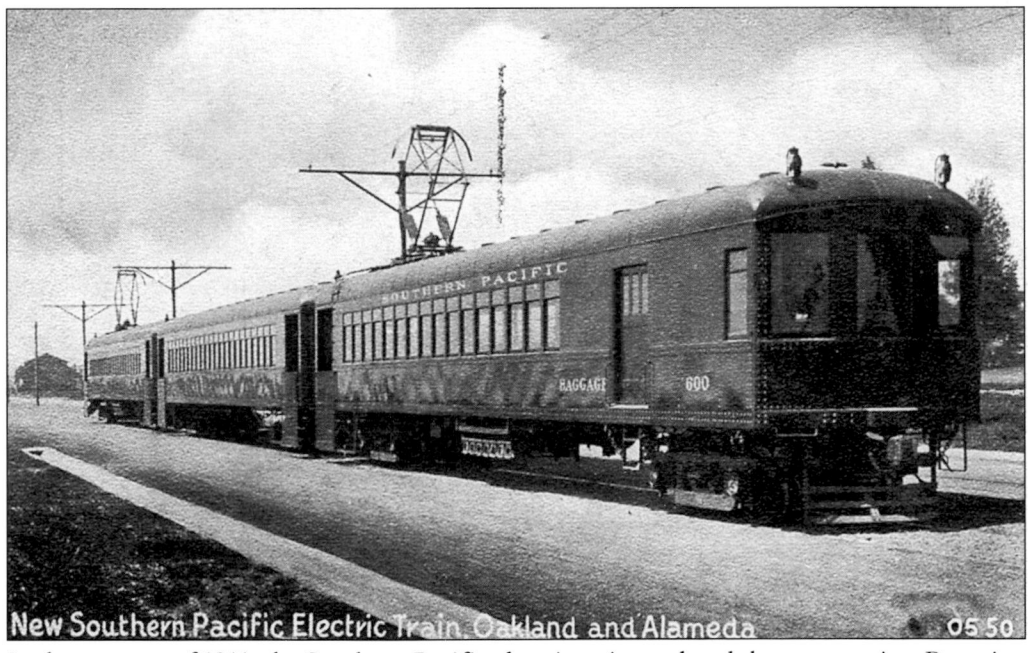

New Southern Pacific Electric Train, Oakland and Alameda

In the summer of 1911, the Southern Pacific electric trains replaced the steam trains. Running every 30 minutes during the day and every 45 minutes in the evening until midnight, the cars were called Red Trains due to their color. Maintenance facilities for the trains were also located in Alameda. (Published by Souvenir Publishing Company, San Francisco, *c.* 1912.)

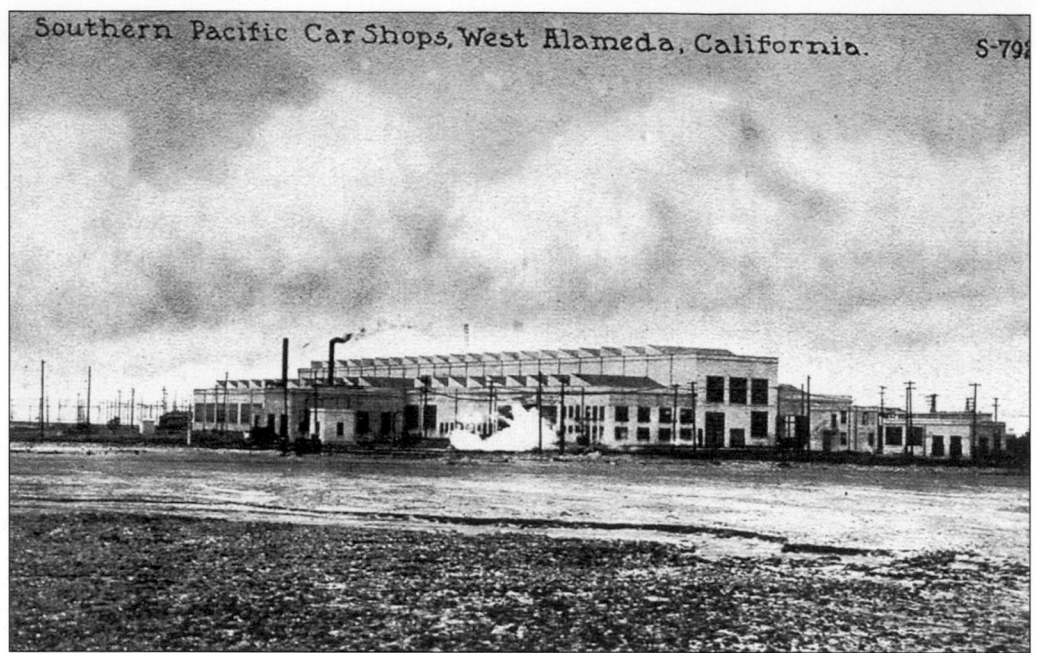

A *c.* 1912 postcard shows the Southern Pacific car shops and the Sawtooth Building, named for its unusual roof. This facility was used for storage and maintenance on the Southern Pacific Red Trains until 1941, when it was moved to West Oakland. (Published by Souvenir Publishing Company, San Francisco.)

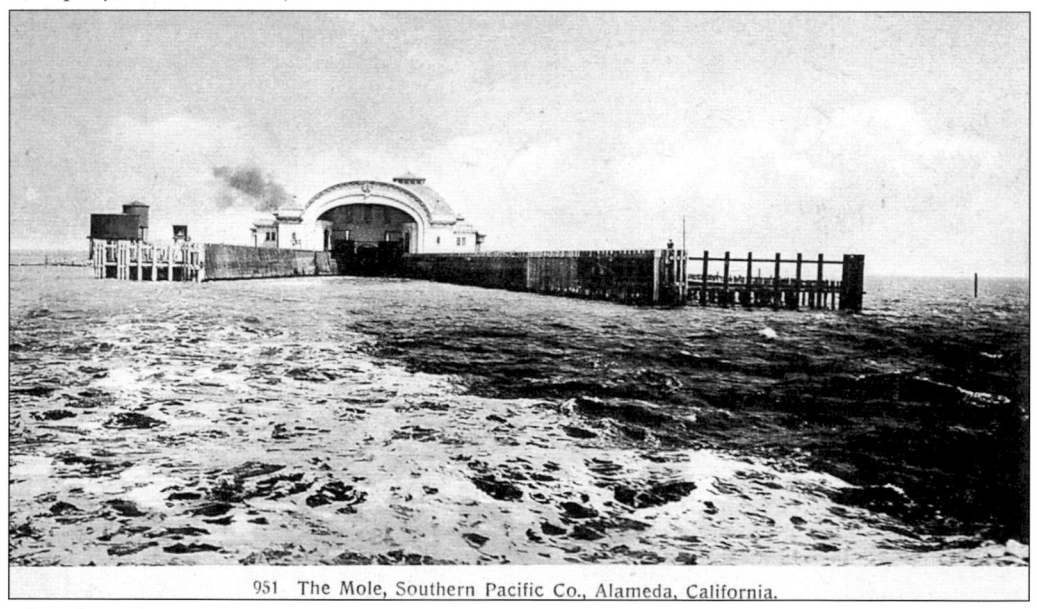

The Alameda Mole was the name of a piece of land created by filling in the Alameda pier with dredged materials during the 1890s. The first depot on that land burned in 1902, and the elaborate and beautiful ferry depot seen here was built to replace it in 1905. Its construction required over six million feet of lumber. After the Bay Bridge opened in 1936, ferry operations were curtailed. The structure was closed in 1939, demolished in 1941, and replaced with the Naval Air Station's runways. (Published by the Cardinell-Vincent Company, Oakland, *c.* 1908.)

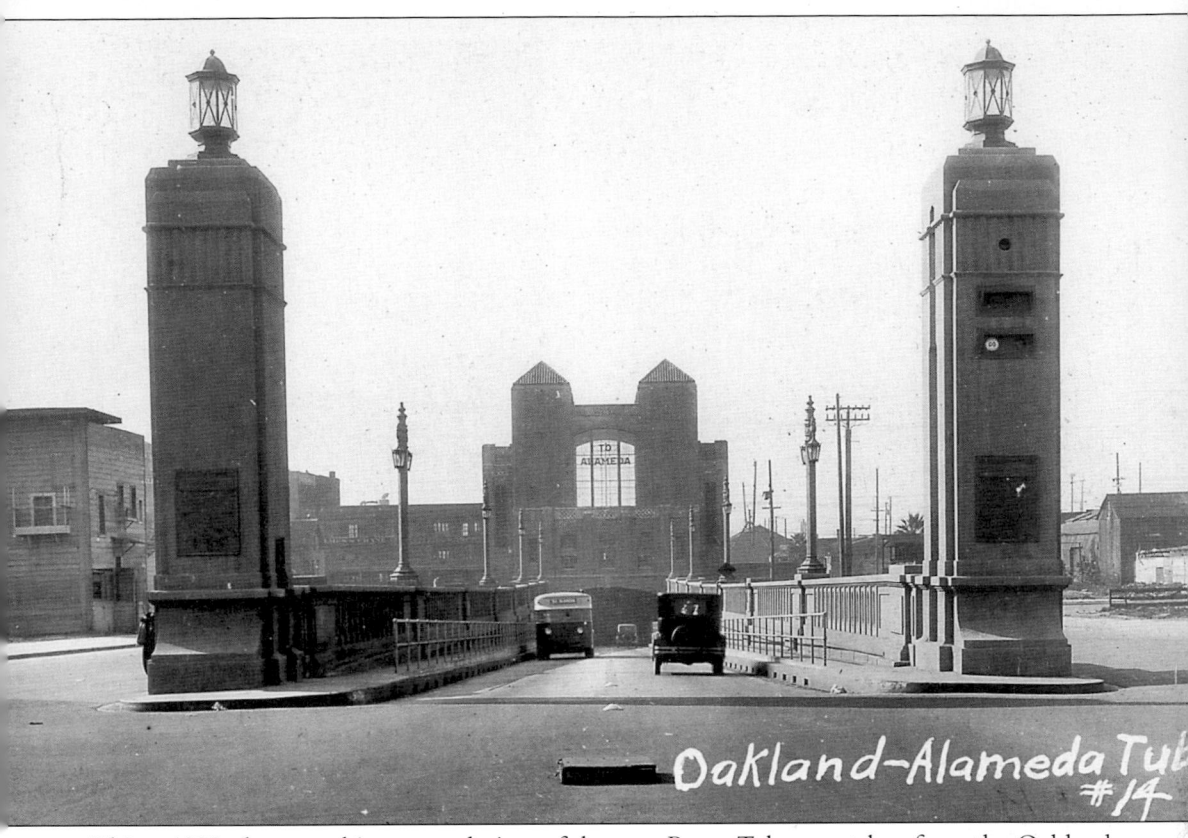

This *c.* 1929 photographic postcard view of the new Posey Tube was taken from the Oakland side. Notice the bus on the left side, leaving Alameda. The first vehicle to pass through the tunnel on opening day was an empty AC Transit bus, driven by Carl H. Brooks at 5:00 a.m. Brooks repeated the same feat on February 13, 1963, in the new Webster Tube.

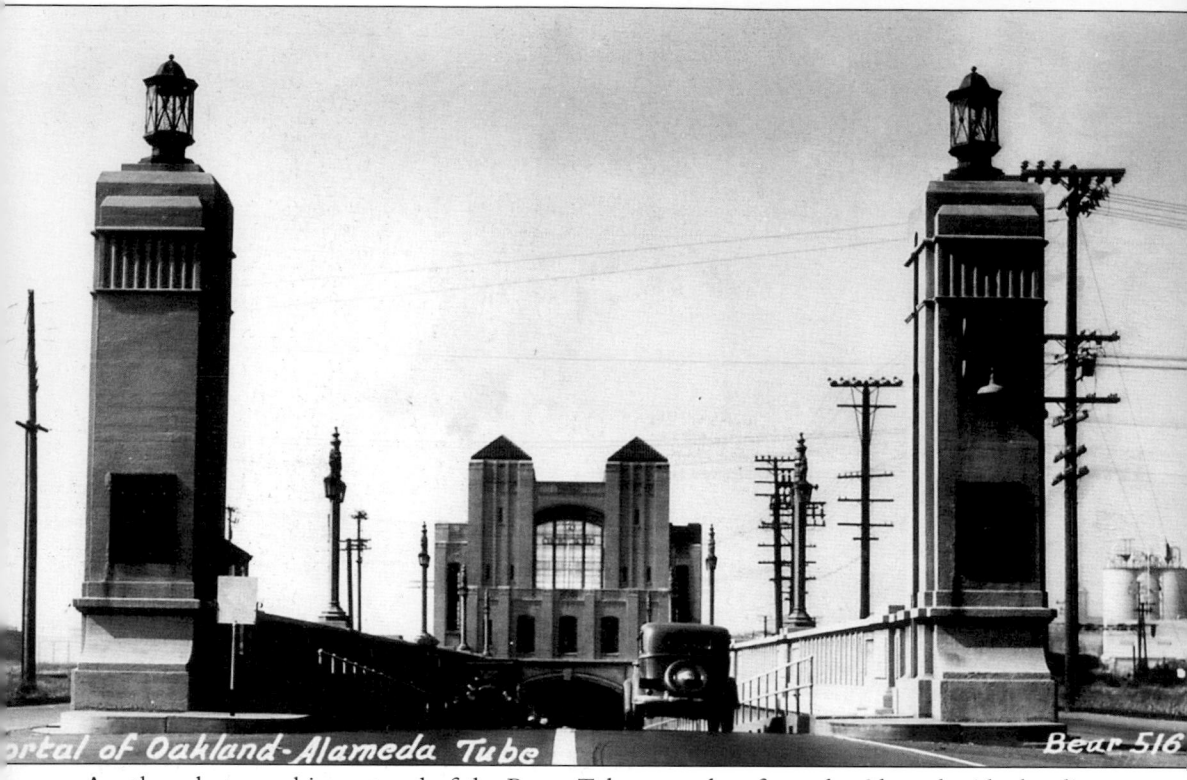

Portal of Oakland-Alameda Tube

Bear 516

Another photographic postcard of the Posey Tube was taken from the Alameda side, heading toward Oakland, *c.* 1935. According to a 1928 pamphlet, horse-drawn vehicles, honking of horns, whistles and other noise-making devices, and smoking were banned inside the tunnel. The speed limit at the time was 20 miles per hour.

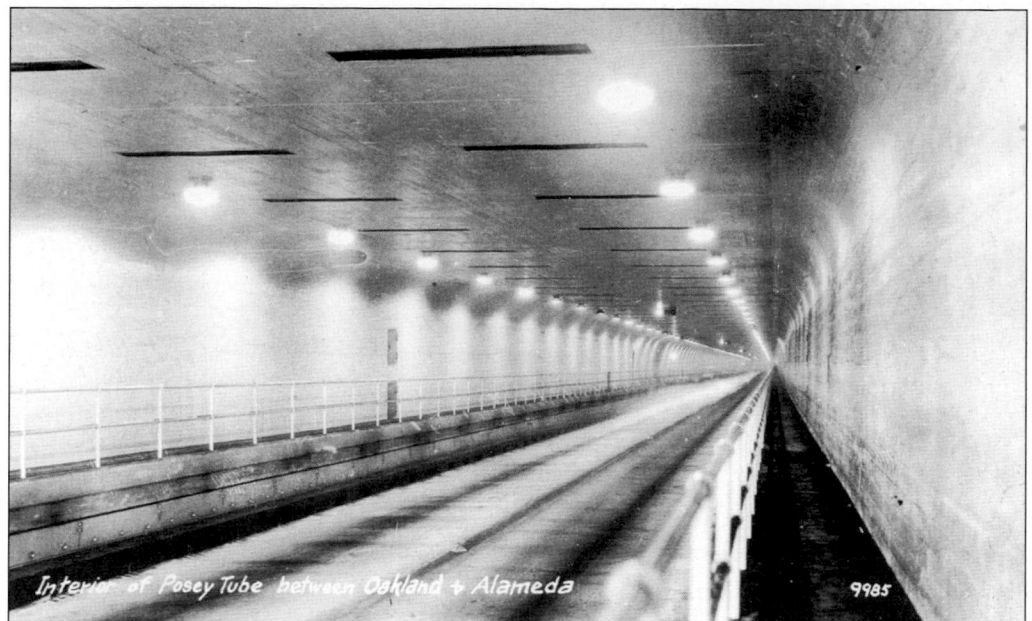

Interior of Posey Tube between Oakland & Alameda   9985

This *c.* 1930 photographic postcard provides an interior view of the Posey Tube. Penciled on the back, in part, is the message, "It's quite an experience going through the first time when one realizes that ships are passing above your head, but one gets used to it very soon."

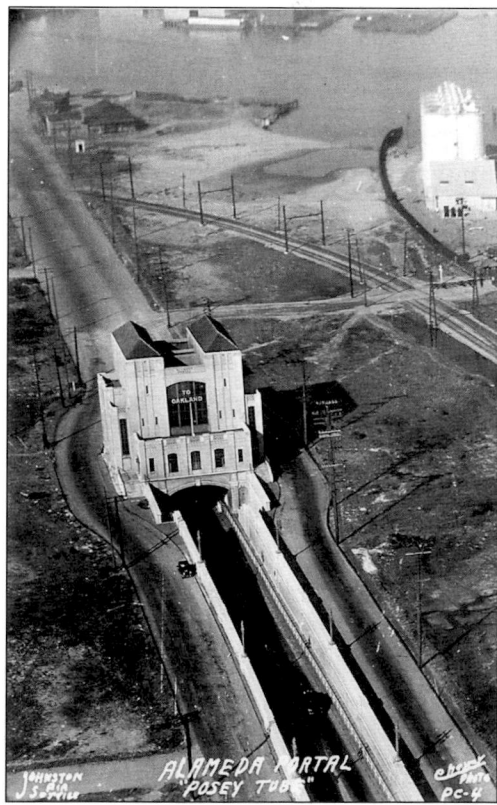

This early 1930s aerial view of the Posey Tube was taken heading toward Oakland. The tunnel was named for Alameda County Surveyor George Posey, who was involved in the original design and construction of this unusual entrance to the island city. Planned in stages between 1908 and 1923, construction on the Posey Tube began in 1925. The opening took place on October 27, 1928, contrary to a sign near the tunnel's entrance dating it to 1927.

ALAMEDA PORTAL "POSEY TUBE"

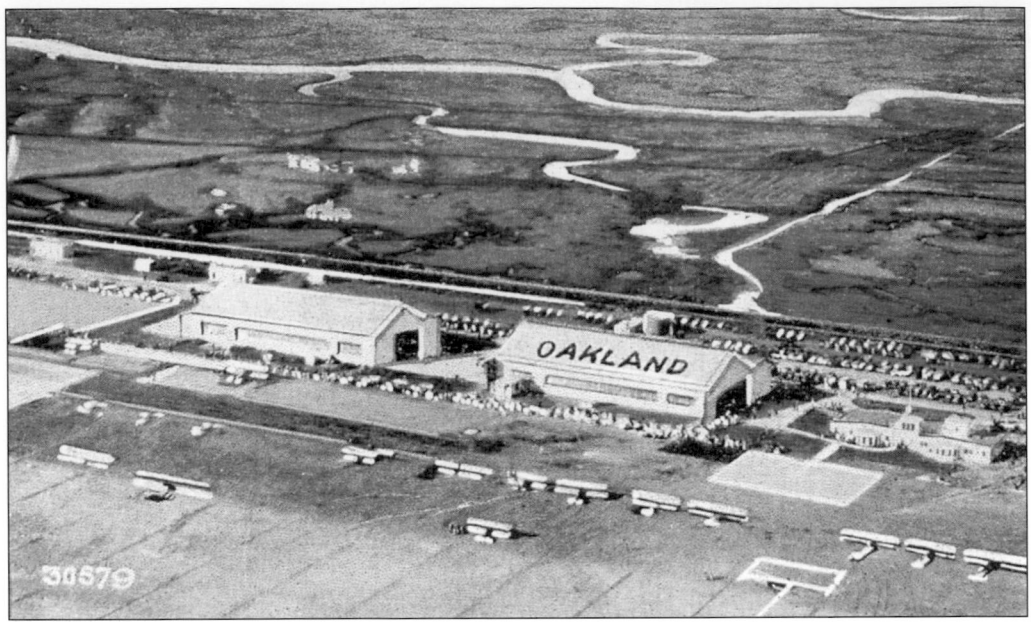

The administration building can be seen on the right side of this aerial view, along with hangars No. 1 and 2, in this 1928 postcard. Beyond lies marshland and the San Leandro Bay. Subsequent to the construction, Alameda was briefly known as "the Airport City," one of many short-lived nicknames. (Published by Western Notion and Novelty Company, Oakland.)

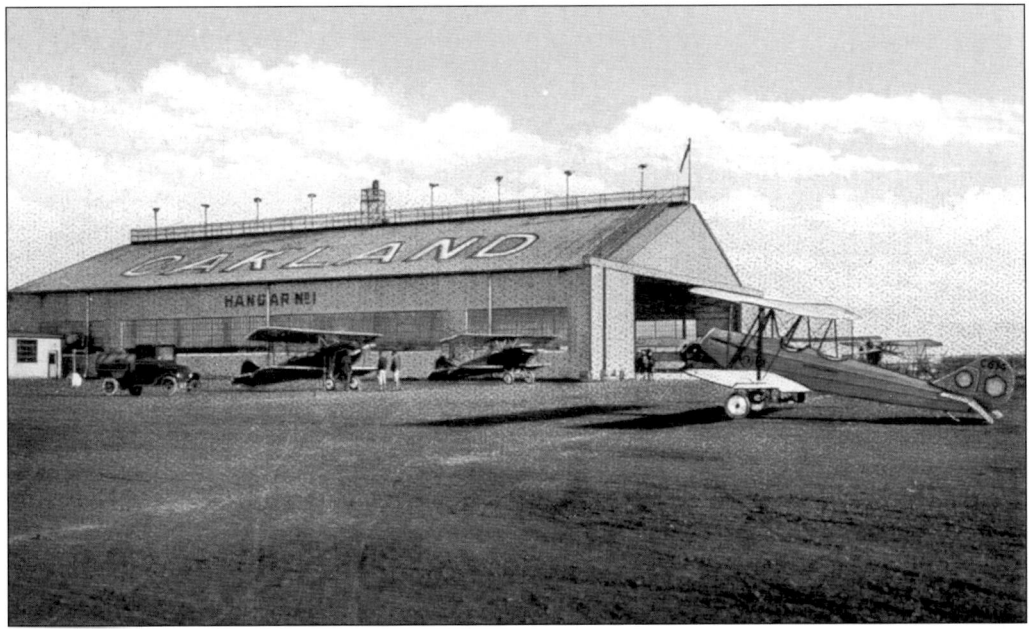

In 1927, construction crews built the longest runway at that time, 7,020 feet, used for the first flight from the mainland to Hawaii. Later that year, Col. Charles A. Lindbergh attended the dedication ceremonies in his *Spirit of St. Louis* airplane. This 1920s postcard shows biplanes, and hangar No. 1. (Published by the Pacific Novelty Company, San Francisco.)

Ten

THE NAVAL AIR STATION AND GOVERNMENT ISLAND

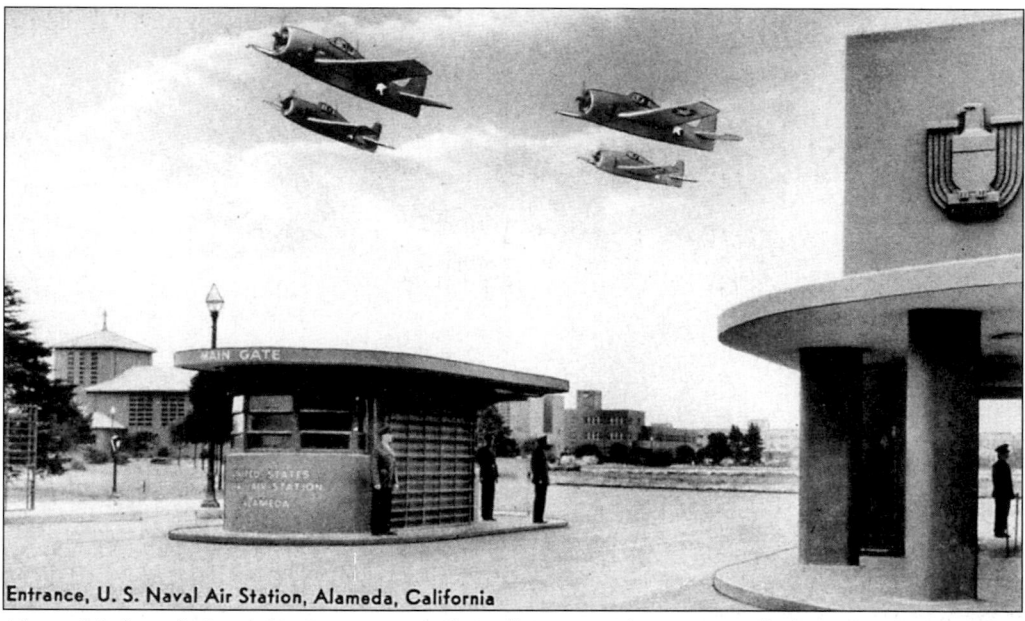

Entrance, U. S. Naval Air Station, Alameda, California

Alameda's famed Naval Air Station started small, as a simple airstrip called Benton Field, which first opened in 1934. Although used by Pan American Airways for practical purposes, it was also constructed to attract the Navy to Alameda. Obviously, the plan worked. Construction on the Naval Base began in 1938 and was so extensive that it was not yet complete when the United States went to war in 1941. Nevertheless, the base began operations with all available facilities. March 1942 brought the *Hornet,* an aircraft carrier that transported the B-52s of Gen. Jimmy Doolittle's Raiders in April 1942. These planes were used in the bombings of Tokyo on April 18, 1942, and the *Hornet* now functions as an offshore museum at the base. This *c.* 1944 postcard shows the Streamline Moderne–style entrance to the base and compliments its "modern buildings" and beautiful landscaping. The U.S. Naval Air Station, Alameda, was one of the Navy's busiest during World War II, and thrived for years after that. (Published by Greenwood Printers Ltd., Oakland.)

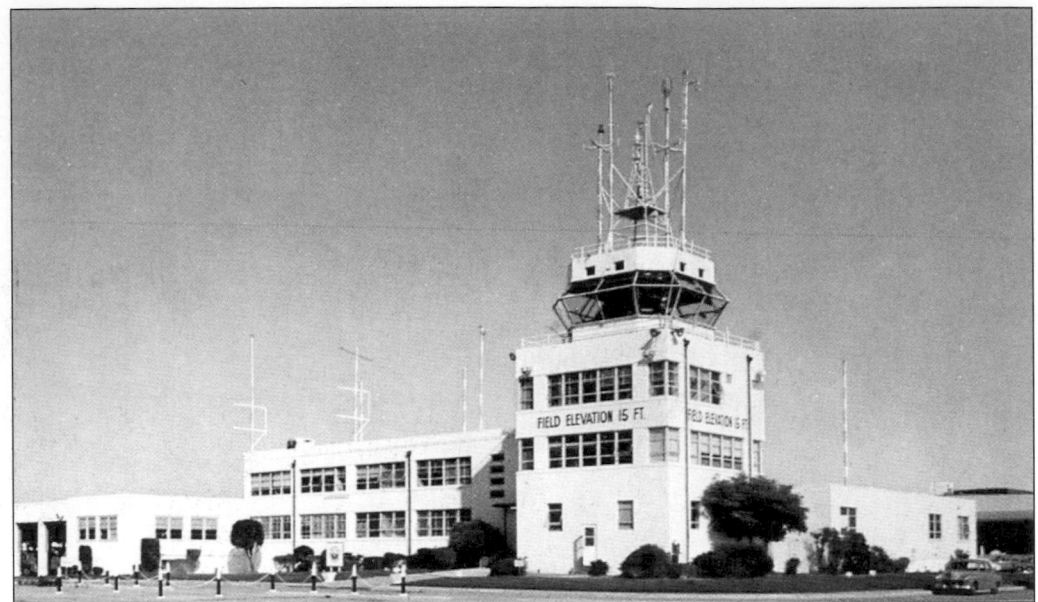

This *c.* 1956 postcard shows the Naval Air Station Operations Building, the "hub of all flight planning and aircraft control activities." Operating 24 hours a day, this facility included the control tower, operations offices, a photographic lab, and emergency rescue teams. After years of service to this country, the Naval Air Station, Alameda, was unfortunately closed in 1997 by the Base Realignment and Closure Commission. (Published by Smith News Company, San Francisco, California.)

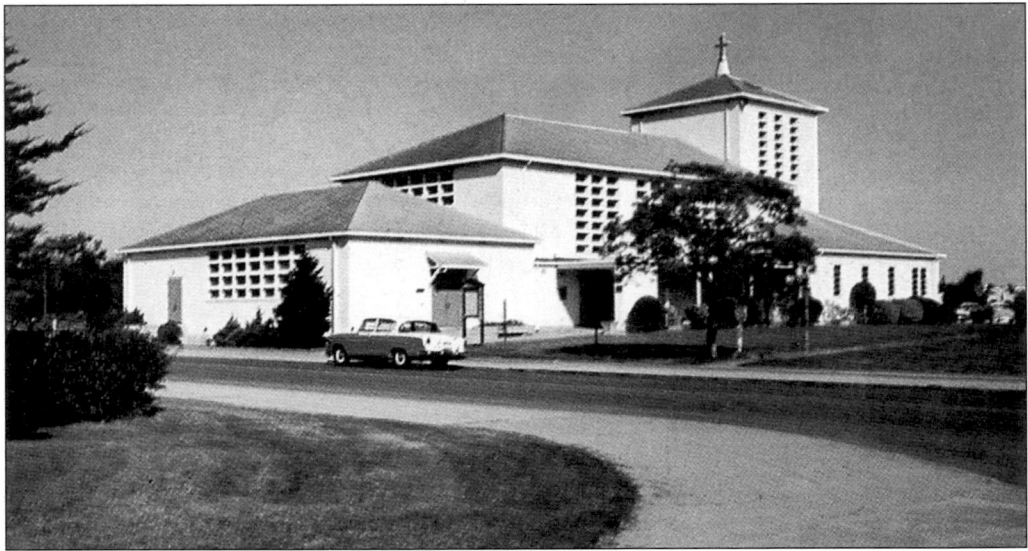

The Naval Air Station Chapel was dedicated in 1943 and served numerous denominations. Actually three chapels in one, it consisted of the Blessed Sacrament Chapel for Roman Catholics, the Shannon Chapel for non-Catholics, and as the back of the card proudly announces, "the Main Chapel, seating approximately 400, which is shared by all faiths in the spirit of 'Cooperation without Compromise.'" The church still stands at the corner of West Red Line Avenue and Saratoga Street, but given its current condition and general appearance, seems to be abandoned, like much of the dilapidated military housing that surrounds it. (Published by Smith News Company, San Francisco, *c.* 1956.)

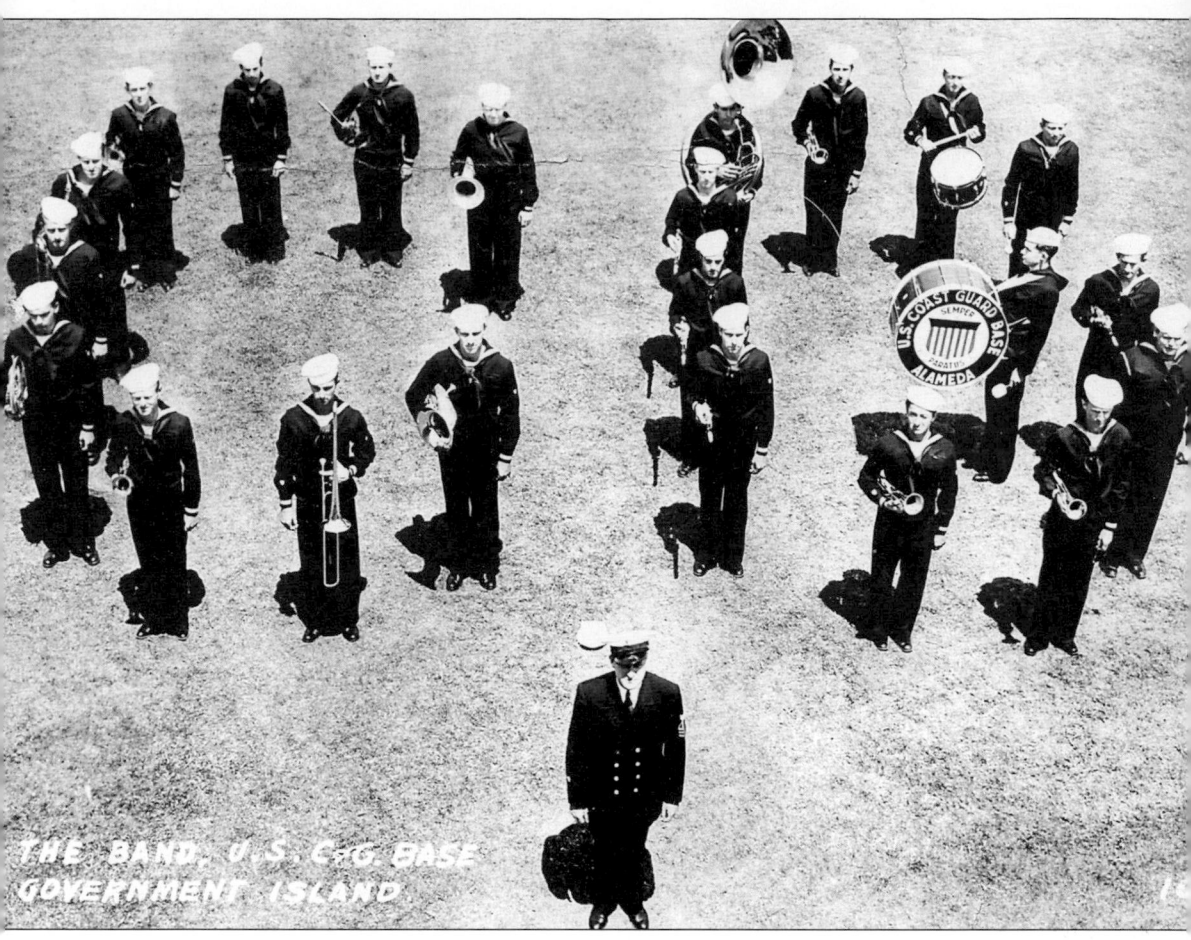

Government Island was established in 1913 in the Oakland estuary and expanded in 1939, after more land was acquired from Alameda. Although accessible only from Oakland, it is within the Alameda city limits. The U.S. Coast Guard Base band poses for this early 1940s photographic postcard. The band still performs to this day.

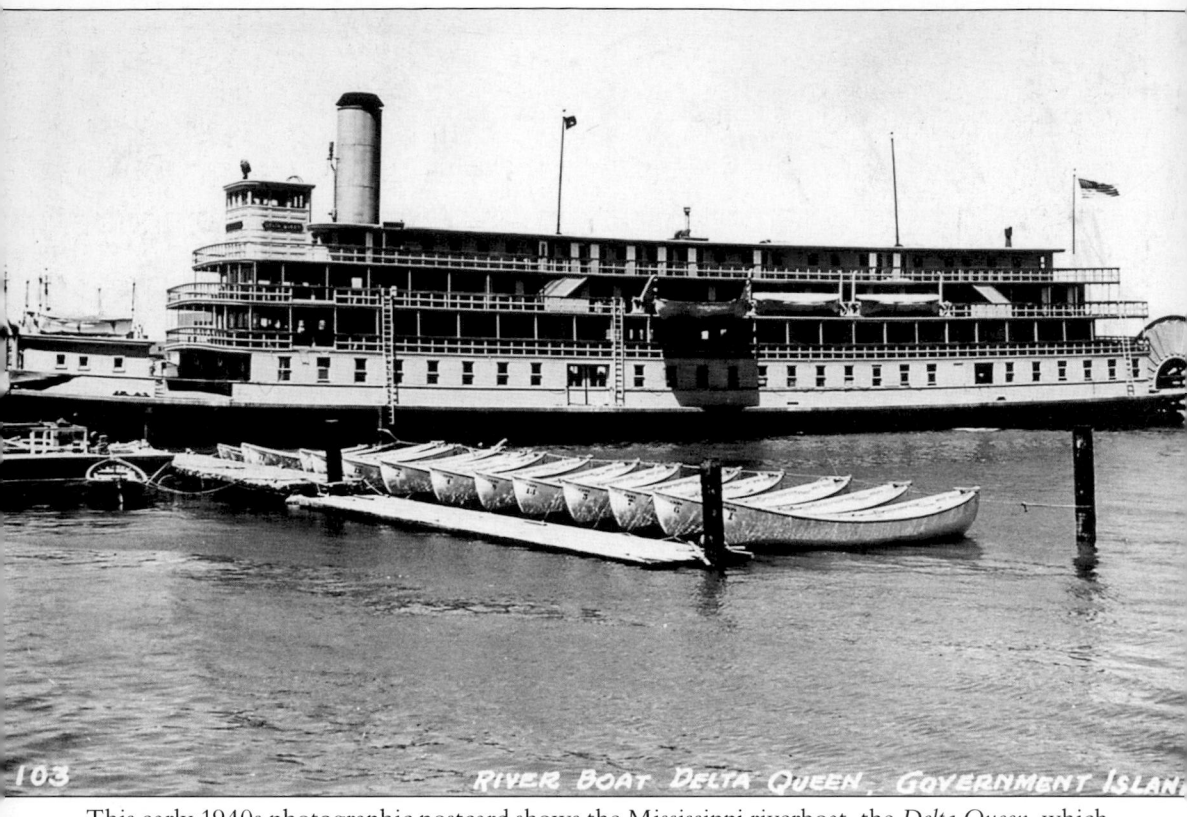

103 RIVER BOAT DELTA QUEEN, GOVERNMENT ISLAN.

This early 1940s photographic postcard shows the Mississippi riverboat, the *Delta Queen*, which was used as temporary barracks and training center in the early days of Government Island, before the school was built. The satisfied sender of this card states it is "a fine place," with "lots to eat."

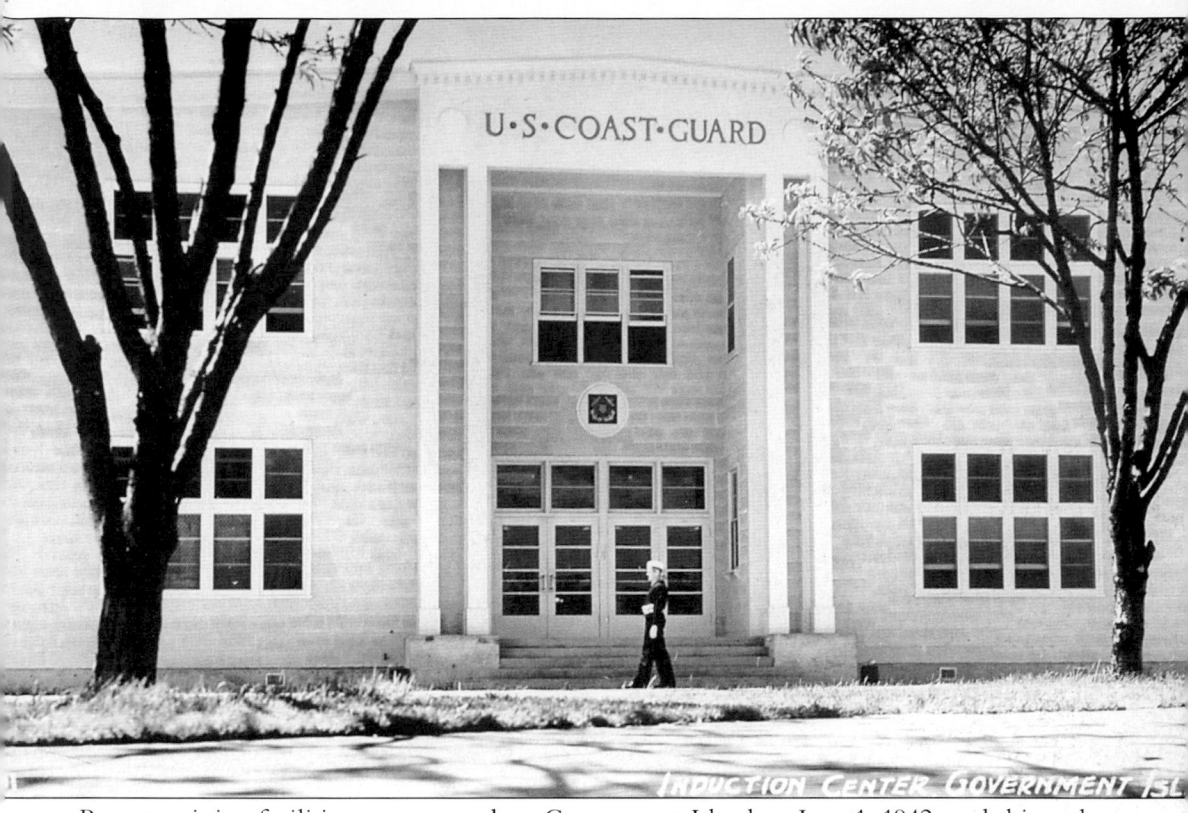

Proper training facilities were opened on Government Island on June 1, 1942, and this early 1940s photographic postcard shows the entrance to the induction center. "I sure can't say much for Calif.," writes this card's dissatisfied author. "We hardly see the sun. I think Minnesota is much nicer."

SELECTED READING

Gunn, George. *Documentation of Victorian and Post Victorian Residential and Commercial Buildings, City of Alameda 1854–1904.* Alameda: self-published, revised edition, 1988.

———. *Buildings of the Edwardian Period, City of Alameda, 1905 to December 31, 1909.* Alameda: self-published, 1988.

Merlin, Imelda. *Alameda: A Geographical History.* Alameda: David Printing Company, 1977.

Minor, Woodruff. *Historic Commercial Buildings of Alameda.* Alameda: Historical Advisory Board, 1993.